MW00586372

A GEOLOGY OF MEDIA

Electronic Mediations

Series Editors: N. Katherine Hayles, Peter Krapp, Rita Raley, and Samuel Weber
Founding Editor: Mark Poster

(continued on page 207)

A
GEOLOGY
OF
MEDIA

JUSSI
PARIKKA

Electronic Mediations, Volume 46

University of Minnesota Press
Minneapolis • London

A version of chapter 2 was published as *The Anthrobscene* (Minneapolis: University of Minnesota Press, 2014). Portions of chapter 4 appeared in "Dust and Exhaustion: The Labor of Media Materialism," *CTheory*, October 2, 2013, http://www.ctheory.net. The Appendix was previously published as "Zombie Media: Circuit Bending Media Archaeology into an Art Method," *Leonardo* 45, no. 5 (2012): 424–30. Portions of the book appeared in "Introduction: The Materiality of Media and Waste," in *Medianatures: The Materiality of Information Technology and Electronic Waste*, ed. Jussi Parikka (Ann Arbor, Mich.: Open Humanities Press, 2011), and in "Media Zoology and Waste Management: Animal Energies and Medianatures," *NECSUS European Journal of Media Studies*, no. 4 (2013): 527–44.

Copyright 2015 by Jussi Parikka

All rights reserved. No part of this publication may be reproduced, stored in a retrieval system, or transmitted, in any form or by any means, electronic, mechanical, photocopying, recording, or otherwise, without the prior written permission of the publisher.

Published by the University of Minnesota Press
111 Third Avenue South, Suite 290
Minneapolis, MN 55401-2520
http://www.upress.umn.edu

Library of Congress Cataloging-in-Publication Data
Parikka, Jussi.
    A geology of media / Jussi Parikka. (Electronic mediations ; volume 46)
    Includes bibliographical references and index.
    ISBN 978-0-8166-9551-5 (hc : alk. paper)
    ISBN 978-0-8166-9552-2 (pb : alk. paper)
    1. Mass media. 2. Mass media—Social aspects. 3. Mass media and culture.
    I. Title. P90.P3355 2015
    302.23—dc23

                                    2014028047

Printed in the United States of America on acid-free paper

The University of Minnesota is an equal-opportunity educator and employer.

27 26 25 24 23 22 21   10 9 8 7 6 5 4

CONTENTS

PREFACE

In *Principles of Geology,* Charles Lyell offers one of the early definitions of the discipline:

> Geology is the science which investigates the successive changes that have taken place in the organic and the inorganic kingdoms of nature; it enquires into the causes of these changes, and the influence which they have exerted in modifying the surface and external structure of the planet.[1]

This iconic take from 1830 outlines geology as one of the main disciplines of planetary inquiry, leaving the regime of morals to the humanities. It is both an emblem of the division of labor in the academia and a genealogical record that could not be more central to our concerns. The geological manifests in earthquakes, mass extinction of species, pollution of the globe, and the debates about the Anthropocene, which demonstrates that morals, culture, and geology after all have something to do with each other. The book argues that the world of thought, senses, sensation, perception, customs, practices, habits, and human embodiment is not unrelated to the world of geological strata, climates, the earth, and the massive durations of change that seem to mock the timescales of our petty affairs. And yet, the human affairs have demonstrated an impact. Science and engineering has a significant impact on the earth. The idealized object of knowledge itself registers the observing gaze that was supposed to be at a distance. Geoengineering is one practice of intertwined naturecultures, and our continuous trespassing over the boundaries of sciences and humanities cannot be neglected by closing our eyes and thinking of semiotics. The relations to the earth are also part of the social relations of labor and exploitation that characterized emerging industrial capitalism of the nineteenth century as much as they characterize contemporary digital capitalism of the twenty-first century from mining minerals, geopolitics of the hunt for energy, and material resources to the factories of production of computational equipment.

This short book is about scientific cultures, technological reality, and artistic perspectives. It engages with science and technology as one pertinent multidisciplinary context for media studies and media art history. It does not claim to be a full-fledged account of the relations of geology and technology. However, it offers an insight relevant to many of us working in the field of media, arts, and contemporary technology studies, including media archaeology.

There is more mining than data mining in *A Geology of Media*. More specifically, it is interested in the connections of media technologies, their materiality, hardware, and energy, with the geophysical nature: nature affords and bears the weight of media culture, from metals and minerals to its waste load. The official Geological Surveys might be an odd place to start media analysis, but they do reveal the backstory of technological culture: the geopolitically important scientific mapping of resources from copper to uranium, oil to nickel, bauxite (necessary for aluminum) to a long list of rare earth minerals. One also finds a mix of nation-state interests, scientific institutions, and, of course, military needs ever so tightly interlinked since the nineteenth century. One is led to consider the systematic laboratorization of everyday culture: even the mundane is produced through a mix of the archaic underworld and the refined scientific process. Even if cultural and media theorists are now aware of the importance of minerals such as coltan (tantalum), it was actually already before digital culture that this specific mineral (often mined in the war-ridden territories of Congo) became mapped as part of the geophysical politics of the twentieth century: "The U.S. Bureau of Mines observed that these materials were 'among the rare metals most vital in 1952 to the United States defense program'"[2] because of tantalum's (and columbium's) usefulness for special "high-strength steel alloys."[3]

The book was finished primarily in Istanbul in 2013 and early 2014, a city where one has a privileged view to some of the issues that we face with technological projects and disastrous environmental consequences. Such are often underpinned by shortsighted and just blatantly exploitative violent politics. The story, and the book, was started during the Gezi protests of summer 2013, sparked off by an environmental protest but resonant of a wider political situation where issues of capitalism, religion, technology, knowledge, and the environment folded into a complex historical event. Istanbul is a tectonic city, sitting on top of geological formations promising another major earthquake in the future. It is a city branded by massive geologically significant building projects. Some are already ready, some are in planning. The recently opened Marmaray tunnel connected the two continents through a tunnel under the Bosphorus; a canal project suggests to link the Black Sea with the Marmara Sea; a lot of the projects are reminiscent of the national engineering of modernity but also now the corporate capital investment in this geopolitically important region. But the protests were also highlighting the aspects that tie location to politics, the life of the earth with increasingly authoritarian ruling powers with corporate interests in the construction business and other businesses. The events demonstrated the impossibility of detaching the political from the natural, the geopolitical from the geological. The short-term political struggles had to do with political freedoms as much as with the awareness of what would happen if some of the massive building projects, including a new airport and a third bridge, would wipe out important parts of the forestry around Istanbul as well as creating extremely dangerous risks to the underground water resources of the city.

This political situation and its link with capitalism was present already in the nineteenth-century evaluation of the changing modes of production. Of course the environmental catastrophe is not merely a capitalist aftereffect. We should not ignore the impact "real socialism" of the twentieth century left in the natural record as radioactive radiation and industrial traces in soil and rivers. But there is a connection to the capitalist intensification of modes of production with the necessity to expand into new resource bases to guarantee growth. What we now perceive as the environmental catastrophe at times branded as the "Anthropocene" of human impact on the planet matches in some periodization also what

Marx and Engels narrativize as a crucial political economic shift. From *The Communist Manifesto*, in 1848:

> The bourgeoisie, during its rule of scarce 100 years, has created more massive and more colossal productive forces than have all preceding generations together. Subjection of nature's forces to man, machinery, application of chemistry to industry and agriculture, steam-navigation, railways, electric telegraphs, clearing of whole continents for cultivation, canalisation of rivers, whole populations conjured out of the ground—what earlier century had even a presentiment that such productive forces slumbered in the lap of social labour?[4]

Marx and Engels's political characterization of capitalism as a mode of mobilizing science and engineering into productive forces is also what now we live as the aftereffect coined the "Anthropocene." The modern project of ruling over nature understood as resource was based on a division of the two—the Social and the Natural—but it always leaked. Bruno Latour constantly has reminded of the impossibility of dividing Nature from Culture. We have various names for the entanglements of the natural–geophysical, including Gaia and the Anthropocene; but both indicate the arrival of something new that points out as insufficient any Modern attempt to name the two, Nature and Culture, separately.[5]

Yet we need to remember that nothing necessarily *arrived*. The geological past in its persistent slowness; the earlier accounts of the Anthropocene before its time in the nineteenth century by Antonio Stoppani (the Anthropozoic) and by George P. Marsh;[6] the early phases of the scientific and technological systems, such as metereology, that visualized and modeled the natural planet as a global system—they were already there.[7] In 1873, in his *Corso di Geologia*, Stoppani paints an image of the human as an inventor who penetrates the earth, the sea, and the air with his technologies and builds from and on the earth's already existing strata.[8] The future fossil layer is already in Stoppani's analysis branded by human technological and chemical traces. Humans leave their mark, and the earth carries it forward as an archive.

The supposedly unexpected event of the Anthropocene had already arrived beforehand. These sudden revelations embedded in geological slowness offer a view both to the historical layers of discourse concerning technology, waste, and time and the geological realities where we collect and dispose of resources. Stoppani's vision of the earth archive is the afterglow of the scientific and technological culture. It's the trash in midst of which we live. And it's the trash we have to sort out in case there would be a human future, in the midst of our constitutive nonhuman fellows.

ACKNOWLEDGMENTS

A Geology of Media forms the third and final part of the trilogy of media ecologies: from the viral worlds of *Digital Contagions* (2007) to the swarms of *Insect Media* (2010), the focus has been on the digital materialism that tied animals and ecology as part of theory and narratives of history. *A Geology of Media* is more focused on the nonorganic and yet connects with the concerns of the two: how to think the continuum between nature and technology?

This book owes its existence to so many friends and colleagues I have met, worked with, and talked with over the years. A lot of my inspiration comes from Sean Cubitt's work on related topics.

The colleagues at Winchester School of Art offered great support, and discussions with Ryan Bishop were especially instrumental in forming some of the arguments. Several people read the text or offered other insights and sources, knowingly or unknowingly. Thanks go (in no particular order) to Garnet Hertz, Steven Shaviro, Sean Cubitt, Ed D'Souza, Seb Franklin, Tom Apperley, Michael Dieter, Benjamin Bratton, Alison Gazzard, Darren Wershler, J. R. Carpenter, Ed Keller, Jordan Crandall, Richard Grusin, Geoffrey Winthrop-Young, Till Heilmann, Paul Feigelfeld, Florian Sprenger, Robin Boast, Kelly Egan, Gary Genosko, Greg Elmer, Ganaele Langlois, Ebru Yetiskin, Olcay Öztürk Pasi Väliaho, Ilona Hongisto, Katve-Kaisa Kontturi, Teemu Taira, Milla Tiainen, Matleena Kalajoki, Rosi Braidotti, Trevor Paglen, Gregory Chatonsky, Jonathan Kemp, Martin Howse, Ryan Jordan, Jamie Allen, David Gauthier, and YoHa. The

University of Minnesota Press has again been a pleasure to work with. Doug Armato and Danielle Kasprzak are two people I want to name in particular, but the entire team deserves a warm thank-you. Similarly, I thank the editors of Electronic Mediations for including this book as part of the series. Thank you also to Diana Witt for preparing the index.

I benefited from a visiting scholar position at Bahçeşehir University in Istanbul during autumn 2013. The book was finalized with help from a senior fellowship at the Leuphana University MECS–Institute in early summer 2014. Preliminary ideas for this book were presented at many events, conferences, and other talks, including at transmediale, Bochum University, Slade School of Art at University College London, Cornell University, Goldsmiths College, Giessen, Mnemonics Cultural Memory summer school in Stockholm, Winchester School of Art, and the Canadian Communication Association Annual Congress.

I would like to dedicate this book to my mother and my father, both in their own ways such a solid ground and support.

1

MATERIALITY

GROUNDS OF MEDIA
AND CULTURE

The future is out there on the permafrost.

—THOMAS PYNCHON, *THE BLEEDING EDGE*

Technology . . . constitutes the abyss of the Anthropocene.

—ERICH HÖRL

An Alternative Media Materialism

To label yourself a materialist does not necessarily by itself mean much. The term is something that demands explication, instead of explaining by its own powers. The long histories of materialism and idealism in philosophy are one reference point, but so are the everyday uses of the term: do we refer to it as the opposite of spiritual or ethical (as in expressions of disgust toward the materialist aspects of consumer society) or refer to the reality of machines and technology that structure our life. The Marxist legacy in political thought and theory has given us indication what historical materialism is, but so have scholars in media theory: media materialism refers to the necessity to analyze media technologies as something that are irreducible to what we think of them or even how we use them. It has come to refer to technology as an active agent in the ontological and epistemological sense. In other words, media structure how things are in the world and how things are known in the world. In fact, media analysis is an excellent way of "giving material specificity to our descriptions of . . . abstract concepts"[1] of which materiality is oddly enough too easily one.

Cultural and media theory have benefited in the past years from an emergence of several accounts of materiality. In media theory, materialism has often been attached to the term *German media theory*—a term that has brought unity to a wider field of scholars engaging with material accounts of media culture in rather different ways.[2] Friedrich Kittler is the most famous reference in this context. Kittler inaugurated various provocations regarding computer culture, hardware, and the technological framing of our contemporary life, which implied a certain nonhuman perspective: the human being is primarily a "so-called Man" formed as an aftereffect of media technologies. At times, Kittler was even branded a media archaeologist because he picked up on Michel Foucault's archaeological and archival cultural history in a new way in his early work.[3] There's a truth to that label: Kittler was adamant that we need to make sure that Foucault's understanding of what governs our contemporary life—its archive—is not only about the statements and rules found in books and libraries. Instead, it is to be found in technological networks of machines and institutions, patterns of education and drilling: in the scientific-engineering complex that practices such forms of power that the traditional humanities theory is incapable of understanding or grasping if it continues to talk about hermeneutic meanings or persists to operate with traditional sociological concepts. Kittler was a *provocateur* in a theoretical psy-ops operation who believed that humanities scholars should work with technology. He himself did. Kittler left behind unpublished writings but also software manuals and hardware, to be part of his *Nachlass*. His early synthesizer from the 1970s was resurrected and included in an art performance by Jan-Peter Sonntag to demonstrate this metamorphosis of Kittler: the Goethe scholar turned synth-geek and tinkerer.

At times in accusing, pejorative ways, and at times in more celebratory tones, the likes of Kittler became an emblem of media materialism: to study media, you need to have a proper understanding of the science and engineering realities that govern the highly fine-structured computer worlds in which we live—without ignoring the fact that technical media did not start with the digital. Older technical media play an important part in the histories and genealogies, the archaeological layers conditioning our present. Media archaeology has been one field to constantly emphasize this point.

For Kittler, media studies was never to be reduced to the play of interpretations, semiotic connotations, or modes of representation, which were only secondary effects, second-order phenomena. Media work on the level of circuits, hardware, and voltage differences, which the engineers as much as the military intelligence and secret agencies gradually recognized before humanities did. This mode of argumentation ignored, however, a wide range of politically engaged work that tried to make sense of why media govern us humans on a semiotic level too. Such creeping suspicions that any inclusive account of materiality definitely filtered out many competing ones triggers the question, what is being left out? What other modes of materiality deserve our attention? Issues of gender, sex, embodiment, and affect? Of labor, global logistics, modes of production? In other words, from where do our notions of materiality stem, and what is their ground?

What if there is another level of media materialism that is not so easily dismissed as we would think? What if media materialism is not something that hones in on the machines only? Where do machines come from, what composes technology in its materiality and media after it becomes disused, dysfunctional dead media that refuse to die? This book is structured around the argument that there is such a thing as *geology of media*: a different sort of temporal and spatial materialism of media culture than the one that focuses solely on machines or even networks of technologies as nonhuman agencies. It echoes John Durham Peters's point that the axis of time and space—familiar also from the Canadian media theory tradition of Harold Innis and Marshall McLuhan—is not restricted to traditional ideas about media as devices but can refer back to cosmology and geology: that the geological sciences and astronomy have already opened up the idea of the earth, light, air, and time as media.[4]

This is a green book—in the sense of referring to the ecological contexts in which we should make arguments about media technological culture—as well as a book covered in dirt and soil. Instead of leafy metaphors of animals, technology, and ecosystems, it insists on a particular aspect of this relation between media and the geophysical environment. Scholars such as Douglas Kahn have recently made the same point that

Kittler's agenda could have been more radical and continued from the circuits to what enables hardware: the environmental contexts, questions of energy consumption, and, one could add, the electronic waste that surround our contemporary worries of what transmission, calculation, and storage mean in a material context.[5]

The guiding conceptual ground of this book refers to geology: the science about the ground beneath our feet, its history and constitution, the systematic study of the various levers, layers, strata, and interconnections that define the earth. It implies the work of geoengineering and geotechnics as specific ways of interacting with the solidity of the earth but also the fine measurements that relate to a wider awareness of the environmental constitution of our lives. Hence geology is not only about the soil, the crust, the layers that give our feet a ground on which to stumble: geology is also a theme connected to the climate change as well as the political economy of industrial and postindustrial production. It connects to the wider geophysical life worlds that support the organic life as much as the technological worlds of transmission, calculation, and storage. Geology becomes a way to investigate materiality of the technological media world. It becomes a conceptual trajectory, a creative intervention to the cultural history of the contemporary.

Geology and various related disciplines and fields of knowledge, such as chemistry and, indeed, ecology, frame the modern world and give it one possible scientific structure. Such disciplines are strongly implied in the emergence of the technological and scientific culture, which feeds to our media cultural practices. It is in this sense that I am interested in finding strains of media materialism outside the usual definition of media: instead of radio, I prefer to think what components and materials enable such technologies; instead of networking, we need to remember the importance of copper or optical fiber for such forms of communication; instead of a blunt discussion of "the digital," we need to pick it apart and remember that also mineral durations are essential to it being such a crucial feature that penetrates our academic, social, and economic interests. Consider, then, lithium as such a premediatic media material that is essential to the existence of technological culture but also as an element that traverses technologies. This chemical element (Li) and metal is essential for laptop batteries as well as future green technologies (again, battery technology, but for hybrid cars). Platinum-grouped metals might be familiar from jewelry but are as important for "computer hard drives, liquid crystal displays, and miniaturized electronic circuits"[6] as for hydrogen fuel cells. Lots of critical materials are in a crucial position in relation to a variety of civilian and military technologies, including what we tend to call just bluntly "media": screens, networks, computers, and more. Tracking chemicals, metals, and minerals is one aspect of this book, extending traditional notions of media materialism into a more environmental and ecological agenda.

Artist Robert Smithson spoke about "abstract geology," referring to how tectonics and geophysics pertain not only to the earth but also to the mind; abstract geology is a field where a geological interest is distributed across the organic and nonorganic division. Its reference to the "abstract" might attract those with a Deleuzian bent and resonate with the concept of "abstract machines." But before the philosophical discourse, Smithson's interest was in the materiality of the art practice, reintroducing metals (and hence geology) to the studio. What's more, Smithson was ready to mobilize his notion emerging in the artistic discourse of land art in the 1960s to a conceptualization of technology that we can say was nothing less than anti-McLuhanian: instead of seeing technology as extensions of Man, technology is aggregated and "made of the raw materials of the earth."[7] From our current twenty-first-century perspective approximately fifty years later, it starts an imaginary alternative media theoretical lineage that does not include necessarily McLuhan, Kittler, and the likes in its story but materials, metals, waste, and chemistry. These materials articulate the high-technical and low-paid culture of digitality. They also provide an alternative materialism for the geophysical media age.

So how does a media theorist turned pseudo-geologist operate? To where does such a hybrid and hyphenated scholar turn? At least in this book, this leads us to track the importance of the nonorganic in constructing media before they become media: the literal deep times and deep places of media in mines and rare earth minerals. It looks at aesthetic discourses and practices, such as psychogeophysics—a sort of speculative aesthetics for the connection of technology and society with a special view to the geophysical—that offer insights to earth media arts.[8] The amount of material would be endless if one were to start looking meticulously at the work of national institutions and geological methods. Geological surveys have moved on from the early work contributing to agriculture and mining to being an essential part of global geopolitics. One can track specific genealogies of geology, politics, and technology even through single institutions, such as the influential scientific agency the U.S. Geological Survey.[9] Since its founding in the latter half of the nineteenth century, it has served an essential role in mapping the necessary natural resources part of nation building into a technologically advanced country—and now, one can see how the role has widened to a global scale; for instance, in Afghanistan, in parallel to the military operations of the war against terrorism, geologists are mapping the resource basis of the country. It promises, besides copper, iron, and gold, also lithium—even enough for Afghanistan to be branded the "Saudi Arabia of lithium." Old geological surveys and methods are being complemented with aerial surveys by geologists collaborating with the Pentagon by using new gravity and magnetic measuring techniques.[10]

To summarize the preceding preamble, this is a book about technical media culture—digital and analog—that starts from the geophysical. It investigates, employs, and mobilizes terms that refer to the geophysical—that is, not just geopolitical—spheres of media culture in a manner that is a combination of conceptually speculative but thematically and media historically grounded. In other words, a part of the book works through historical sources and examples, but with an emphasis on media arts. Indeed, it is the lens of media art practices and theoretical discourse that offers us a specific way to look at the recent years of climate change, the Anthropocene, and geophysics-embedded work: the ideas about deep time of the media,[11] psychogeophysics, e-waste, the Anthropocene, chemistry, and the earthly as a media history that works in nonlinear ways. This idea of media (art) histories as one of nonlinear strata pushes even the media archaeological agenda of media history to its extreme. Human history is infused in geological time.[12]

Temporality and Medianatures

Among the variety of theories and methods in media studies debates of the past years, media archaeology has become a way to multiply and bend traditional media historical methods to incorporate new ways of grasping the history of oddities, losers, and, more generally, conditions of media culture. It maps the real imaginary of how fantasies of media become part of the real technological projects and how media aesthetics contributes to new forms of political design of culture. Media archaeological writings from Erkki Huhtamo to Wolfgang Ernst, Friedrich Kittler to Siegfried Zielinski, Thomas Elsaesser and many others have offered an exciting tool kit that expands what we even think of as media technologies.[13] But media theory relates to notions of temporality as well: the various different approaches are not only about material objects but how we think of (media cultural) temporality—media time that is recurring and based on topoi; the idea of deep times that will be addressed and radicalized in this book; the focus on microtemporalities that define technical media culture on the level of machines and technological processes; the recursive methodology of time and the expansions of new film history into media archaeology in ways that offer new sets of questions and bootstrap a new sense of media historical time. All of these are examples of media archaeology as executed media philosophies of time, which offer an important subcurrent to thinking about materiality.

In Wolfgang Ernst's media archaeology and media archaeography, the focus is on microtemporalities and time-critical aspects of especially computational media. Ernst's focus on the agency of the machine as a temporal regime that forces a reconsideration of media historical macronarratives works in alternative ways. The methodological mode of media history based on writing has to encounter the specific *Eigenzeit*[14] of the machine: how technological culture and its specific instance in machines are not just *in* time but also fabricate time. The revolution speeds of hard drives, clock times of computers, network pings, and so forth are examples of the temporalities in which machines themselves are embedded and which they impose on the human social world. Machines don't just write narratives: they calculate. In Ernst's words, the difference between this sort of media archaeology and media history is this: "A computing culture, from a media-archaeological view, deals not with narrative memory but with calculating memory—counting rather than recounting, the archaeological versus the historical mode."[15]

But then there is the other pole of extremely long durations. As we engage with in more detail in chapter 2, Zielinski's adoption of the concept of deep time to media art discourse has offered a way to think and operate like a geologist of media art culture. For Zielinski, this concept has been a way to bypass the short-term "psychopathological" capitalist media discourse to understand that the interactions between media, art, and science have long roots. Indeed, Zielinski was after ways of modulating seeing and hearing before we historically rather recently thought to call them media.[16]

In stories of inventions by Empedocles, Athanasius Kircher, and many others, Zielinski uncovers the layered history that offers a way to engage with the past that is suddenly animated in front of our eyes and more alive than the repetitious advertising-based digital media innovations. Zielinski's deep time is a methodology that bypasses the narrative of definite origins and is interested in the quirky variations within media history. There is an archaeological urge to dig out the uncovered, the surprising, the anomalous, and in Zielinski's hands, this digging takes on the geological and paleontological concepts. But what if this notion based in geological time needs further radicalization? Indeed, what if we should think more along the lines of Manuel Delanda's proposition of thousands of years of nonlinear history and expand to a geology of media art history: thousands, millions of years of "history" of rocks, minerals, geophysics, atmospheric durations, earth times, which are the focus of past decades of intensive epistemological inquiry and practical exploitation as resources—things we dig from the (under)ground, the harnessing of the atmosphere and the sky for signal transmissions, the outer space for satellites and even space junk, as a new extended geological "layer" that circles our planet, like Trevor Paglen reminds us in his photographic performance/installation *The Last Pictures*, which takes place in the orbit around the Earth[17] (see Figure 1; see also chapter 5). If the emergence of industrialization since the nineteenth century and the molding of the environment with mines, smelting facilities, and sulfur dioxide from coal energy was addressed by poets who either in adoring ways or critically narrativized the dramatic aesthetic and ecological change, our contemporary technological arts do similar work, although often also engaging directly with the material world of geophysics in their practice.

This geophysical media world manifests itself in contemporary arts. This book covers examples of projects from Paglen to microresearchlab

Figure 1. Trevor Paglen, *Spacecraft in Perpetual Geosynchronous Orbit, 35,786 km above Equator,* 2010 (detail, part 2 of diptych). The artist was also interested in orbital technologies as an extension of the geologic in his earlier *Artifacts* series. Courtesy of the artist; Metro Pictures, New York; Altman Siegel, San Francisco; Galerie Thomas Zander, Cologne.

(Berlin), from technological fossil installations to the work of earthquake sonification. Indeed, sound is one way to characterize the deep time media aesthetics and its epistemological background. The earth roars and has a sound. It was something realized already in the 1950s when Emory D. Cooke released his *Out of This World* vinyl LP containing earthquake soundscapes[18] and then later by media artists as well as theorists such as Kittler. The following quotation from Kittler illustrates that with the technologies of time-axis manipulation, also the long duration slowness of geophysics—often too slow, or otherwise working in frequencies inaudible and invisible for human perception—becomes part of our aesthetic experience:

> Take an earthquake like the one in Kobe with thousands of casualties, seismographically record its inaudible slow vibrations, replay

the signals of the entire horrific day in ten seconds—and a sound will emerge. In the case of earthquakes that, like those in the Pacific, result from the clash of two tectonic plates, the sound will resemble a high-pitched slap, in the case of those that, like those in the Atlantic, are the result of the drifting apart of two continental plates, it will, conversely, sound like a soft sigh. Thus, the spectrum, that is, a frequency composition, gives the violent events timbre or quality: America becomes Asia. A short time ago I was privileged to hear the timbre of such quakes and I will not forget it for the rest of my life.[19]

Geophysics was already earlier adopted as part of the aesthetic practices and vocabularies of the avant-garde. With a meticulous documentation with a special emphasis on the electromagnetic, Douglas Kahn demonstrates how this connection of the earth and the avant-garde composers ranged from Alvin Lucier's experiments to Pauline Oliveros's *Sonospheres*. Electronic music studios became allies with nature—or at times also demonstrated the obsolescence before their time of even having the need for an electronic music studio: it's all existing already, in our brains, in nature.[20] An aesthetics that comes from the vibrations of nature is a theme running through certain Deleuzian-inspired accounts—foremost among them Elizabeth Grosz's[21]—but it is also a way to tap into the geophysical as an affordance for what we call "media." Indeed, no wonder that we can summon the ideas of such physical nature like the Schumann resonances—a concept that "ties low-frequency electromagnetic resonances of the entire earth"[22] with New Age discourse: the earth is a living entity with a specific frequency range. This obviously is one variation of the more scientific arguments for the Gaia hypothesis, which offers one important background for any conceptualization of the earth, of life, and which was preceded by the much older idea of terra mater: "From classical antiquity to the eighteenth century it was widely believed that stones and metals grow beneath the earth like organic matter."[23]

But still in our scientific worldview, the idea of organic and nonorganic life entwined resurfaces. In poetic words of paleontologists such as Richard Fortey—"life made the surface of the Earth what it is, even while it was Earth's tenant"[24]—we must underline the interaction of biological and physical determinants in molding the planet. We can also extend to a realization that pertains to cultural reality and media cultural practices and techniques. Such are earth's tenants, and yet effectively contributing to the way in which the planet is being seen, used, and modified. We need to be aware how carefully grafted concepts are able to catch the variety of practices that work across traditional disciplines and connect issues of nature and culture. The effect of the planet earth as seen from space since late 1960s space travel started demonstrates how visual media contribute to scientific concepts. The planetary vision—of a holistic organism as much as an object of military and scientific technologies of transportation and visualization—was part of why scientists from James Lovelock to Lynn Margulis contributed to the wider discussions of feedback mechanisms. But it also signaled a shift from James Hutton's *Theory of the Earth* (1788) to media of the earth, executed by means of technologies and media—of visualization techniques revealing the earthrise from the moon but also the galaxy from new perspectives. What's more, the trip to the moon included the Apollo lunar module bringing back geological samples,[25] a dream not altogether disappeared: the promise of mining helium-3 important for another energy revolution could be seen only as a natural continuation of the planetary politics of nation-states and corporations such as Google into interplanetary dimensions.[26] Such speculative accounts have even spoken of Russian moon colonies established by 2030 as part of the current geopolitical race for resources.[27]

The mediated vision turned back on the earth itself was instrumental to a whole new range of social and scientific agendas. Visions of the earth from the moon since the 1960s but also the technological gaze toward deep space with Hubble were never *just* about space and its interplanetary objects but as much about mapping such entities as part of the corporate and national interest. Geographical surveys benefited from the developed lenses and image processing of satellite-enabled remote sensing.[28] The perspective back to the globe has prompted the existence of corporate maps such as Google Earth and a massive military surveillance system too. And in ecological contexts, it enabled a way to capture the Gaia concept's force as a way to understand the various layers where the biological and the geophysical mix. In Bruce Clarke's words,

> from the co-evolution of living systems with the totality of their terrestrial environment, Gaia emerged as a meta-system of planetary self-regulation maintaining viable conditions of atmospheric

composition, temperature, oceanic pH and salinity, and of the global distribution of organic nutrients such as nitrogen, sulfur, and potassium. The biosphere performs like any living organism with a complement of homeostatic feedback mechanisms for maintaining geophysiological functions at healthy levels. Gaia theory is an indispensable framework for thinking about global climate change because it is only by recognizing Gaia's multi-systemic self-regulation that we can fully understand what we are now facing—the imminent failure of those regulating systems.[29]

From systems emblematic of the post–World War II cybernetic culture to earthquakes: what might be an unforgettable aesthetic experience for a German media theorist is an important epistemological framework for geophysical research. Such media and aesthetic methods prepare the earth to become knowable and intelligible. I want to underline the following argument: there is a double bind between the relations of media technologies and the earth conceived as a dynamic sphere of life that cuts across the organic and the nonorganic. It is also increasingly framed as standing reserve in the Heideggerian vocabulary: a resource for exploitation, and viewed as resource, *ordered* to present itself.[30] This is where dynamics of vibrant life meet with the corporate realities of technologized capitalism that is both a mode of exploitation and an epistemological framework.

Our relations with the earth are mediated through technologies and techniques of visualization, sonification, calculation, mapping, prediction, simulation, and so forth: it is through and in media that we grasp earth as an object for cognitive, practical, and affective relations. Geological resources used to be mapped through surveys and field observation, now through advanced remote sensing technologies.[31] They are in a way extensions of Leibniz's universal calculus, which offered one way to account for the order of the earth, including its accidents like earthquakes (such as the infamous 1755 in Lisbon). But as Eyal Weizmann suggests, this calculation of the earth is now less divine and more about the "increasingly complex bureaucracy of calculations that include sensors in the subsoil, terrain, air, and sea, all processed by algorithms and their attendant models."[32] Similarly, practices of meteorology are mediatic techniques that give a sense of the dynamics of the sky;[33] geology is an excavation into the earth and its secrets that affords a view not only to the now-moment that unfolds into a future potential of exploitation but also to the past buried under our feet. Depth becomes time. A tape recorder tracks the slow roar of the earthquake—like already in the 1950s practices of measurement, fascinating in regard to the effects of nuclear detonations as well as earthquake trembles, making them a media object: "Through the tape recorder, earthquakes and explosions became portable and repeatable."[34] In some ways, we can also say that this means the portability and repeatability of the Real: the geophysical that becomes registered through the ordering of media reality.[35]

And conversely, it is the earth that provides for media and enables it: the minerals, materials of(f) the ground, the affordances of its geophysical reality that make technical media happen. Besides the logic of ordering, we have the materiality of the uncontained, and the providing, that is constantly in tension with the operations of framing. This double bind—which I call the sphere of medianatures—is the topic of this book, with a special focus on geology and the geophysical.

Despite some references, I am not really opting for the Heideggerian route, however useful his comments on standing reserve and ordering might be. Instead, medianatures is a variation on Donna Haraway's famous and influential concept of naturecultures.[36] The term is for Haraway a way to understand the inherently interconnected nature of the two terms that in Cartesian ontology were separated across the field of the infamous binaries: nature versus culture, mind versus matter, and so on. In Haraway's terms, we are dealing with a more entangled set of practices in which it is impossible to decipher such spheres separately. Instead, naturecultures implies the ontological need to take into account the co-constituted relationships in which

> none of the partners pre-exist the relating, and the relating is never done once and for all. Historical specificity and contingent mutability rule all the way down, into nature and culture, into naturecultures.[37]

This topological conceptualization that remains sensitive to "historical specificity" is an important way to talk about the related notions of "material-semiotic" and "material-discursive" spheres as underlined in recent new materialism.[38] Medianatures is meant to incorporate a similar drive but with a specific emphasis on (technical) media culture. It is a concept that crystallizes the "double bind" of media and nature as co-constituting spheres, where the ties are intensively connected in material nonhuman realities as much as in relations of power, economy, and work. Indeed, it is a regime constituted as much by the work of micro-organisms, chemical components, minerals, and metals as by the work of underpaid laborers in mines or in high-tech entertainment device component production factories, or people in Pakistan and China sacrificing their health for scraps of leftover electronics. Medianatures is a useful concept only when it scales down to the specific instances of material-discursive events.

Ties and relations of medianature are often revealed in some of the extreme contexts of exploitation and environmental damage. Electronic waste, resource depletion, and globally unevenly distributed relations of labor are such instances where art vocabularies turn to medianatures. This is a refashioning of the underground from avant-garde to geology, geophysics, and political economy. To use Sean Cubitt's words referring to planned obsolescence: "the digital realm is an avant-garde to the extent that it is driven by perpetual innovation and perpetual destruction."[39]

The underground is another important topographical site for geology of media (arts). The underground is the place of hell—itself defined in Western mythology by its chemistry: the smell of sulfur, and the killing poisons of carbon dioxide, which is why since Virgil's *Aeneid* the Underworld is marked by death to any animal approaching it.[40] The underground is at the crux of technological imaginary of modernity—a place of technological futures since the nineteenth century as well as the artistic avant-garde outside the mainstream.[41] Going underground happens in spy stories as well as in postapocalyptic scenarios, whether earlier ones such as Gabriel Tarde's *The Underground Man* (1904/1905)[42] or post–World War II nuclear anxiety. Lewis Mumford sees mining and the underground as ideal cases to understand modern technology: he names this turn toward nonorganic technological nature as paleotechnics. It starts so in the foundational scenes of modern capitalism, where mining is inherently linked to projects demanding extensive amounts of capital, as well as itself enabling the further buildup of significant technological industries. Scenes of burrowing down to the earth and digging penetrate now also the urban sphere in constant upheaval, a constant rebuilding and opening of depths. Rosalind Williams points this out: "Between the late 1700s and early 1900s, the ground of Britain and Europe was dug up to lay the foundations of a new society. Subterranean images became familiar sights during that period: workers sinking picks into the soil, city streets slashed down the middle, whole industrial regions turned into minelike terrains."[43] A new infrastructural world was born, one that recircuits as part of the contemporary planetary moment, which weaves together labor and the earth.

For Mumford, paleotechnics refers specifically to the age of coal mining and its social and aesthetic consequences preceding the neotechnic age of electricity characterized by much lower energy transmission costs and a different scientific setup of society. However, one can say that in a different way, the paleotechnic persists from the eighteenth and nineteenth centuries into the twenty-first. New forms of energy distribution, synthetic materials with the advancement of chemistry, as well as the new methods in metallurgy that Mumford sees as a shift from the paleotechnic to the neotechnic gradually since the late nineteenth century and gradually during twentieth century[44] are still, I argue, grounded in the wider mobilization of the materiality of the earth as part of industrialization, technology, and also media technological culture.

As a perspective of the modern variations of the underworld as a place of hard work, approach it through Mika Rottenberg's video piece *Squeeze*, featured at the Istanbul Biennial 2013. The video is a single-screen narrative that unfolds into a spatial underground machine of sorts in which female workers of different ethnicities participate without direct relation or knowledge of each other. As a classic depiction of a capitalist mode of production and alienation, Rottenberg's video is effective. But it also engages with the materialities and spatialities in such a way to merit special attention: the work of lettuce pickers on the field leads through the lettuce rolls to an underground factory, where different departments, work practices, and surreal procedures (a tongue sticking out of the wall, just to be sprayed with water in regular intervals to keep it wet) combine into a machine articulating heterogeneous elements of an oddly functioning assemblage. The machine is itself a processing of materiality just to produce it as a piece of waste in the end, consisting of blush, rubber, and lettuce. Here the underground becomes a spatial arrangement to highlight the separated sphere of production that underlies our feet and is detached from our direct perception but maintaining the everyday practices. The underground is the place of repetitious, exploitative, and even absurd work of arrangements and rearrangements of partial objects without a view of the big picture. Labor alienation is expressed in terms of aesthetics of odd parallel realities. It is the sphere of material processing, and both of the earth and the human labor as standing reserve. It is a gendered zone as well, and Rottenberg's work is an important guide and an analogy to what I pursue in *A Geology of Media*: starting the excavations of contemporary materiality of media arts from beneath your feet, from the Underworld.

Rottenberg's video constitutes a recap of something that was expressed in *Punch* magazine in 1843 in a satirical image "Capital and Labour," which shows what orchestrates the modern life: the hidden underground machinery of workers (Figure 2). It expresses a link between the imaginary of the underground in the nineteenth century and the more recent versions of aesthetics of labor and the down under. The visible reality is sustained by complex and absurd arrangements of work and infrastructure that is itself an arrangement of human and technological components. However, the underground of industrialization and capitalism rests as part of the geology of the earth.

The Anthrobscene

The Anthropocene is one of the leading concepts that brought a geological awareness to climate change discussions of the past years and decades. Suggested by the Nobel Prize–winning chemist Paul J. Crutzen more than ten years ago[45] and preceded more informally by Eugene Stoermer in the 1980s, the term is a sort of placeholder for the contemporary moment that stretches from the 1700s or the 1800s to the current time. It performs this cartography from a geological perspective, which argues for a sort of a holistic but analytical view to the changes in our life world. Following the Holocene, the accepted term for the geological period of the past ten thousand to twelve thousand years, the Anthropocene refers to the massive changes human practices, technologies, and existence

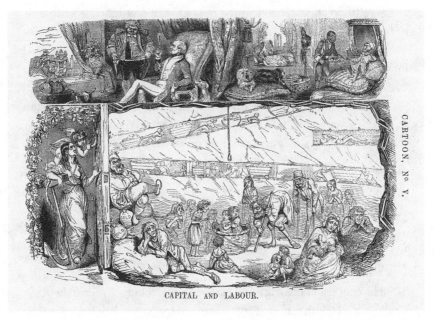

CARTOON, Nº V.

CAPITAL AND LABOUR.

Figure 2. "Capital and Labour, Cartoon, No. V." A satirical image from 1843 in *Punch* (volume 5) underlines the ontology of labor as one of underground: capitalism works in the depths to find an infrastructural level that sustains the pleasant consumerized life above the ground and yet stays invisible. Reprinted with permission of *Punch* magazine.

have brought across the ecological board. The concept, which is not scientifically universally accepted,[46] takes aboard the cross-species and ecological ties human activity has been developing: the concept speaks to the relations with other animals—for instance, domestication of the dog—and the various techniques of living, primarily agriculture and fire, which have had massive influence over thousands of years. But the Anthropocene—or the *Anthrobscene*, to use a provocative combination of the term with the addition of a qualifying "obscene"[47]—starts to crystallize as a systematic relation to the carboniferous: the layers of photosynthesis that gradually were being used for heating and then as energy sources for manufacture in the form of fossil fuels. In China, the use of coal and the emergence of significant coal mines go back to the Song Dynasty (960–1279), only later followed up by key centers such as in England.[48] More significantly, the move from local and regional use of such resources emerges with industrialization and the triangulation of fossil fuels as energy source, technology, and wealth creation related to the new capitalist order. The economic order was from its start an energetic one, reliant on the slowly accumulated resources of coal, oil, and gas. Fossil fuels such as oil were essential for the smoother and quicker planetary movement of energy compared to coal. In this sense, globalization, too, as a form of transported planetarization, has been based on logistics of energy.[49] In short, one could claim that capitalism had its necessary (but not sufficient) conditions in a new relation with deep times and chemical processes of photosynthesis:

> Hitherto humankind had relied on energy captured from ongoing flows in the form of wind, water, plants, and animals, and from the 100- or 200-year stocks held in trees. Fossil fuel use offered access to carbon stored from millions of years of photosynthesis: a massive energy subsidy from the deep past to modern society, upon which a great deal of our modern wealth depends.[50]

The concept of the Anthropocene features technology from the start: Crutzen starts with James Watt's steam engine as one key feature of the Anthropocene, illustrating how it is a concept where geophysics ties in with cultural techniques. What's more is the link of escalating proportions that one can follow up with technology and energy as some of the driving forces of geological proportions. This actually quickly cascades into realization of the economic and social ties but also toward the interlinks between energy, technology, and chemistry. Indeed, we should not neglect the list of chemical issues that the notion of the Anthropocene marches onto the stage, from Crutzen's first text moving swiftly from Watt to issues of methane, carbon dioxide, sulfur dioxide, nitrogen, nitric oxide, and more.[51] Indeed, the mythological smell of Sulfur of Hell is replaced by a twentieth- and twenty-first-century version of acid rain, consisting of sulfur dioxide that results, among other processes (including volcanic eruptions), from smelting of metal ores and the use of fossil fuel.[52]

I am fascinated with the possibilities of unfolding media and technology through chemistry: an elemental "periodic table" approach to modern scientific materiality. It is clearly one of the issues that any exposition of the relations of the Anthropocene and (media) technologies should take into account. This is a theme crystallized by Steffen, Crutzen, and McNeill:

Fossil fuels and their associated technologies—steam engines, internal combustion engines—made many new activities possible and old ones more efficient. For example, with abundant energy it proved possible to synthesize ammonia from atmospheric nitrogen, in effect to make fertilizer out of air, a process pioneered by the German chemist Fritz Haber early in the twentieth century. The Haber-Bosch synthesis, as it would become known (Carl Bosch was an industrialist)[,] revolutionized agriculture and sharply increased crop yields all over the world, which, together with vastly improved medical provisions, made possible the surge in human population growth.[53]

The metal, chemical, and mineral agents of history become pushed from mere contextual insights to agents of a different sort of genealogy. Besides being observable through the scientific eye, and the apparatus of measurement, which gives verifiability to the analyses in geology, ecology, and the environmental sciences, such aspects have implications for how we approach technology in the humanities. In history-disciplines, the methodological and thematic expansion of topics has already included nonhuman issues through environmental concerns, primarily William McNeill's work, as well as John McNeill's.[54] Environmental themes become a way to articulate a global history that offers a complementary narrative to globalization, as told through the media technological and capitalist expansion of trade, travel, and communication routes over the past centuries, accelerating the past decades. And it offers a way to account for the scientific definition of media in the environmental disciplines: this completely different understanding of media of land, air, and water is, however, a necessary aspect of our more arts and humanities way of understanding media technologies, as this book demonstrates.

In more theoretical terms, I already mentioned the work of Delanda as a way of looking at the assemblages of nonhuman kind that work through Deleuze and Guattari's geological arguments. More recently, Dipesh Chakrabarty has influentially argued for a renewed and shared agenda between natural history and the more human-centered histories (which we could say include cultural history and media history). In Chakrabarty's words, it is crucial that we interrogate the horizon of the Anthropocene as having effects on our historical sense of being too.

This humanities approach is now also recognizing the importance of biological and geological contributions as part of the social collective. This includes the realization that humans are also biological and geological agents[55] but also that, to understand the wider patterns of the social, we need to resist the old-fashioned methodological dualisms haunting disciplinary thinking of the past. But Chakrabarty's elegant and important text includes a further twist that brings such insights into proximity with postcolonial critiques of globalization as well as analysis of the political economy of capitalism. In short, we need to be able to find concepts that help the nonhuman elements contributing to capitalism to become more visible, grasped, and understood—as part of surplus creation as well as the related practices of exploitation. This historical mapping of the environmental is also a mapping of the historical features of capitalism as a social and technological planetary arrangement.

This critical mapping is a matter of vocabularies we use (the insufficient manner of using the term *species* to refer to the human impact on the earth system) and the necessity for a specification of the scientific concepts too:

> At the same time, the story of capital, the contingent history of our falling into the Anthropocene, cannot be denied by recourse to the idea of species, for the Anthropocene would not have been possible, even as a theory, without the history of industrialization.[56]

The stories we tell imply more than just their words; they tell stories of media and mediation, of materiality and the earth. The stories are themselves of a scale of geological durations that are at first too slow to comprehend. This demands an understanding of a story that is radically different from the usual meaning of storytelling with which we usually engage in the humanities. This story is more likely to contain fewer words and more a-signifying semiotic matter[57] that impose a presence especially in the current era of crisis to which we refer as the climate change.

Concepts in crisis seek to make sense of change while signposting the necessity for different vocabularies.[58] Hence use of surprising perspectives as well as provocations is needed, as is the work of concepts that travel across disciplines.[59] One implicit concept behind this book is

Deleuze and Guattari's pre-Anthropocene notion of "geology of morals." It is part of the set of geophilosophy that the French duo mobilized as a way to offer nonlinguistic concepts for cultural reality entangled with other regimes of the material. More accurately, such sets offered ways to bypass the linguistic accounts of making sense of cultural reality with different concepts, including the abstract machine and the geologically tuned ones. Notions of strata, sedimentations, double articulations, and an alternative to the signifier-signified-model are introduced as a way for a postanthropocentric theory.[60] The geological thought that one finds in *A Thousand Plateaus* and later in *What Is Philosophy?* is a way of accounting for the material production of meanings in relation to their a-signifying parts: a sort of assemblage theory of material practices. Deleuze and Guattari's philosophy maps the geology of thought, which moves from the geophilosophical territories in which thinking happens in relation to the grounds, undergrounds, and territories where the immaterial events of thinking and affect are always tied to stratified assemblages.[61] "Thinking is neither a line drawn between subject and object nor a revolving of one around the other. Rather, thinking takes place in the relationship of territory and the earth."[62] Thinking is here stretched as more of a movement of multiplicities that pertains to territories rather than as a cognitive faculty restricted to already formed human subjects. This notion of geophilosophy attaches thinking to its conditions of existence, which are, however, always immanent to the event of thought itself.

Such geologically oriented ways of understanding thinking resonate with the wider thrust of "ecosophy" one finds in Guattari's writing and which has been mobilized in the recent media ecology discussions.[63] The notion of geology and (un)grounds has triggered important recent philosophical discussions from Deleuze and Guattari to the nineteenth-century thought born in the midst of emerging mining cultures, for instance, F. W. J. Schelling or the "chemical thought" of Friedrich Schlegel.[64] The early nineteenth century lived in an enthusiasm for the mine, mining, and the underground—both poetically across England and Germany and in political economy of mining.[65]

In philosophical terms, the geological becomes a way to interrogate in a material and non-human-centered way the constitutive folding of insides and outsides and the temporal regimes involved in (media) culture.[66] What is interesting is how, across the various debates, in all their differences, what is being carved out is, besides a geological-ontology (geontology?), also something that can be rolled out as a methodology. For instance, in Iain Hamilton Grant's Schelling-focused writings, it is spelled out in a manner that relates it to a material stratification of genealogy turning geology:

> Thus the earth is not an object containing its ground within itself, like the preformationists' animal series; but rather a series or process of grounding with respect to its consequents. If geology, or the "mining process," opens onto an ungroundedness at the core of any object, this is precisely because there is no "primal layer of the world," no "ultimate substrate" or substance on which everything ultimately rests. The lines of serial dependency, stratum upon stratum, that geology uncovers do not rest on anything at all, but are the records of *actions* antecedent in the production of consequents.[67]

The seemingly stable groundedness of the earth reveals through the modern practices of mining (and one should not neglect their relation to the hypercapitalist exploitation of the earth itself on a massive technological level) another sort of an ontology that resonates with the logic of capitalism as articulated by Deleuze and Guattari: the shifting ungrounds that they call the axiomatics of capitalism, which work through a constant deterritorialization of established territories, like a massive geoengineering project burrowing through formed lands, territorializing them in novel ways. No wonder that the geological itself turns out to be more defined by its holes, mines, and the lack of one final determining stratum; instead, what one finds are the various "records of actions," which, in the case of this book, are translated as the epistemological and technological workings on/with the geophysical.[68]

The metallurgical is another geocentric concept Deleuze and Guattari mobilized as a form of "minor science" of new materialism that teases out the potentialities in matter. It is offered as a counterexample to the hylomorphic models where matter is expected to be inert and the form animating it immaterial. Instead, notions of vital materialism (Bennett), metallic affects (Delanda), and in general new materialism all assume a different sort of material assemblage.[69] The metallurgical refers to an ambulant, nomad science that contrasts with the form-seeking Royal Science that extracts constants and categories from its observations. The metallurgist is a figure of someone who *"follows* the flow of matter"[70] and invests in giving a reality to the variations and potentials in the object. Metal is the privileged example and is inspiring to such vital materialists as Bennett because of its seemingly stable solidity, which, however, is in metallurgist perspective and practice revealed as teeming with material potentials that can be teased out in different constellations, temperatures, and conditions; this applies to the atomic level, where a metallurgist has a practical "know-how" relation to metal that applies to the wider role metals play in cultural assemblages as nonhuman agents.[71] Hence, to follow Bennett's adaptation of Deleuze and Guattari's ethological idea about bodies defined by their unfolding potential, where "ethology" refers to experimental relationality, "the desire of the craftsperson to see what a metal can do, rather than the desire of the scientist to know what a metal is, enabled the former to discern a life in metal and thus, eventually, to collaborate more productively with it."[72]

This stance should not be confused with a practice–theory division. Indeed, I want to insist that there is a metallurgical way of conducting theoretical work: ambulant flows, transversal connections, and teasing out the materiality of matter in new places, in new assemblages of cultural life in contemporary technological media.

The cartography of geocentric cultural theory is definitely not only about philosophical references. From the James Hutton of *The Theory of the Earth* to philosophy (Hegel, Schelling, and contemporary speculative realist discussions involving Grant, Graham Harman, and Steven Shaviro), we can also move toward the media geological contexts, which this book tackles. Despite references to the ongoing debates in theory, this book does not attempt to create a primarily philosophical argument; more accurately, it argues the case for a geology of media that tries to pin down the often rather broad notion of "nonhuman" agency to some case studies concerning the assemblages in which the grounds of media are ungrounded through the actual geologies of mining, materiality, and the ecosophic quest becoming also geosophic.

Indeed, the earth of media finds itself displaced from geography to geophysics. This is why Pynchon's latest book, *The Bleeding Edge* (2013), refers to the future media landscapes of permafrost: the natural cooling systems of northern climates (or by rivers in abandoned paper mill factories acting as remnants of the industrial era serving as corporate housing for the server farms) are perfect for the servers and data storage that release heat. Data processing needs energy, which releases heat, of course. Data demand their ecology, one that is not merely a metaphorical technoecology but demonstrates dependence on the climate, the ground, and the energies circulating in the environment. Data feeds of the environment both through geology and the energy-demand. What's more, it is housed in carefully managed ecologies. It's like the natural elements of air, water, fire (and cooling), and earth are mobilized as part of the environmental aspects of data. Data mining is not only about the metaphorical big data repositories of social media.

In a great summarizing phrase in Andrew Blum's book *Tubes*, a Facebook data center manager speaks to this elemental part of data: "This has nothing to do with clouds. It has everything to do with being cold."[73] The manager summons the same world as a character in Pynchon's novel. Cool, cold data are not just a linguistic or visual metaphor, despite that elegant modernism that still lives inside the architectures of data—at least in the images Google released of its data server factories. Coolness is not a media theoretical attitude in this context but a media management issue that ties the earth to the escape velocity of data.

Data need air. "Cool outside air is let into the building through adjustable louvers near the roof; deionized water is sprayed into it; and fans push the conditioned air down onto the data center floor,"[74] explains Blum. Coolness of cyberpunk transforms from a rhetorical trope to the coolness of the building's climate control. Fans surround the terabytes of data. The manager of the data center continues about the building: "The air hits this concrete floor and roils left and right. This whole building is like the Mississippi River. There's a huge amount of air coming in, but moving really slowly."[75] It's important to notice the persistence of issues of ecology from air to the soil as well as noncognitive work: that we still talk of factories and rather physical processes having to do with our hardware and how we manage and work with data at their material level. Blum: "The cloud is a building. It works like a factory. Bits come in, they get massaged and put together in the right way and sent out."[76]

Such journalistic narratives as Blum's are useful in highlighting the alternative rhetoric to the cyberpunk immateriality, which has persisted since the 1980s up until the present day. Now a geopolitical turn is happening that takes into account that data have a material and legal territory and that we can speak of geophysics of information. This is another sort of a context that justifies the use of the hybrid expression "geology of media." This differs from the literary genre of steampunk that follows a cyberpunk aesthetics of the 1980s and 1990s and offers a literal steampunk for the twenty-first century: the steam of the data center somewhere up north, preferably on the permafrost, cooling down the heat of data crunching. The Anthrobscene logic: the North affords the Cool, the South provides the Cheap (labor).

The Chapters

The chapters of this book are strata themselves. They stratify and condense themes that intertwine and build on each other as dynamic apparatuses mobilizing different sorts of material: historical sources, theory, and, importantly, references to contemporary media art projects and practices.

One could call this approach a media history of matter: the different components, minerals, metals, chemicals, and other things involved in media are considered as essential to media history and archaeology. Media technologies can be understood as a long story of experimenting with different materials—from glass plates to chemicals, from selenium to silicon, from coltan to rare earth minerals, from dilute sulfuric acid to shellac silk, different crystals in telegraphic receivers, and gutta-percha for insulation in earlier transatlantic wired communication. Also Mumford notes this in his analysis of the emergence of modern materiality of technology: technological phases, or "epistemes" as Foucault might have it, are themselves functions of the ways in which materials and energy are channeled, appropriated, and exploited:

Just as one associates the wind and water power of the eotechnic economy with the use of wood and glass, and the coal of the paleotechnic period with iron, so does electricity bring into wide industrial use its own specific materials: in particular, the new alloys,

the rare earths, and the lighter materials. At the same time, it creates a new series of synthetic compounds that supplement paper,
glass and wood: celluloid, vulcanite, Bakelite and the synthetic res-
ins, with special properties of unbreakability, electrical resistance,
imperviousness to acids, or elasticity.[77]

What for Mumford marks the passage from paleotechnics to neo-
technics is for my purposes in *A Geology of Media* altogether a passage
of different ways of mobilizing the earth into and as media. The march of
aluminum came with its own material affordances of lightness, feeding
into new forms of speed and transport. And rare earth minerals are not
a discovery only of the digital media age: tantalum, tungsten, thorium,
cerium, iridium, manganese, and chromium are among the materials
that Mumford sees as essential to understanding the twentieth-century
technological culture.[78] We can add that it is this list that also works as
true "transmedia": useful elements from gadgets and systems of electricity to mechanical technology to digital media, essential in different ways.

Besides the materials of production, media history is a story of
relations between the organic and nonorganic and the waste products
emerging from the use and misuse of materials. Media history participates in stories of global expansion through colonialism and the rush for
resources: the invaluable materials from minerals to oil and other energy
sources such as uranium—a global mapping of territories increasingly
exhausted.[79] Besides historical examples, we are living a new geopolitical
rush now: military, corporate, and scientific operations hand in hand
in the Arctic regions, dangerous areas of Africa, Afghanistan, and, for
instance, the deep seas, looking for deeper hidden resources of petroleum
and critical materials from metals to uranium.[80] Besides materials and
waste, media deal and function through energy. The transistor-based
information technology culture would not be thinkable without the various meticulous insights into the material characteristics and differences
between germanium and silicon, not only in their "pure" state but mixed
with just the right dose of impurities. Currently in the long networks of
media operations—and media in operation—energy is an essential part of
the circuit where the geopolitical race for resources meets the geophysical
needs of advanced technologies.[81] This means shifting our focus with the

help of media arts and design projects to the other stuff of media materialism: the metals, minerals, and chemicals in which we can develop the aforementioned ecosophical and geosophical perspective.

This book aims to take up these issues in five main chapters. This chapter acted as a theoretical introduction to the context and the issues. In the next chapter, I focus on deep times. The concept has already been effectively used by Siegfried Zielinski in his take on the paleontology and geology of media arts, but my point is to remind of the need for an *alternative* deep time. In this account, we take deep times more literally and look at geology of media in and through the mines and (un)grounds.

The third chapter follows suit and continues developing specific aesthetic concepts for the geophysical media world. It picks up on the idea of psychogeophysics—a version of the Situationist psychogeography—and offers a radical aesthetics of the media technological world that maps the relations between subjectivity, capitalism, and the earth in long-term durations and geophysical assemblages. In the chapter, we focus on projects by the Berlin and London–placed microresearchlab, Martin Howse's earthcomputing, and the *Crystal World* project by Kemp, Jordan, and Howse: speculative media arts that addresses in assays and technological assemblages the substrate as part of our media systems.

Running through the book is the aim to talk about the variety of materialisms and temporalities of media. In the fourth chapter, I address these themes through a nonhuman particle: dust. Dust is carried forward as a rhetorical device too, mobilizing the entangled materialities of global labor and residue materialism. Dust is found as residue of polished iPads as well as attached to workers' lungs from coal mines to contemporary factories of information technology. The art projects by Yokokoji–Harwood (YoHa; from the United Kingdom) are good examples of addressing this notion of residue, from coal to aluminum. They reveal an alternative side to the discourse of cognitive capitalism: the world of hardwork and hardware that persists as a defining factor of digital media culture.

Chapter 5 picks up on (media) fossils. The paleontological insight to the history of the planet might put special interest on fossils, but similarly it is a figure that one finds resurfacing in Walter Benjamin's analysis of advanced capitalism as well as in contemporary projects such as Grégory Chatonsky's art and Trevor Paglen's extension of the geophysical sphere of technological fossils to the dead media orbit of satellites circulating the earth. Issues of deep space become part of the geological agenda and expanded into thoughts about the temporality of the Anthropocene.

In addition to the main chapters, and after the meditations offered in the afterword, we decided to add an appendix because of its centrality to all the issues addressed in the book. "Zombie Media: Circuit Bending Media Archaeology into an Art Method" is a text cowritten with the artist–theorist Garnet Hertz. It stems from our shared theoretical interests in media archaeology and electronic waste as well as circuit bending and hardware hacking as practice-based design interventions into contemporary technological culture.

Throughout the book, I use art projects not merely as ways to illustrate the main thesis but also for the converse: many of the things and arguments in this book have been first mapped by artistic methods. I refer to projects such as iMine (by Baruch Gottlieb, Horacio González Diéguez, and Cocomoya); the microresearchlab group; Trevor Paglen's visual art, Katie Paterson; YoHa's work on aluminum and coal; various hardware-hacking and circuit-bending practitioners, including Garnet Hertz but also, for instance, Benjamin Gaulon's Recyclism; Grégory Chatonsky's art installations, Jonathan Kemp's and Ryan Jordan's work, Jamie Allen's, and David Gauthier's geosurveys of media infrastructures; and many more. It was initially through many of these projects that I gained insight into and inspiration for many particular aspects of the book. The artistic projects were able to demonstrate the issues of this new materialism of geophysical kind: a different sort of materiality and an alternative digital media arts culture, irreducible to the enthusiasm for software.

2

AN ALTERNATIVE DEEP TIME OF THE MEDIA

They penetrated to the bowels of earth and dug up wealth, bad cause of all our ills.

—OVID, *METAMORPHOSES*

The Submerged Cloud

The debates about the Anthropocene and electronic waste underline a necessity to engage with the geophysical stakes of media cultural infrastructure. Much of recent years' focus has been on the cloud and its promise of disappearance of hardware and the immaterial embeddedness in data. However, the cloud brings with it a demand to develop new political vocabularies that address the double bind of technical materiality and conceptual immateriality, as Seb Franklin argues.[1] The issue of the cloud extends to software cultures and their disappearance into a branch of the service industries;[2] it brandishes the importance of the hardware in new ways but seems to be limited to being the vessel of the service in attractive mobile forms, such as the investment in different sorts of tablets and smartphones evinces; it attracts the circulation of discourses of movement and immateriality, of the imaginary and dreams that fulfill the necessary gaps in the actual user experience when encountering a lack of wireless signal or some other physical disturbance. It was in a very different way that the geopolitical aspects of the physical Internet were highlighted in 2013. In the wake of revelations of NSA's spy program PRISM, the world saw images of lonely data server farms and other institutions of the geopolitical surveillance agencies—the mute monolith structures, also pictured recently in *Time* magazine (December 23, 2013) by Trevor Paglen.

But after Edward Snowden's whistle-blowing, what also surfaced was the case of seemingly random places such as Brazil: why was Brazil so much on the map of the surveillance operations of the American agency? What was so interesting about Brazil? The reason was quickly exposed: it was about the submarine cables. The paranoid surveillance mechanisms of the post-9/11 world of U.S. terror are also highlighting the extensive infrastructural arrangements of networks on the physical level. One of the main lines, Atlantis-2, connects South America to Europe and Africa,[3] allowing for a crucial interruption node to exist when *data arrive ashore*, to put it poetically. We need to look at the underground as well as at submerged realities, which are not that much different from the laying of the Atlantic cables in the mid-nineteenth century. Back then, the submerged media were escorted by an enthusiasm of interconnectedness. Now it is a secret enthusiasm for interruptedness. The grounds, ungrounds, and undergrounds of media infrastructures condition what is visible and what is invisible. Under the ground, one finds the subterranean infrastructures of modernity: telecommunications cables as much as sewage systems, metro trains, and electricity. For instance, the Parisian underground galleries became even a tourist attraction.[4] Nineteenth-century urbanization meant a move underground, whereas we seem to live a twenty-first-century move to the heavens. Yet clouds reach back to the land and sea territories and the geopolitical.[5] The earth is part of media both as a resource and as transmission. The earth conducts, also literally, forming a special part of the media and sound artistic circuitry.[6] It is the contested political earth that extends to being part of military "infrastructure": the earth hides political stakes and can be formed as part of military strategy and maneuvers.

The underground is addressed in this chapter through an investigation of deep time. Besides a geological concept, it has been adopted in media arts discussions by the German media (an)archaeologist and variantologist Siegfried Zielinski. However, in the context of the materiality of media, we need to ask, do we need more strongly to underline the geophysical aspects of this geology of media and deep time? Do we need to go underground, submerge, and dig out cables submarine and subterranean to understand further hidden depths of materiality of media?

And the Earth Screamed, Alive

What if your guide to the world of media would not be the usual suspect—an entrepreneur or evangelista from Silicon Valley or a management school scholar aspiring to catch up with the smooth crowd-sourced clouding of the network sphere? What if your guide would be Professor Challenger, the Arthur Conan Doyle character from the 1928 short story "When the World Screamed"? The story appeared in *Liberty* magazine and offered an odd insight into a mad scientist's world, with a hint of what we would nowadays call "speculative realism." Professor Challenger, whose dubious and slightly mad reputation preceded him, offered an insight into what later philosophers such as the French writing duo Gilles Deleuze and Félix Guattari happily picked up on: that the earth is alive and its crust is tingling with life. But the idea of the living earth has a long cultural history too: from antiquity, it persists as the idea of terra mater and, in the emerging mining cultures of the eighteenth and nineteenth centuries, becomes embedded as part of romantic philosophy; later, in the twentieth century, the emergence of Gaia theories brings a different connotation to the holistic life of the planet.

The narrative of geology and strata starts with a letter: an undated letter addressed to Mr. Peerless Jones, an expert in artesian drilling. The letter is a request for assistance. The nature of what is required is not specified, but the reputation of the mad scientist, the slightly volatile personality of Professor Challenger, promises that it would not be a normal operation. Escorted with suspicion and curiosity, it soon becomes evident that Mr. Jones's drilling expertise is needed. In Sussex, United Kingdom, at Hengist Down, Professor Challenger is engaged in a rather secret drilling operation, although it remains for a longer period unclear for what sort of a job the special drills are needed. Even the sort of material to be penetrated reveals only later to be different from what is usually expected when we speak of mining operations: not so much chalk or clay or the usual geological strata but more of a jellylike substance.

The professor had for a longer time drilled deeper and deeper through the earth's crust until he had finally ended up so deep so as to find a layer that pulsates like a living animal. He needed help and contacted Jones for the project that gradually had shifted from geology to something else. The earth is alive, and that this vitality can be proved with experimental means was actually the true objective of Challenger's mission. Instead of drilling and mining for petroleum, coal, copper, iron ore, and other valuables for which men usually dig holes in the ground, Challenger's mission is driven by a desire to prove a new speculative position that concerns the living depths of the earth: beyond the strata of "sallow lower chalk, the coffee-coloured Hastings beds, the lighter Ashburnham beds, the dark carboniferous clays, and . . . gleaning in the electric light, band after band of jet-black, sparkling coal alternative with the rings of clay,"[7] one finds the layers, which did not adhere to the classical geological theories of Hutton or Lyell. It seemed suddenly as if undeniable that even nonorganic matter is alive: "The throbs were not direct, but gave the impression of a gentle ripple or rhythm, which ran across the surface,"[8] Mr. Jones describes the deep surface they found. "The surface was not entirely homogenous but beneath it, seen as through ground glass, there were dim whitish patches or vacuoles, which varied constantly in shape and size."[9] The whole layers, the core and the strata, throbbed, pulsated, and animated. It should not even be necessary to go to similar lengths as Professor Challenger does, in one of the most bizarre rapelike scenes in literature, when he penetrates that jellyesque layer just to make the earth scream. This scientific sadism echoes in the ears of the audience and much further. It is the sound of "a thousand of sirens in one, paralyzing all the great multitude with its fierce insistence, and floating away through the still summer air until it went echoing along the whole South Coast and even reach our French neighbors across the Channel."[10] All this was observed and witnessed by an audience called by the professor—peers and interested international crowd, by invitation only.

The interest for "the bowels of the earth"[11] was not restricted to the writing of fiction and the vibrant language of Conan Doyle returning merely to the scientific discourse of geophysics. Professor Challenger was predated by nineteenth-century fiction characters, like Heinrich in Novalis's Heinrich von Ofterdingen (1800/1802) asking, "Is it possible that beneath our feet a world of its own is stirring in a great life?"[12] The poetic thrust toward the living, pulsating earth opened it up: for coal, for minerals, for precious material. Jules Verne's Les Indes Noires (1887; The Black Indies) told the story of an exhausted coal mine where, however, a new discovery is made, leading into a whole underground Coal Town.[13] Theories of the Hollow Earth might not have persisted except in popular fiction, but the idea of the underground artificial infinity—now as a seemingly infinite resource too—gained ground.[14]

The earth had become a resource. Metals and minerals were tightly linked to the emergence of modern engineering, science, and technical media. For instance, copper has been a crucial material feature of technical media culture since the nineteenth century. A lot of the early copper mines were, however, exhausted by the start of the twentieth century, leading into new demands both in terms of international reach and depth: new drills were needed for deeper mining, which was necessary to provide the materials for an increasing international need and systematic—and yet environmentally wasteful—use in wires and network culture. In addition, the increasing demand and international reach resulted in the cartelization

Figure 3. The underground became both a poetic and an engineered realm of technology, from romanticism to twentieth-century industrialization. The mines never disappeared but persist as effective geological scars even in advanced technological culture. Bingham Canyon copper mine in Utah, Rio Tinto, Kennecott Utah Copper Corp. Photograph by Spencer Musik.

of the copper business from mining to smelting.[15] Indeed, besides such contemporary contexts of mining where Challenger's madness starts to make sense, one is tempted to think of an imaginary of horrors of the underground from Lovecraft to Fritz Leiber. Leiber preempts a much more recent writer of the biopolitics of petroleum, Reza Negarestani, both highlighting the same theme: petroleum is a living subterranean life-form.[16] One should neither ignore the earth screams caused by hydraulic fracturing—fracking that, besides the promise that it might change the geopolitical balance of energy production, also points toward what is often neglected in the discourse of geopolitics, that is, *geos*, the earth, the soil, and the crust. By pumping pressurized water and chemicals underground, the procedure forces gas out from between rocks, forcing the earth to become an extended resource. Rocks fracture, benzene and formaldehyde creep in, and the planet is primed to such a condition to expose itself. Fracking is, in the words of Brett Neilson, perfectly tuned to the capitalist hyperbole of expansion beyond limits: "Whether it derives from the natural commons of earth, fire, air, and water or the networked commons of human cooperation, fracking creates an excess that can be tapped."[17]

Perhaps Professor Challenger's current versions are not found only in fiction either. Besides mining operations, such scientific missions as the Kola superdeep borehole in the ex–Soviet Union was such a hyperbolically sounding attempt that stayed true to the Challenger spirit. It held the depth record for a long while, at 12,262 meters. Scientists found in the early 1980s, after years of patiently, slowly drilling through the crust, an odd reality of geophysical phenomena, chemical surprises such as boiling hydrogen gas, and the sheer existence of water much deeper than expected in the rock minerals.[18]

Inside the earth one finds an odd chemical, rocky, and metallic reality, which feeds into metal metaphysics and digital devices. Besides the speculative stance, one can revert back to empirical material too. In short, of direct relevance to our current media technological situation is the reminder that according to year 2008 statistics, media materiality is very metallic: "36 percent of all tin, 25 percent of cobalt, 15 percent of palladium, 15 percent silver, 9 percent of gold, 2 percent of copper, and 1 percent of aluminum"[19] go annually to media technologies. We have shifted from being a society that until the mid-twentieth century was based on a very restricted list of materials ("wood, brick, iron, copper, gold, silver, and a few plastics"[20]) to the fact that even a computer chip is composed of "60 different elements."[21] Such lists of metals and materials of technology include critical materials, including rare earth minerals that are increasingly at the center of both global political controversies of tariffs and export restrictions from China. They are also related to the debates concerning the environmental damage caused by extensive open-pit mining massively reliant on chemical processes. Indeed, if the actual rock mined is likely to contain less than 1 percent of copper,[22] it means that the pressure is on the chemical processes of teasing out the Cu for further refined use in our technological devices.

The figures about metals of media seem astounding but testify to another materiality of technology that links with Conan Doyle but also with contemporary media arts discourse of the deep time of the earth. However, I will move on from Professor Challenger to Siegfried Zielinski, the German media studies professor, and his conceptualization of deep times of media art histories. In short, and what I shall elaborate in more detail soon, the figure of the deep time is for Zielinski a sort of a media archaeological gesture that, though borrowing from paleontology, actually turns out to be a riff to understanding the longer-term durations of art and science collaboration in Western and non-Western contexts. However, I want to argue that there is a need for a more literal understanding and mobilization of deep times—in terms of both depth and temporality—in media technological discourse and in relation to media art histories too. Professor Challenger is here to provide the necessary, even if slightly dubious, point about geological matter as living: this sort of a media history is of a speculative kind in terms of referring to a completely different time scale than usually engaged with in terms of our field. It borrows from the idea of dynamics of nonlinear history that Manuel Delanda so inspirationally mapped in terms of genes, language, and geology but which, in this case, can be approached even more provocatively as not just thousands but millions and billions of years of nonlinear stratified media history.[23] Media history conflates with earth history; the geological materials of metals and chemicals gets deterritorialized from their strata and reterritorialized in machines that define our technical media culture.

The extension of life to nonorganic processes follows from Deleuze and Guattari's philosophy. Life consists of dynamic patterns of variation and stratification. Stratification is a living double articulation that shows how geology is much more dynamic than just dead matter. This is obviously an allusion to the reading one finds in Deleuze and Guattari's *A Thousand Plateaus*, in which the whole philosophical stakes of this enterprise are revealed. The intensities of the earth, the flows of its dynamic unstable matter, are locked into strata. This process of locking and capture is called *stratification*, organizing the molecular nonorganic life into "molar aggregates."[24]

Hence, as a minor rhetorical question detouring via Deleuze and Guattari, what if we start our excavation of media technologies and digital culture not from Deleuze's so-well and often quoted "Postscript on the Societies of Control" text but from their joint texts on geology and stratification?[25] This is the implicit task of this chapter, with a focus on the emerging critical discourse of resource depletion, minerals, and the even harder materiality than just hardware. Hardware perspectives are not necessarily hard enough, and if we want to extend our material notions of media thoroughly toward deeper materialities and deeper times, we need to be able to talk of the nonmediatic matter that contributes to the assemblages and durations of media as technology. This comes out most clearly in two ways. First is the research and design, fabrication and standardization, of new materials that allow for mediatic and high-technology processes to emerge. This relates to history of chemistry as well as product development, aluminum and other synthetic materials that characterize modernity, alongside the work on material sciences that enabled so much of computer culture. Silicon and germanium are obvious examples of discoveries in chemistry that proved to be essential for computer culture. More recently, to take an illustrative example, the minuscule twenty-two-nanometer transistors that function without silicon are made of indium, gallium, and arsenid and demonstrate that a lot of science happens way before discursive wizardry of creative technology discourse. The MIT research project is allowing "evaporated indium, gallium, and arsenic atoms to react, forming a very thin crystal of InGaAs that will become the transistor's channel,"[26] a short quotation that suffices to narrativize that materiality of media starts much *before media become media.* Second, in a parallel fashion, we need to be able to discuss the media that are not *anymore* media. This is the other pole of media materiality that is less high tech and more defined by obsolescence:[27] the mined rare earth minerals essential to computers and in general advanced technology industries from entertainment to the military, as well as, for instance, the residue products from the processes of fabrication, like the minuscule aluminum dust residue released from polishing iPad cases to be desirably shiny for the consumer market[28] (see chapter 4).

An Ecology of Deep Time

Zielinski's notion of *Tiefenzeit,* deep time, is itself an attempt to pick up on the idea of geological times to guide the way in which we think of the humanities-focused topics of media arts and digital culture. Deep time carries a lot of conceptual gravity and is employed as a way to investigate the "Deep Time of Technical Means of Hearing and Seeing." Zielinski's approach kicks off as a critique of a teleological notion of media evolution that assumes a natural progress embedded in the narratives of the devices—a sort of a parasitical attachment, or insistence on the rationality of the machines and digital culture, that of course has had its fair share of critique in the past decades of media and cultural studies. We could call this "mythopoesis"[29] (to borrow a notion from a different context of the Ippolita group), which as a critical perspective, focuses on the narratives of and on technology as the site of political struggle. Zielinski's media archaeological and more so *anarchaeological* approach, however, hones in on geological time.

For Zielinski, earth times and geological durations become a theoretical strategy of resistance against the linear progress myths that impose a limited context for understanding technological change. They relate in parallel to the early modern discussions concerning the religious temporal order vis-à-vis the growing "evidence of immense qualitative geological changes"[30] that articulated the rift between some thousands of years of biblical time and the millions of years of earth history.

This deep temporality combined the spatial and temporal. Indeed, in James Hutton's *Theory of the Earth* from 1778, depth means time: under the layers of granite, you find further strata of slate signaling the existence of deep temporalities. Hutton is proposing a radical immensity of time, although it comes without a promise of change; all is predetermined as part of a bigger cycle of erosion and growth.[31] Despite his use of terms such as *continual succession* for time of the earth and its geological cycles discovered in its strata (the reading of strata, "stratigraphy"), time of immense durations does not, however, change in the historical fashion. More specifically, and in Hutton's words,

> the immense time necessarily required for this total destruction of the land, must not be opposed to that view of future events, which is indicated by the surest facts, and most approved principles. Time, which measures every thing in our idea, and is often deficient to our schemes, is to nature endless and as nothing; it cannot limit that by which alone it had existence; and, as the natural course of time, which to us seems infinite, cannot be bounded by any operation that may have an end, the progress of things upon this globe, that is, the course of nature, cannot be limited by time, which must proceed in a continual succession.[32]

Hutton continues to discuss and consider "the globe of this earth as a machine, constructed upon chemical as well as mechanical principles," as well as an organized body that proceeds through times of decay and repair. Hutton proposes a view and a theory of the earth as one of cycles and variations:

> His theory posited that the earth was constantly restoring itself. He based this concept on a fundamental cycle: erosion of the present land, followed by the deposition of eroded grains (or dead ocean organisms) on the sea floor, followed by the consolidation of those loose particles into sedimentary rock, followed by the raising of those rocks to form new land, followed by erosion of the new land, followed by a complete repeat of the cycle, over and over again. Hutton was also the first to recognize the profound importance of subterranean heat, the phenomenon that causes volcanoes, and he argued that it was the key to the uplifting of formerly submerged land.[33]

As becomes clear later, in Lyell's classic account of geology, this articulates a division in terms of the geological versus the historical.[34] For
Lyell, Hutton's assumption of the cyclical deep times becomes a research
tool to understand the radical temporality of the earth. Lyell was definitely interested in change in ways that did not pertain to Hutton,[35] but
this historicity was still of a different order to that of the emerging history
disciplines focused on the hermeneutic worlds of the human. The different sets of knowledge formations pertaining to the natural and to the
moral are also the context for two different modes of temporal order. The
time of the human concerns differs from the geological, which, however,
is argued to be a radical dynamic force that affects life across the boundaries of the organic and the nonorganic. And yet it was a necessity to
keep these separated, despite that modern institutions were increasingly
interested in such durations that surpassed the human: geological and
biological (in sciences of the evolution). In creative cultural theory, we
have recently seen inspiring accounts that connect feminist ontology with

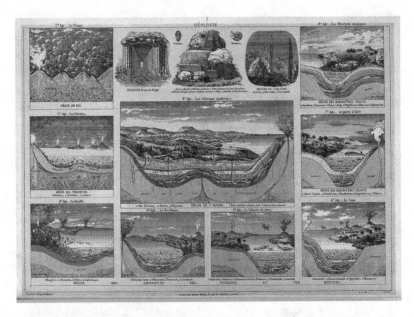

Figure 4. A lithograph featuring a visualization of geology through the ages of the earth
and details of types of stone. Colored lithograph by Bethmont, 1911, after himself.
Wellcome Library, London.

Charles Darwin's temporal ontology of open-ended becoming through evolution.[36]

Influential thinkers such as Rosi Braidotti have built on the Anthropocene discussions to connect it to a wider geocentric perspective, which prompts us to rethink fundamental notions of subjectivity, community, and political attachment. For Braidotti, the notion is, however, to be connected to ongoing struggles on the level of postcolonial and feminist agendas as well as avoiding technophobia and holistic, nostalgic fantasies of the earth. One could claim that some of the radicalization of the temporal ontology started with Hutton and Lyell already[37]—a time beyond biblical restrictions but tied to a view of a grand cycle that with Lyell led to the master trope of uniformitarianism.[38]

But neither Hutton's nor Lyell's theory is a stable ground for a more radical and nonlinear account of time for contemporary cultural and media theory. Indeed, it might have displaced biblical time but introduced the earth in an odd way almost as if a transcendent entity outside historical change. Hutton's worldview was deistic, and for him the world was a perfectly designed machine.[39] Hutton's geological world is also without change and difference and works in cyclical temporeality.[40] It is no wonder, then, as Simon Schaffer points out, that Hutton's account inspired Adam Smith's ideas concerning the invisible hand of capitalism in the emerging industrial system.[41] Both seemed to believe in universal laws governing the empirical world. The embedded cyclicality, of course, offers a fruitful view to erosions and renewals. For Zielinski, geological metaphors offer a way to investigate technological culture, but for Hutton, the planet *is* a machine. It is, however, one modeled according to the steam engines of his age, primarily the Newcomen engine, which, in its principles of expansion of steam, also gives the idea of elevation of the crust directly to inspire Hutton.[42] This machine is also one of organic unity and cyclical renewal, which feeds off the heat at its core.[43]

Such ideas inspired various visualizations of the deep time of the earth that machinates through the life-enabling media of the soil. The deeper strata and their remaining layers, including fossils, signal time as well: the planet is structured according to a depth of the temporal past. These layers structure animal and human life but also the industrial system of production and the technological culture of human civilization.

But this is exactly where Zielinski also departs. Paradoxically, the inspiration of Hutton (and one should remember that he was only one of the geotheorists working on this topic in his time) goes both toward the universalizing and standardizing logic of the industrial factory system and toward Zielinski's exactly opposite account of variantology that, however, finds a different tune with Stephen Jay Gould. Indeed, through Gould, Zielinski is able to carve out a more detailed account of what the geological idea affords to media art history and media analysis as variantology.

To achieve this, Zielinski has to turn from Hutton to more contemporary readings of geology and paleontology. Zielinski picks up on Gould's paleontological explanations and ideas that emphasize the notion of variation. It is in Gould's *Time's Arrow, Time's Cycle* that Zielinski finds a suitable account for a critique of progress in media culture. As a reader of Gould, Zielinski notes that the quantifying notion of deep time is itself renewed with a qualitative characteristic that produces a critique of myths of progress, which present a linear imagination of the world. Both discover the necessity to abandon divinity from the cosmological picture, whether one of the earth or the media. Instead, one has to develop such images, metaphors, and iconography that do not reproduce illusions of linear progress "from lower to higher, from simple to complex."[44] A resurging emphasis on diversity takes the place of the too neatly stacked historical layers.

Without going too much into the geologic debates, we need to understand how Gould's note itself is based on his arguments against uniformitarianism. Gould's argument for the "punctuated equilibrium" is targeted against the false assumption of continuity of a uniform evolution that persisted in the various geological and evolutionary accounts for a long time. It includes Lyell's views as much as Darwin's beliefs.[45] The series of arguments and academic discussion Gould started together with his cowriter Niles Eldredge stems from the early 1970s and included, besides a new way of approaching the fossil record, also a different sort of an understanding of the temporal ontology of geology.[46] In short, against the view that one can read a slow evolutionary change from the geological records, which at times are with gaps and missing parts, one has to approach this "archive" in a different way. This imaginary starts already in the nineteenth century: processes of transmission and recording are already present in the earth itself, a vast library waiting to be deciphered.[47] However, the idea of punctuated equilibrium suggested that instead of the constant uniform speed of change and evolution, the fossil record might show different speeds of changes: from slow to sudden jolts. The processes of speciation and variation are not necessarily one speed only but more of a multitemporal mix with singular points that punctuate the evolution in specific ways.

Already this short elaboration reveals the wider scientific stakes in Gould and Eldredge's account that was to offer a different theoretical understanding of time in geology. For Zielinski, this enabled a way to understand media archaeology as related to a notion of deep times of the ways in which we modify, manipulate, create, and re-create means of hearing and seeing. Zielinski introduces inspirational deep times of apparatuses, ideas, and solutions for mediatic desires that take inventors as the gravity point. He himself admits this approach as being even romantic and focused paradoxically on human heroes. It includes figures such as Empedocles (of four elements fame), Athanasius Kircher, and, for instance, the operatic dreams of Joseph Chudy and his early audiovisual telegraph system from the late eighteenth century (he composed a one-act opera on the topic, *The Telegraph or the Tele-Typewriter*). It also includes the opium-fueled media desires of Jan Evangelista Purkyne, a Czech from the early nineteenth century in the habit of using his own body for various drug- and electricity-based experiments to see how the body itself is a creative medium. What we encounter are variations that define an alternative deep time strata of our media culture outside the mainstream. It offers the anarchaeology of surprises and differences, of the uneven in the media cultural past revealing a different aspect of a possible future. Zielinski's project is parallel to imaginations of "archaeologies of the future"[48] that push us actively to invent other futures.

Zielinski's methodology offers a curious paradox in terms of the general paleontological framing. The deep time metaphor acts as a passage to map different times and spaces of media art history. Even the term connotes the darker underground of hidden fluxes that surface only irregularly to give a taste of the underbelly of a deep media history.[49] They offer variation in the sense Zielinski is after in media variantology: media do not progress from simple to complex, there are no blueprints for prediction, and we need to steer clear of the "psychopathia medialis" of standardization and find points of variation to promote diversity. This is not meant to signal conservation but active diversification as tactics of a living cultural heritage of technological pasts in the present-futures.[50]

In any case, though this is fascinating, I would carefully suggest picking up on the more concrete geological implications of Zielinski's metaphorics. With a theoretical hard hat on, I wonder if there is actually more to be found in this use of the notion of deep time both as temporality and geological materiality. Perhaps this renewed use is what offers a variation that attaches the concepts back to discussions concerning media materialism and the political geology of contemporary media culture reliant on the metals and minerals of the earth. Hence the earth time gradually systematized by Hutton and other geotheorists of his period sustains the media time in which we are interested. In other words, the heat engine cosmology of earth times that Hutton provides as a starting point for a media art historical theory of later times is one that also implicitly contains other aspects we need to reemphasize in the context of the Anthropocene: the machine of the earth is one that lives of its energy sources, in a similar way that our media devices and political economy of digital culture are dependent on energy (cloud computing is still to a large extent powered by carbon emission–heavy energy production[51]) and materials (metals, minerals, and a long list of refined and synthetic components). The earth is a machine of variation, and media can live off variation—but both are machines that need energy and are tied together in their dynamic feedback loop. Electronic waste is one of the examples of the ways in which media feed back to the earth history and future fossil times.

The main question that Zielinski's argument raises is this: besides the media variantological account concerning the design of apparatuses, users, desires, expressions, and different ways of processing the social order and means of seeing and hearing, there is this other deep time too. This sort of an alternative is more literal in the sense of returning to the geological stratifications and a Professor Challenger type of an excavation deeper into the living ground. The geological interest since the eighteenth and nineteenth centuries produced what was later coined "deep time," but we need to be able to understand that a new mapping of geology and the earth's resources was the political economic function of this emerging epistemology. This is where the archaeological and geological interests of knowledge reveal the other sides of the deep times as exposing the earth as part of new connections. Indeed, the knowledge of the planet through geological specimens (demonstrated, for instance, in Diderot and D'Alembert's "Mineral Loads or Veins and Their Bearings" in volume 6 of *l'Éncylopedie*, 1768) and its newly understood history meant a new relation between aesthetics and the sciences. This link is also beneficial for new ways of extracting value: "As a result of eighteenth-century archeological and antiquarian activities, the earth acquired a new perceptual depth, facilitating the conceptualization of the natural as immanent history, and of the earth's materials as resources that could be extracted just like archeological artifacts."[52]

The media theoretical deep time divides into two related directions:

1. Geology refers to the affordances that enable digital media to exist as a materially complex and politically economically mediated realm of production and process: a metallic materiality that links the earth to the media technological.

2. Temporalities such as deep time are understood in this alternative account as concretely linked to the nonhuman earth times of decay and renewal but also to the current Anthropocene of the obscenities of the ecocrisis—or to put it in one word, the *Anthrobscene.*

Deep temporalities[53] expand to media theoretical trajectories: such ideas and practices force media theory outside the usual scope of media studies to look at the wider milieu in which media materially and politically become media in the first place. This relates to Peters's speculative question about cosmology, science, and media, which turns into a short historical mapping of how astronomy and geology can be understood as media disciplines of sort.[54] Continuing Peters's idea, we can further elaborate geophysics as degree zero of media technological culture. It allows media to take place and has to carry their environmental load. Hence this geology of media perspective expands to the earth and its resources. It summons a media ecology of the nonorganic, and it picks up from Matthew Fuller's notes on "media ecology as a cascade of parasites"[55] as well as an "affordance," but itself afforded by a range of processes and techniques that involve the continuum of the biological-technological-geological.

A Media History of Matter:
From Scrap Metal to Zombie Media

Throughout this book, I am interested in alternative accounts of how to talk about materiality of media technology. One aspect, with again a concrete ecological edge to it, is the acknowledgment of the growing waste problem resulting from discarded media technologies. And another aspect relates to energy and power: for example, cloud computing is still rather dependent on nonrenewable energy with heavy CO_2 emissions.[56] Indeed, what I want to map as the alternative deep time relates to geology in the fundamental sense of the Anthropocene. Crutzen's original pitch offered it as a transversal map across various domains: from nitrogen fertilizers in the soil to nitric oxide in the air; carbon dioxide and the condition of the oceans; photochemical smog to global warming. Already Crutzen had initiated the expansive way of understanding the Anthropocene to be more than about geology. In Crutzen's initiating definitions, it turned into a concept investigating the radical transformations in the living conditions of the planet.

The Anthropocene can be said to be—in the way the German media philosopher Erich Hörl suggests referring to Deleuze—a concept that maps the scope of a transdisciplinary problem. So what is the problem? Hörl's suggestion is important.[57] He elaborates the Anthropocene as a concept that responds to specific questions posed by the technological situation. It is about the environmental aspects but completely tied to the technological: the concept as well as its object are enframed by technological conditions to which we should be able to develop a further elaborated insight with the humanities tools and conceptual arsenal. Indeed, this is where a geology of media offers the necessary support as a conceptual bridge between the materials of chemical and metallic kind and the political economy and cultural impact of media technologies as part of the ongoing global digital economy discourses.

The concept of the Anthropocene becomes radically environmental. It does not mean purely a reference to "nature" but an environmentality understood and defined by the "technological condition."[58] The environmental expands from a focus on the natural ecology to an entanglement with technological questions, notions of subjectivity and agency (as a critique of a human-centered worldview), and a critique of such accounts of rationality that are unable to talk about nonhumans as constitutive of social relations. The Anthropocene is a way to demonstrate that geology does not refer exclusively to the ground under our feet. It is constitutive of social and technological relations and environmental and ecological realities. Geology is deterritorialized in the concrete ways that metal and minerals become themselves mobile, enabling technological mobility: Benjamin Bratton's words could not be any more apt when he writes how we carry small pieces of Africa in our pockets, referring to the role, for instance, of coltan in digital media technologies[59] and when the visual artist Paglen sees the geo-orbital layers of satellite debris as outer reaches of earth's geology and the Anthropocene (*The Last Pictures* project; see chapter 5).

Besides Africa, iPhones are, in the words of *mammolith*, an architectural research and design platform, "geological extracts" drawing from the planet's resources and supported by a multiplicity of infrastructures. The geological bits you carry around are not restricted to samples of Africa but include the material from Red Dog pit mine in Alaska, from where zinc ore is extracted and refined into indium in Trail, Canada. But that's only a small part of it all, and such sites where material turns gradually closer to media are "scattered across the globe in the aforementioned countries, as well as South Korea, Belgium, Russia, and Peru."[60] An analysis of dead media should also take into account this aspect of the earth and its relation to global logistics and production.

More concretely, let's focus for a while on China as a territory part of the global chains of production and abandonment of media technologies. This geopolitical China is not solely about the international politics of trade and labor, which are not to be dismissed from the picture. However, we need to be able to think about the *geos* in this geopolitics too: the soil, the earth, the waste. In a sense, we can focus on the material production of what then ends up as the massive set of consumer gadgets and the future fossil record for a robot media archaeologist (see chapter 5 on future fossils of media culture), but also as discarded waste: both electronic waste and in general scrap metals, necessary for the booming urban building projects and industrial growth.

Adam Minter's journalistic report *Junkyard Planet* offers a different story of hard metals and work and looks at the issue from the perspective of geology of scrap metals.[61] China is one of the key destinations not only for electronic waste but for scrap metals in general, offering a different insight to the circulation of what we still could call geology of technologies. China's demand for materials is huge. Part of the country's continuing major construction projects from buildings to subways to airports was the need to be able to produce—or reprocess—more metals: scrap copper, aluminum, steel, and so on:

> On the other side of the mall, in all directions, are dozens of new high-rises—all under construction—that weren't visible from the subway and my walk. Those new towers reach 20 and 30 stories, and they're covered in windows that require aluminum frames, filled with bathrooms accessorized with brass and zinc fixtures, stocked with stainless steel appliances, and—for the tech-savvy households— outfitted with iPhones and iPads assembled with aluminum backs. No surprise, China leads the world in the consumption of steel, copper, aluminum, lead, stainless steel, gold, silver, palladium, zinc, platinum, rare earth compounds, and pretty much anything else labeled "metal." But China is desperately short of metal resources of its own. For example, in 2012 China produced 5.6 million tons of copper, of which 2.75 million tons was made from scrap. Of that scrap copper, 70 percent was imported, with most coming from the United States. In other words, just under half of China's copper supply is imported as scrap metal. That's not a trivial matter: Copper, more than any other metal, is essential to modern life. It is the means by which we transmit power and information.

The wider picture of technological culture is not restricted to worried comments about the rare earth minerals essential to iPhones. The bigger picture becomes clear when we realize the extent to which, by the phase technical media end up disused, they reveal their geology. The material history of media—for instance, telecommunications—extends to the copper extracted from the wires, removing the outer covers to find this mini-mine of valuable media materials. The history of mining of copper, with its environmentally dangerous effects, is extended to the re-mining from wires for the repurposing of supposedly dead objects. One could say, following Minter's narrative, that such a technological history of materials and material history of media as matter does not really follow the logic of from life of use to death of disuse, but in places such as Foshan's Nanhai District, technologies and media materials never die: it is the place where scrap metal gets processed.[62] So despite networking infrastructure having gradually abandoned copper for materials such as extruded glass or plastic to compensate for the informationally lossy metals, the latter have not entirely disappeared in the lighter, glass-based, "transparent" cloud computing culture.

In "Zombie Media" (see the Appendix), with Garnet Hertz, we address the wider context and impact of the "dead media" that refuse to disappear from the planetary existence.[63] It's the heavier residue of metal technological communication media culture. Building on Sterling's work, we argue that there is a need to account for the undead nature of obsolete media technologies and devices in at least two ways: to be able to remember that media never die but remain as toxic waste residue, and also that we should be able to repurpose and reuse solutions in new ways, as, for instance, circuit bending and hardware hacking practices imply. The zombie media angle builds on two contexts not specific to digital media but present in such accounts as Goldberg's and the wider micropolitical stance that ties consumer desires with design practices. Planned obsolescence is one such feature art/hacking projects combining hardware hacking and circuit bending, such as Benjamin Gaulon's Recyclism, critically highlight as a persistent feature of contemporary design of technological objects and systems. Similarly, such approaches take into account the current issue of abandoned hardware, which even in functional devices reaches amounts of hundreds of millions of screens, mobiles, and electronic and computing technologies that still are not properly dealt with after their use. A couple of years' old U.S. Environmental Protection Agency statistics talk of 2.37 tons of electronics ready for their afterlife management, which represented "an increase of more than 120 percent compared to 1999."[64] The primary category is related to screen technologies, but we can safely assume that the rise of mobile technologies would soon contribute a rather big share of this dead media pile, of which only 25 percent was collected for any sort of actual management and recycling in 2009. The amount of operational electronics discarded annually is one sort of geologically significant pile that entangles first, second, and third nature:[65] the communicational vectors of advanced digital technologies come with a rather direct link to and impact on first natures, reminding that the contemporary reliance on swift communicational transactions is reliant on this aspect of hardware too. Communicational events are sustained by the broader aspects of geology of media. They include technologies abandoned and consisting of hazardous material: lead, cadmium, mercury, barium, and so on.

National, supranational, and nongovernmental organizational bodies are increasingly forced to think the future of media and information technologies as something "below the turf." This means both a focus on the policies and practices of e-waste as one of the crucial areas of concern and planning toward raw material extraction and logistics to ensure supply. As the preceding short mention of scrap metal China illustrated,

Figure 5. The April 2014 excavation in Alamogordo, New Mexico, of the 1983 abandoned and buried Atari games became a widely publicized form of "media archaeology," with connotations relating it to the much bigger problem of dumping electronic waste and the residuals of game and electronic culture in heaps of rubbish. Photograph by Taylor Hatmaker.

the usual practices of mining are not considered the only route for a future geology of media. In any case, the future geo(physical)politics of media circulate around China, Russia, Brazil, Congo, and, for instance, South Africa as key producers of raw materials. It connects to a realization that the materiality of information technology starts from the soil and the underground. Miles and miles of crust opened up in drilling. This depth marks the passage from the mediasphere to the lithosphere. An increasing amount of critical materials are found only by going down deeper into the crust or otherwise difficult-to-reach areas. Offshore oil drilling is an example, in some cases in rather peculiar circumstances and depths: the Tupi deposits of oil off the coast of Brazil, beneath one and a half miles of water and another two and a half miles of compressed salt, sand, and rock;[66] new methods of penetrating rocks, fracturing them, or of steam-assisted cavity drainage; deep sea mining by countries such as China; and the list could be continued. Corporations such as Chevron boast with mining depth records—tens of thousands of feet under the ocean bottom[67]—in search for oil and minerals. Suddenly an image comes to mind, one familiar from an earlier part of this chapter: Professor Challenger's quest to dig deeper inside the living crust that is alive.

Depth becomes not only an index of time but also a resource in the fundamental sense of Martin Heidegger's standing-reserve: technology reveals nature in ways that can turn it into a resource. For Heidegger, the writer of trees, rivers, and forest paths, the River Rhein turns from Hölderlin's poetic object into a technological construct effected in the assemblage of the new hydroelectric plant. The question of energy becomes a way of defining the river and, in Heideggerian terms, transforming it:

> The revealing that rules throughout modern technology has the character of a setting-upon, in the sense of a challenging-forth. That challenging happens in that the energy concealed in nature is unlocked, what is unlocked is transformed, what is transformed is stored up, what is stored up is, in turn, distributed, and what is distributed is switched about ever anew. Unlocking, transforming, storing, distributing, and switching about are ways of revealing.[68]

This notion of transformation becomes a central way to understand the technological assemblages in which metals and minerals are mobilized as part of technological and media contexts. Technology constructs such new pragmatic and epistemological realms where geology turns into a media resource. And similarly, geology itself transforms into a contested technologically conditioned object of research and a concept that we are able to use to understand the widespread mobilization of nature. It also transforms issues of deep times from a merely temporal question of pasts to one of futures of extinction, pollution, and resource depletion, triggering a huge chain of events and interlinked questions: the future landscape of media technological fossils (see chapter 5).

This transformation of geology of media, and media of geology/ metals, works in a couple of directions. Theorists, policy makers, and even politicians are increasingly aware of the necessity of cobalt, gallium, indium, tantalum, and other metals and minerals for media technological ends, from end-user devices like mobiles and game consoles to capacitors, displays, batteries, and so forth. In short, the geophysics of media consists of examples such as the following:

cobalt: (used for) lithium-ion batteries, synthetic fuels

gallium: thin layer photovoltaics, IC, WLED

indium: displays, thin layer photovoltaics

tantalum: microcapacitors, medical technology

antimony: ATO, microcapacitors

platinum: fuel cells, catalysts

palladium: catalysts, seawater desalination

niobium: microcapacitors, ferroalloys

neodymium: permanent magnets, laser technology

germanium: fiber-optic cable, IR optical technologies[69]

Moments of deep time are exposed in such instances as Clemens Winkler's 1885–86 discovery of germanium (named, of course, after his home country) and being able to distinguish it from antimony.[70] Winkler's discovery in Freiberg sits as a part of history of chemistry and elements for sure, but it also initiates insights into computer culture, where the semiconducting capacities of this specific alloy were in tough competition with what we now consider a key part of our computer culture: silicon. But such deep times are also telling a story of the underground that is not to be confused with discourse of underground art and activism, as we so often revert back to in media art historical discourse. This new definition of media deep time is more in tune with mining and transportation, of raw material logistics and processing and refining of metals and minerals. The underground haunts the military imaginary and reality through the geography of bunkers, guerrilla trenches, and passages (such as the Vietcong) as well as the nuclear silos that are burrowed into the landscapes of the United States, for instance;[71] it haunts the technological reality of modernity. The underground has since the nineteenth century at least been the site of an imaginary of technological future, as Rosalind Williams demonstrates,[72] but it is also the actual site of technological production.

To reiterate the argument of the chapter, the extensively long historical durations of deep time in the manner introduced to media art discussions by Zielinski take place in antique times, with medieval alchemists, and in nineteenth-century science–art collaborations as exemplary events of deep time media artistic techniques and ideas. But what if we need to account for an alternative deep time that extends more deeply toward a geophysics of media culture? This is a possibility not to be missed: an alternative media history of matter. Such extends the historical interest in alchemists to contemporary mining practices, minerals, and the subsequent materialities. Would this sort of an approach be something that is comfortable to tackle with materiality below the ground level,[73] stretched into a continuum between political economy of resources and art practices (as we see in the next chapter in more detail)?

The geology of media that nods toward Zielinski but wants to extend deep times toward chemical and metal durations includes a wide range of examples of refined minerals, metals, and chemicals that are essential for media technologies to operate in the often audiovisual and often miniaturized mobile form, as we have grown to expect as end users of content. A usual focus on Understanding Media is complemented with the duration of materials as significant for media temporality. Hence media history of matter as well is in its own way another aspect of the geological deep time.[74]

The interactions of chemicals, material sciences, and technical media were never really forgotten in such accounts as Kittler's. His media historical insights were often aware that material sciences and discoveries have a grounding role in terms of enabling not only media technologies but also military operations. Hence his attention to such details as a blockade of Chilean nitrate to Germany[75] by the telegraphically effective British naval troops in World War I unravels as a story the geopolitical importance of sodium nitrate mining in Chile, the necessary substitute of synthetic ammoniac by the German chemical innovation of Haber and Bosch, needed for munitions production. Technologies are matters of war and logistics, which are ways to mobilize the particular Kittler perspective to a media history of matter:

> For over a century, wars and technologies have dreamed of being ahead of their day. In reality, however, they are forced to engage in recursions that burrow into ever deeper pasts. Lack of nitrate scuttled Alfred von Schlieffen's ingenious plan of attack. Just as up-to-date computer design is steadily closing in on the big bang, the logistics of war (irrespective of wishful ecological thinking) consume ever-older resources. The Second World War began with the switch from coal and railroads to tank oil and airplane fuel, the Pax Americana with the exploration of uranium (in Germany, the task was assigned to Hans-Martin Schleyer).[76]

In this chemical conjunction, history of fertilizers meets history of war and technological culture. The thousands of years of cultural techniques of manipulating the soil for purposes of agriculture reach one sort of a singular point by World War I but also show how histories of the Anthropocene entangle with war and technology, where only the latter have been discussed in media theory and history. But in this context, as already hinted at some points earlier, the chemical constitution of technological culture is not to be neglected. Industrialization becomes a point of synchronization of the various lineages of cultural techniques. The agricultural metaphor of "culturing" is in the scientific age part of the development of chemical means of manipulation of the soil. The soil can be made fertile, and the history of the geological impact of humans is also about the isolation of ingredients such as phosphorus (1669), nitrogen (1772), potassium (1807), and, later, nitrogen. The years constitute recent events in the nonlinear history of the earth becoming adapted to technical cultural history. The technical–scientific ties together with the Anthrobscene too:

"The arrival of industrialization, ushering in the Anthropocene, is marked by the human ability to move vast quantities of geologic material."[77]

Nation-states and their media-supported wars are themselves fueled by material explorations and, to put it simply, energy. But these are wars with a punctuated imbalance. As Sean Cubitt notes, much of contemporary geological resource hunt and energy race is conditioned by neocolonial arrangements: their targets are in territories traditionally belonging to indigenous people and "geological resources are sourced in lands previously deemed worthless and therefore earmarked as reservations for displaced indigenous peoples during the period of European imperial expansion from the 18th to the 20th centuries."[78] This is a good way of demonstrating that, in some ways, contemporary states—and corporations—are still obscenely modern in their manner of operations. Eviction, massacre, and conquering are part of the normal repository of actions allowed in guaranteeing resources, as Geoffrey Winthrop-Young writes.[79]

Oil is the usual reference point for a critical evaluation of earth fossils, modern technological culture, and the link between nation-state and corporate interests in exploiting cheap labor and seemingly cheap resources. But of course, it is not the only one. Other materials are also moved on an increasingly massive level and as an important function in the militarily secured energy regimes of the globe. Genealogies of logistics, media, and warfare are particularly "Kittlerian," even if what is missing from his media materialism is often the theme of labor. Indeed, instead of merely war, we could as justifiably track down genealogies of media materials to labor processes, exploitation, and dangerous conditions that characterize also the current persistence of *hard work* alongside persistence of *hardware*[80] (see chapter 4). Perhaps these two are better indexes of digital culture than software creativity or immaterial labor.

Conclusions: Cultural Techniques of Material Media

In Thomas Pynchon's *Against the Day* (2006), a novel set before the digital and more focused on the modulation and standardization of processes of light for the use of technical media such as photography, one gets a sense of the chemistry of media. Pynchon's status as part of a theoretical mapping of history of media and technology has become consolidated ever since *Gravity's Rainbow* (1973) tied together war, technology, and a weird narrative mix of paranoia, conspiracy, and mental states. The V-2 rocket motivated insights into technology, and science as an essential part of power relations inspired Kittler and a range of other scholars in Germany and internationally. In *Against the Day*, the theme is similar, but with a focus on light, optics, and chemistry, where especially the latter is what connects to our need to understand media history through its materials. It is an account that persists from the early histories of photography, such as geologist–photographer W. Jerome Harrison's *History of Photography* (1887), which, if you read it through the perspective of geology of media, becomes a story of chemicals instead of merely the inventor–experimenters such as Niepce, Daguerre, or Talbot: bitumen (in lithography); tin or, for instance, iodide; lactates and nitrates of silver; carbon processes; uranium nitrates; and chlorides of gold.[81] The history of technical media is constantly being reenacted in different ways in contemporary media arts. For photochemical artists, getting their hands dirty with gelatin and silver nitrates, this is part of the artistic methodology infused in chemistry: cyanotypes' aesthetic effect comes down to chemicals (ammonium iron [III] citrate and potassium ferricyanide). A film artist with a media archaeological bent knows the amount of combination needed in testing and experimenting with chemicals or materials.[82] But this knowledge is more of the sort a metallurgist might hold than a scientist: experimentation in dosage and practice-based learning of the materials' characteristics.[83]

In Pynchon's own version of media materialism and optical media, the list of objects constitutes a sort of a pre–media technological media materialism, a list of voluntary or involuntary participants in the process of technical imaging circa the nineteenth century:

> After going through all the possible silver compounds, Merle moved on to salts of gold, platinum, copper, nickel, uranium, molybdenum, and antimony, abandoning metallic compounds after a while for resins, squashed bugs, coal-tar dyes, cigar smokes, wildflower extracts, urine from various critters including himself, reinvesting what little money came in from portrait work into lenses, filters, glass plates, enlarging machines, so that soon the wagon was just a damn rolling photography lab.[84]

Besides the object worlds with which the narrative continues—a world a speculative realist might call "flat,"[85] including a litany from humans to lampposts to trolley dynamos and flush toilets—so much has already happened on the level of chemical reactions. In other words, the media devices are not the only aspects of "materialism," but we are as interested in questions of what enables and sustains media to become media.

In this sort of perspective of deep time geologies and chemistries of media, one cannot avoid at least a brief mention of the long history of alchemy. Isn't it exactly the lineage of alchemy that is of relevance here? It has meant imbuing a special force to the natural elements and their mixes, from base to precious: from realgar, sulfur, white arsenic, cinnabar, and especially mercury to gold, lead, copper, silver, and iron.[86] The history of alchemy is steeped in poetic narratives that present their own versions of sort of deep times (e.g., in pre-Christian Chinese alchemy[87]) as well as occupying a position between arts and sciences.[88] In a way, as Newman notes, alchemy prepared much of later technological culture in its own experimental way. Developers included a variety of such cases: Avicenna with his *De congelatione* (at one point mistaken for a writing by Aristotle) and scholastic writers such as Vincent of Beauvais, Albertus Magnus, and Roger Bacon are main examples of early-thirteenth-century practitioners. In Vincent's *Speculum doctrinale,* written between 1244 and 1250, one gets a sense of alchemy as a "science of minerals," a sort of practice-based excavation into their transmutational qualities. In Vincent's words, alchemy "is properly the art of transmuting mineral bodies, such as metals and the like, from their own species to others."[89]

In *Against the Day,* Pynchon presents his own condensed narrative prose lineage from alchemy to modern chemistry and technical media. According to his way of crystallizing the chemistry of technological culture, this transformation in knowledge and practices of materials corresponds to the birth of capitalism, which is characterized by a regularization of processes of material reaction and metamorphosis. In *Against the Day,* a dialogue between two characters, Merle and Webb, reveals something important about this turning point from alchemy to modern science:

> "But if you look at the history, modern chemistry only starts coming in to replace alchemy around the same time capitalism really gets going. Strange, eh? What do you make of that?"

Webb nodded agreeably. "Maybe capitalism decided it didn't need the old magic anymore." An emphasis whose contempt was not meant to escape Merle's attention. "Why bother? Had their own magic, doin just fine, thanks, instead of turning lead into gold, they could take poor people's sweat and turn into greenbacks, and save that lead for enforcement purposes."[90]

What Pynchon brings into play in this admittedly short quotation is labor. Besides media histories of matter, such issues link up with histories of exploitation and capture of surplus value. Indeed, besides a material history of media before it becomes media, Pynchon is able to highlight the magical nature of the commodity production related to the novel forms of "alchemy": the new magic explicated by Marx as the fetish of the object hiding the material forces of its production is characteristic of this aspect, which is usually defined as the material history understood as a history of labor and political economy. However, we need also to understand the technological and the media elements in this mix, which also returns to the issue of geology, the earth.

In short, techniques of experimenting with different reactions and combinations of elements and materials are also media practices. Our screen technologies, cables, networks, technical means of seeing and hearing, are partly results of meticulous—and sometimes just purely accidental—experimentation with how materials work: what works, what doesn't, whether you are talking of materials for insulation, conduction, projection, or recording. The sciences and the arts often share this attitude of experimentation and the experiment—to make the geos expressive and transformative. The transistor-based information technology culture would not be thinkable without the various meticulous insights into the material characteristics and differences between germanium and silicon—or the energetic regimes—whether that involves the consideration of current clouds (as in server farms) or the attempts to manage power consumption inside computer architectures.[91] Issues of energy are ones of geophysics too—both in the sense of climate change accelerated by the still continuing heavy reliance on polluting forms of nonrenewable energy production and through the various chemicals, metals, and metalloids such as germanium and silicon, media cultural aftereffects of the geological strata. That is also where a deep time of the planet is inside our machines, crystallized as part of the contemporary political economy: material histories of labor and the planet are entangled in devices, which, however, unfold as part of planetary histories. Data mining might be a leading hype term for our digital age of the moment, but it is enabled only by the sort of mining that we associate with the ground and its ungrounding. Digital culture starts in the depths and deep times of the planet. Sadly, this story is most often more obscene than something to be celebrated with awe.

In the next chapter, we turn to crystallization as well as continue on the topic of aesthetics of the geophysics, or, more accurately, the psychogeophysical method of mapping relations of the earth, capitalism, and technology.

3

PSYCHOGEOPHYSICS OF TECHNOLOGY

The strata of the Earth is a jumbled museum. Embedded in the sediment is a text that contains limits and boundaries which evade the rational order, and social structures which confine art. In order to read the rocks we must become conscious of geologic time, and of the layers of prehistoric material that is entombed in the Earth's crust. When one scans the ruined sites of pre-history one sees a heap of wrecked maps that upsets our present art historical limits.

—ROBERT SMITHSON

A lesson from the early geological discourse of the eighteenth century: earth is a massive heat engine. Inside it lies the bursting hot molten core as a seemingly eternal and yet historically formed source of energy. The rise and movement of landmasses from the seas is the breath of the earth. What sounds like the later Gaia theory of the earth as a living entity is already in limited ways part of the earlier geological discourse. Inhale, exhale. The soil is a central mediating element. Agriculture cultivates life, but soil is media—or like the currently increasing demand for synthetic soil suggests, "soils are a form of technology."[1] More than two hundred years before the realization that production of soil might be a great business for the increasingly polluted planet, James Hutton's worldview is focused on the idea of the earth as a big machine: it sounds very apt considering that the industrial age is just round the corner. The earth is an old machine and still not devoid of the Christian connotations and a belief in the intelligent design. Nothing is accidental but rather is governed through a higher order.

Depth means time, but it also means heat. Deep down is the hot core. The internal heat is one of life that melts the gravel, sand, and other formations under the seabed and consolidates them into rock, to paraphrase Rudwick.[2] The solids are end results of long processes of a natural historical kind. And yet, it is history, but in the sense Manuel Delanda pitches as a sort of a new materialist metaphysics of metallic affects: metals have to be accounted as chemical catalysts.[3] However, they do not catalyze only chemical reactions but social, political, economic, and, indeed, media technological ones too.

The previous chapter outlined some ideas for an alternative deep time of the media. It was a start at least. My suggestion in this book is to excavate this deep layer of media technologies that, besides connotations of depth (the reality of mines as essential to existence of contemporary technological culture), points toward temporalities: the rethinking of what media historical times count as part of our analysis—the long-term durations of geological formations, of mineralization across millions of years, as well as the millions of years of decomposition of fossils to form the fossil fuel layers essential for the modern technological world. We also have to account for the effects on the climate in broadest terms and the way in which media technologies play a double role. This double role is articulated as follows:

1 Media technologies as an epistemological framework, which enable one to perceive, simulate, design, and plan in terms of the environment and the climate; media compose the framework that allows us to talk about, for instance, climate change in the way in which we do nowadays.[4]

2 Second, we can consider media technologies as the aftereffect, the afterglow,[5] that will remain as the fossilized trace of designed obsolescence and gadget-culture, as well as the massive infrastructures around which media function: energy, raw material production, and mountains of discarded keyboards, screens, motherboards, and other components.

This chapter develops these themes, but with a special connection to art methods and aesthetics. Indeed, this is again characteristic of the just mentioned double bind; the enabling aesthetics of even being able to talk about such scales as "the climate" or even its change on a geological time scale; and the aesthetics of this change as a form of critique that intervenes in and feeds off from the geophysical. This chapter introduces one of the main concepts of the book: *psychogeophysics*. This concept and an art practice or a mix of methods is an expansion of the psychogeographical familiar from the Situationist vocabulary. Psychogeophysics argues that we need to extend beyond the focus on the urban sphere to the geophysical for a more fundamental understanding of the modulation of the subject that is stretched between ecologies of capitalism and those of the earth. This discussion of aesthetics as a pertinent revamping of Situationism—here a nod is in place to McKenzie Wark's recent years of highlighting the relevancy of Situationist theorists, practices, and themes with a particular eye to some of its neglected figures[6]—is taken to a rather extreme direction that talks about geophysics and media technologies in connection.

The chapter discusses the psychogeophysical "manifesto" (published in *Mute* magazine) as an extended "Situationism" of the geophysical media arts.[7] In this context, the conceptual discussion is connected to some recent art and hacktivist projects, which engage with the provocative concept. Such projects include Martin Howse's *Earthbooth* and Florian Dombois's *Earthquake* sonification but also other relevant takes that address earth durations, sounds, and sensations.

Psychogeophysical Dérives

Questions of aesthetics unfold in a different way if you start to ask them from a nonhuman perspective. A question of aesthetics—as a question not necessarily of art and its value but of perception and sensation—unfolds in alternative ways when considering animals. In literature, Josephine the singing mouse (in Franz Kafka's short story) is one curious story of such fictitious animal worlds and aesthetic appreciation, but in biology and experimental psychology, it is a matter of measurable temporal rates and thresholds of perception. The rates of perception of different animals are so very different from the human senses: it is not cognitively or affectively easily accessible how a bird perceives, a fish senses sound, or a bee is embedded in a different world of color sensations. This brings the question from philosophy of aesthetics to the fields of physiology and experimental psychology emerging in the nineteenth century with figures such as Helmholtz and others taking the front stage with their material and empirical investigation: how do you measure the objective and physiological thresholds of animals, including humans?[8] But what happens if you start asking such questions from the perspective of the nonorganic?

The memory of a rock is of different temporal order to that of the human social one.[9] Abbé La Pluche in *Le Spectacle de la nature* (1783) reminded how "the stones and metals have truly preserved for us the history of the world."[10] The capacities, embodied modes of sensation, memory, and time, offer at least partial conditions for a number of aesthetic ideas, which are not restricted to "art" per se but resonate with issues in geology and astronomy.[11] Such broader definitions of media and aesthetics also allow us to consider the connections of the organic human bodies in the organic and nonorganic surroundings.

Of course, there are traditions and examples in twentieth-century art and philosophy eager to engage with the rock world. Land art, environmental arts, but also such a figure as Roger Caillois prove the case in point. The quasi-surrealist Caillois's fascination with stones sets as part of his long-term investment in the mystical but also the wider allegorical relations with nature. This resulted in a nice collection of rocks (systematized according to categories of *bizarre, insolite* [unusual], and *fantastique*) but also a philosophical investigation of the nonorganic, temporality, and myths.[12] Indeed, Caillois's *Writing of Stones* (1970) hints at the transition from admiring stones as objects to their transformative power as well as their archival status as visual media: images of fossil imprints of long lost, imaginary cities as well as the intimation that in the rock and the mineral is another force that the stone itself can produce—a force of alteration.[13] From rocks as objects to minerals, metals, and the geological strata as forces of production—from objects of appreciation and knowledge to enabling catalysts in the way a metallurgical perspective has it—a metal is defined by what it can do.[14]

Postanthropocentric discussions concerning aesthetics, technology, and the environmental necessitate an inclusion of a new ecology of relations between humans, animals, and the nonorganic. Indeed, as Jane Bennett notes as a spokesperson for vibrant materialism, "culture is not our own making, infused as it is by biological, geological and climatic forces."[15] Such an articulation of the postanthropocentric is happening across a range of fields, including, for instance, animal aesthetics. Matthew Fuller's "Art for Animals" is exemplary in this case.[16] But it also happens in other formations of art that take into serious consideration the organic and nonorganic realms of perception and sensation. In other words, perhaps there is an ethical urgency to consider the posthuman—the lack of certainty of what constitutes the human brought about by scientific, technological, and ecological forces. Of an increasing necessity is, as Rosi Braidotti flags, the need to engage with a "planetary, geo-centred" perspective.[17] In other words, in such accounts and in the psychogeophysical focus of this chapter, I do not engage with an Aesthetization of Nature that might separate humans from their environment—a point Tim Morton also raises in *Hyperobjects*[18]—but with the opposite: to establish proximity, map the links, the continuum of medianatures[19] where the natural ecology is entirely entangled with the technological one. Morton refers to this as the *viscous* quality of hyperobjects, but this chapter talks of some similar themes from an art and technology perspective.

So indeed the question: how do the soil, the crust, the rocks, and the geological world sense? It is definitely a dilemma anyone deep into Alfred North Whitehead would find attractive, but let's consider it from the perspective of media and aesthetics. How do things like earthquakes and the tide, electromagnetism and radiation of other sorts, fit in? Those might be Morton's hyperobjects, but they also fit with some ways of speaking and some operations focused on geophysical aesthetics. Perhaps the way to question these is not through a conceptual metaphysical discussion and essays but through excursions, walks, experiments, and assays? Indeed, what if the method is more pertinent to the description of the London Psychogeophysics Summit of 2010 activities. Instead of a metaphysical essay on the nonhuman, take a walk outside, for instance, in East London:

The London Psychogeophysics Summit proposes an intense week-long, city-wide series of walks, fieldtrips, river drifts, open workshops and discussions exploring the novel interdisciplinary frame of psychogeophysics, colliding psychogeographics with earth science measurements and study (fictions of forensics and geophysical archaeology). Centred around SPACE, open events include practical workshops in building simple geophysical measurement devices from scrap materials, fieldtrips for study and long-term use of such devices in the city, measurement and mapping of physical and geo-physical data during city-wide walks, deployment of strategic underground networks, fusion of fiction, dérive and signal excursion, studies of river signal ecologies alongside short lectures and discussions of broad, interdisciplinary psychogeophysical themes.[20]

The concept of psychogeophysics is introduced as a complementary term to that of psychogeography—a much more familiar concept in twentieth-century art vocabularies following up on the Situationists. But if the psychogeographical was an analysis of the specific effects of the urban environment on our senses and affective orientation, then the geophysical twist brings in a stronger nonhuman element that is nonetheless aware of the current forms of exploitation but takes a strategic point of view on the nonorganic too. The method might at first seem rather similar: take a walk. Derive and drift, fuse fiction with the places that you visit, frequent, or just pass by. Approach your surroundings through the eyes and writings of Pynchon and J. G. Ballard. But don't think what you see is the only level of reality—there is also the invisible and the underground. The underground might open a different way of investigating the notion of affordance: what enables things to be perceived as they are designed to be perceived so as to sustain our habits.[21] In a Guy Debord–Situationist manner, originating from the late 1950s, the psychogeographical does not denounce the physical landscapes—after all, the term still carries with it "geography." In fact, Debord does not fail to mention "soil composition or climatic conditions"[22] when progressing toward the speculative methodology of psychogeography. The latter is introduced as a mapping of the habitual patterns of the city life, and it offers ways to find variations to break and short-circuit the media–economic conjunction of the psyche with the urban environment. However, what follows from the psychogeographical mission statement are primarily meditations concerning the urban. Indeed, the urban sphere has been privileged in later instances too, giving it a special place in the critical methodologies that offer cartographies of the late modern capitalism—a capitalism that suits the spectacle so often fixated on the media *cultural* condition.

Wark does an invaluable job in describing the general idea of the psychogeographical and how it relates to 1950s thinking of the city (especially Paris), the Letterist International and the relations to art practice of the dérive. In the hands of Debord and Ivan Chtcheglov, this methodology is not merely a social scientific mapping of the interpersonal stretched between the objective surroundings and the subjective indoors. Instead, it is a more radical take on the subjective as a fold that is guided through such stratified sets of places and vectors. Wark argues how the turbulence of such a geographic is one important condition for the cartography of currents, fixed points, and vortexes.[23] The term and its relation to the dérive contain many implications about productive time and leisure time. However, let's first focus on the primacy of the urban and how it is critiqued in the more recent geophysical variations.

The term *psychogeophysics* is introduced in 2010 by the London Psychogeophysics Summit Collective.[24] In *Mute,* the collective demands in a rather manifest way a rescaling of the psychogeographic focus into a more earthly one: the notion of psychogeophysics is meant to offer a provocative distancing from some aspects of psychogeography. With rather strong articulations that at times resemble Deleuze and Guattari's critique of the interior- and couch-focused mind-set of psychoanalytic theory as opposed to the great outdoors of schizoanalysis, psychogeography is critiqued as being an example of a methodology for the house-dwelling mind-set. It is claimed to be occupied with the civilized urban states of mind and architecture, of indoors and the urban structured sets of living. In the view of psychogeophysics, what is ignored are the wider geological contexts in which habitual life can even start to be structured:

> Psychogeophysics; just as the entire weight of the earth conspire [*sic*] to pull down suspended objects (gravity; a relatively weak but keystone force) the human condition is being shaped by the entire earth: psychology as plate tectonics of the mind.[25]

The text continues to attack the "INMB (In My Back Yard) regionalism and general lack of ambition to look beyond the city and beyond the contemporary" that is seen as characteristic of the psychogeographical bias. After all, to adopt the tone of the Summit's manifesto of psychogeophysics,

cities come and go, neighbourhoods go from bust to boom in cyclical fashion. The psychogeophysical angle, which has everything
going for it, is already deluded by procedural navel gazing (the
big fat belly of the google-jugend) and an irrational belief in the
supreme objectivity of measurement and raw data.[26]

Some of the concepts, especially referring to the plate tectonics of
the mind, remind of Robert Smithson's earthwork art discourse. Especially in his 1960s text "A Sedimentation of the Mind: Earth Projects,"
Smithson introduces language that strongly resonates with the ecological
thought of Gregory Bateson, but in an art and geology context. It's already
in Smithson's ideas that one finds a continuity, a topological twist, and a
connection between the mind and the earth that extends into a dynamic
aesthetic relation: of erosion, wearing away, compositions, and decom-
positions. The brain and the earth share the processual structuration that
expands into what Smithson calls "abstract geology,"[27] which also enables
a different way of understanding technology, unrestricted to the actual
technological devices and systems but encompassing the wider field of
materials.

The London Psychogeophysics Summit uses the language of low-
frequency horror of planetary dimensions alongside connotations of obsolescence to summon the image of the world of psychogeophysics. It relates
to the inadequacy of aesthetic methods rooted in the city, shopping streets,
and cozy indoors to actually address the relations of geology and contemporary capitalist life. The psychogeophysical cartography is meant to
reveal the tension between the human settlements and the environmental. This force and tension is one that is pitched as more radical than of
green politics; it is one of dimensions that mobilize the Kantian sublime
into a contemporary technological culture perspective:

A mountain is more important than Paris, a volcano is more important than Cairo, an earthquake is more important than Dubai, the
geomagnetic north is more important than all cities in the Americas
together. A billion+ years of void, Los Angeles sinks into the ocean
(cataclysm), a billion+ years of void. A billion+ years of void, a garden fence falls to the ground (cataclysm), a billion+ years of void.

Geophysics not geography defines us. Lat/Lon systematics can
not contain earth masses on the move. Mount Fuji does not need
Google.earth.[28]

Psychogeophysics aims for planetary scales of aesthetics. It can be
seen taking the original Situationist city-focus born in the urban sphere
of Paris of the 1950s and 1960s to engage with the geophysical as the
uncontained element beyond the urban. Indeed, what Gary Genosko has
referred to as the new four elements, or the mobilization of the elements
of earth, fire, air, and water[29] in contemporary biopolitics and environmental contexts, is one way of understanding the persistence of the material. The "elemental" is present in Smithson's pitch for an alternative
to McLuhan's human-focused theory of technology, and in Genosko's
hands, it provides a way to understand how the psychogeophysical might
pan out as part of a wider contemporary field of discussion on aesthetics,
the environmental, and the extended ecological politics.

Indeed, whereas posthumanities discourse has been instrumental
in opening up the humanities to the animal as part of the social and economic field (exploited in various industries) as much as the animal inside
us (critique of anthropocentrism with approaches emphasizing the non-
conscious),[30] we might need to figure out more specifically the continuum across the organic and the nonorganic. In recent collections, such
as *Making the Geologic Now*,[31] this cartography is present, but the psychogeophysical seems to trigger an alternative field of inquiry in which
some recent art projects and practices offer their version of the manifesto's message. It is in this sense that psychogeophysics performs the con-
tinuums across the biological, the nonorganic, and the social. It can also
offer an ethico-aesthetic perspective to the minerals inside us and the
metals and rocks out there enabling technological gadgetry—an abstract
geology.

Hence a range of artworks that actually tap into this geological materialism might be in a key position to open our eyes and ears to something
rather different: they offer visuals and sounds of the nonhumans. Even
Félix Guattari's language of ecology of the mind seems to pale next to
such tectonic psychological vocabularies, which, however, do not come
without predecessors.

Art of Geology, Machines of Soil

To which regime of aesthetics do geological formations, earthquakes, the soundscapes of ice melting, or, for instance, the various radiations that form the electromagnetic sphere belong? What sort of aesthetic vocabularies are at our use when we want to interface the geological and the human made? The aesthetic discourse, including Immanuel Kant's *Critique of Judgment*, has set a specific way of relating to the outside world, but more specifically what is of interest is the relation to the geological—such a fashion theme especially in the early nineteenth century in Germany and in Britain, fueling literature and philosophy.[32] The subterranean world of the eighteenth and nineteenth centuries was not merely about geology and mines, but as Rosalind Williams argues, terms such as *the sublime* and *fantasy* were also part of the imaginary of the underworld.[33] This included a fascination with ruins since the eighteenth century, with the archaeological fever entering painting: Giovanni Battista Piranesi's imagery is a good example of the reimagination of the classic Roman Empire in the late eighteenth century; John Martin's "The Destruction of Pompeii and Herculaneum" (1822) is emblematic of the awe-inspiring horrors of geophysical forces as sublime threats to the human civilization and contributing to the mythological status of this famous volcanic eruption. The various images of ruins of abbeys and such are an integral part of British painting alongside other themes that demonstrate this fascination with the archaeological, ruins, and the geophysical decay of the urban.[34] In the more recent decades of artistic discourse, various suggestions have paved the way for a reemergence of geology and the great outdoors as part of critical arts—not least in landscape art, and for instance geopoetics, "concerned, fundamentally, with a relationship to the earth and with the opening of a world."[35]

For sure, a quick glance of the photographic art of landscapes and geology still reminds of the rather classical aesthetic predispositions that one inherited from eighteenth- and nineteenth-century philosophy and the contrasting sentiments of measures of man and the immeasurability of Nature. This was carried over from landscape painting to the technologies of national parks, flagging one sort of a capture of the ideal natural beauty by means of techniques of reproduction. Richard Grusin argues that in the American context, national parks mark a technological mode of reproduction of nature.[36] This is an idealized set of conditions through which nature becomes represented as well as enmeshing geography, geology, nation building, and aesthetic concerns. Places of geophysical uniqueness such as Yellowstone Natural Park or the Grand Canyon became landscapes and environments of geologically loaded aesthetics already in the nineteenth century. Immanuel Kant's aesthetic vocabulary was reemployed by, for instance, Clarence Dutton's 1882 *Tertiary History of the Grand Cañon District,* alongside its Atlas part. In narratives and images, the Grand Canyon is shifted from discourses of beauty to those of the sublime—cognitively inaccessible and well described by Grusin:

> Insofar as it is represented in terms that resemble the accretive operation of erosion and sedimentation, Dutton's account of the epistemology of sublime perception is finally geological. For Dutton, there is no fundamental difference between his geological and his literary passages, between his scientific and his aesthetic purposes.[37]

In Dutton's prose and images, the landscapes become a geological cartography of plateaus and strata, of "Jurassic remnants"[38] now conveyed with such aesthetic description and prescription as a sort of an archive of nature remediated. This idea of the sublime as the aesthetic of the geological deep time is demonstrated by Rosalind Williams: geological thought but also the "aesthetic discovery of industrial technology"[39] are supported by this sort of aesthetics in the nineteenth century. Landscape painting goes hand in hand with birth of geology (as a modern discipline and a mind-set).

But in a longer perspective, a lot of the art of the geologic admits the role of the human in the more than poetic engineering of the planet. This is a point picked up for years now by the Anthropocene discussions, and motoring several important aesthetic interventions too. Indeed, such aesthetic questions are in prime position to raise the substantial ethical question for humanities: can we remain *just-humanities* in an age of planetary scale engineering and massive changes to the very physical ground on which we live?

Instead of the Anthropocene, let's discuss psychogeophysics as a minor concept. I mean "minor" in the sense of its visibility even in artistic discourse, as well as minor in the Deleuze and Guattarian sense of gathering forces of the potential, of variation and of deviation: it is an experimentation finding ambulant potential lines rather than aimed at establishing an axiomatic Master Set of Principles.[40] In our case, the aesthetical question is further removed from sole considerations of art per se and is more closely about the temporal and spatial conditions in which perception becomes possible. This sort of perception is, however, partly removed from the human being into a wider assemblage that takes into account the wider climatological and geophysical spheres. In this context, Katie Paterson's installation piece "Vatnajökull (the sound of)" is a fascinating project, which concretely connects technological infrastructures of transmission with the soundscapes of the geophysical.

Have you ever wondered how glaciers sound? What is the (an)*ruf* of the glacier?

> An underwater microphone lead into Jökulsárlón lagoon—an outlet glacial lagoon of Vatnajökull, filled with icebergs—connected to an amplifier, and a mobile-phone, which created a live phone line to the glacier. The number +44(0)7757001122 could be called from any telephone in the world, the listener put through to Vatnajökull. A white neon sign of the phone number hung in the gallery space.[41]

Dial-a-glacier is a reminder of the acoustic spheres and dislocations of the slowly melting oceans—a weird phone call to the geologic sphere of the planet. Here the transmission media become also a measurement device that allows access to the otherwordly, yet constantly present through the variety of representations concerning climate change. The melting ice and the icebergs are signals of a slow change triggering and triggered by a multiplicity of causalities involving humans, technology, and an odd heritage of industrial culture. Even soundscapes of oceans are an aesthetic measurement device of the climate change and the arts of the *Anthrobscene*. As a parallel to Paterson's piece, consider the scientific news about the rising ocean acid levels causing the change in the acoustic environments too. This is especially affecting whales' methods of communication across the transmission media of water but is a wider aesthetic index of change: the oceans and glaciers as acoustic media are inscription surfaces of the industrial period aftereffects and act also as massive geological amplifier of signals. What's more, especially in the case of acid levels of oceans, it is a sort of a time machine, transporting us back to an earlier Cretaceous period from 145 (±4) to 66 million years ago.[42]

The psychogeophysical fascination with tectonics is anticipated by such artworks as Florian Dombois's *Earthquake* sonifications.[43] Auditory seismology presents itself as a time-critical[44] methodology of understanding the geophysical events through establishing a relation between the ear and the temporal unfolding of earthquakes as sonic processes. But it also lends itself to a media artistic methodology, an apt example of what we nowadays call arts–science collaboration. Psychogeophysics is anyway a rather minor current in the contemporary media arts scene, but it is able to speak to the issues of deep seas and deep crust in ways that actually feel very pertinent. It returns posthuman theory as a sort of planetary venture that summons what Deleuzians might call a Becoming-Earth, and it also challenges the stabilizing and romanticizing notions of the earth.[45]

The earth and its geophysical sphere does not stop with the ground or the underground. It extends as part of the climate and the electromagnetic sphere, brilliantly mapped by Douglas Kahn in his recent *Earth Sound Earth Signal*. Kahn's quirky media history of the electrical arts goes back to the natural electrics as examples of how the earth participates in the much later projects too, from Alvin Lucier's brainwaves art to Joyce Hinterding's work with natural electromagnetic phenomena.[46] Projects emerging in the middle of the twentieth century in the sound arts established more than just talking about nature or the individual human being. Instead, connections between the outer space and the brain were experimentally woven in ways that signal a much earlier phase of what nowadays is branded as a *new* focus on the nonhuman realm. What is more, the media history of early-nineteenth-century technological assemblages of measurement of the atmosphere and the earth is the media archaeological point of departure for so much of later sonic and electromagnetic arts. It is in this context that one finds the double articulation of technological episteme of knowledge concerning the natural sphere and its rearticulation in media artistic–technological practices![47]

Reading Kahn, we can understand how both theoretically and media historically the circuiting of the earth has moved from the underground upward. As Kahn highlights, the underground of technologies starts before the avant-garde of the twentieth century and even outside clandestine military operations clouded in secrecy: "During the nineteenth century, communication went underground—nothing necessarily secretive or subaltern, even the most common telegraph and telephone messages followed a technological circuit that was returned and completed through the earth."[48] The closed metallic circuit is predated by the open earth circuit.[49] The ionosphere became part of international network culture by the 1920s with radio, outer space after World War II with the beginning of the military-enabled satellite age. The geophysical communication culture of technical media is part of an expansion of the circuit: from the underground to above the ground, to the ionosphere where intentional human messages share the signal space with whistlers, and then the space—an extended rim of the Anthropocene (and the Anthrobscene of space junk) that we discuss further in chapter 5.

Kahn's account fits in with the geophysical focus on aesthetics I want to address through the provocations of psychogeophysics. What distinguishes Kahn is his mapping of the energetic history of technical media circuited with the expanded earth. Natural "things" such as radiation, electromagnetism, and Earth magnitudes are leaking into art vocabularies and as such smuggle a bit of the nonhuman into the otherwise often very human-centered focus of aesthetics. Indeed, aesthetics becomes twisted into a different set of questions. It becomes connected to themes usually considered "scientific," begging the Latourian question: what are the aesthetics of matters of fact, and in what sort of social and aesthetic assemblages do we produce something that relates to our usual assumptions concerning knowledge, including scientific?[50] But it also returns the question: what is it that actually affords our sense of aesthetics and media anyway? What is the earth and the ground and the ungrounds of our aesthetics, our perception, our sensation, and the sensibility of the nonhuman subject?

Earth Computing as Psychogeophysic Cartography

Kahn's natural history of media (arts) resonates with the focus of psychogeophysics, although the latter is a rather more unruly practice-based endeavor. In the midst of the Anthropocene discussions and ongoing development of the theme of "materiality" in relation to media studies and new materialism, a range of artists are engaging with this geological materiality of devices and infrastructures also in ways that connect to a politics of digital culture. Jamie Allen and David Gauthier's *Critical Infrastructure* project that stemmed from their transmediale 2014 festival residency is emblematic of this investigation of what sustains media environments (Figure 6). Besides referring to itself as a "media archaeology of the present" and "the post-digital as the infra-digital or infratechnical,"[51] *Critical Infrastructure* adopts the terms and even methods of geology too. Using geological and architectural survey equipment, the artist–technologists investigate what underpins the increasingly invisible realms of technology: both the subterranean realms of the security and surveillance industries and the critical materials and their supply chains, part of the economic security regimes.

More directly related to the manifesto are the experimental projects by the group microresearchlab (Berlin/London) and, for instance, the

Figure 6. The *Critical Infrastructure* installation investigated the conflation of geological machinery and metaphors with the realm of big data mining. Poetically, one could say that the project infused the social mediasphere with the lithosphere–pedosphere. Project by David Gauthier and Jamie Allen. Courtesy of Transmediale/Simonetta Migano Transmediale/Elena Vasilkova 2014.

Crystal World projects by Jonathan Kemp, Ryan Jordan, and Martin Howse.[52] In recent years, we have seen the three iterations of the *Crystal World* ("decrystallization," "recrystallization," and the "*Crystal World*") executed in various ways with chemicals, natural elements, and DIY tinkering that brings out a rougher edge to opening up hardware than just circuit bending. For instance, the *Crystal World* exhibition—with its different versions in Berlin and London—presented a twisted take on the periodic table of Mendelev from the 1860s. Mendelev's table itself was not only empirical but also speculative, suggesting the rhythmicity of chemical elements.[53] Some of these projects are closer to laboratory experiments than an exhibition. But instead of a stabilization of materials as in scientific processes, they aim to look for variations and the strata of the earth reterritorialized as technology (see Figure 7).

Through different methods, Howse, Kemp, and Jordan investigated the process of crystallization and decrystallization as defining digital culture. In this limelight, "computers are highly ordered set of minerals" and the (de/re)crystallization methods backtrack their material lineages just like tracking the deep times of geological stratifications. This details the mineral and metal basis of computational technology (from coltan to gold, copper, etc.) but also the processes of extracting and constructing. Besides reproducing the processes of extraction of valuables from discarded technology, the projects also test as to how far art vocabularies and methods can go. It sets itself beyond the usual institutional prescriptions as a way to elaborate the aesthetic method through "construction of high heat and high voltage synthetic geologies, crystalline signal processing, speculative geophysics, anthropocenic (re-)fossilizations, and diffracted odic imaging,"[54] where the work of computational hacking becomes reattached to lineages of alchemy. This is where the base elements—in this case, from fungi to mud—are connected with the supposedly refined evolved material bits of advanced technologies, such as computers, but ones whose insides are exposed to what they consist of, for example, copper and aluminum in a constellation of elements of postapocalyptic mood. Besides workshops, the *Crystal World* projects such as the one in London are weird installations of computer culture, which, however, feature the odd inside-outs of "rust and lumps of scavenged copper and zinc in a solution of silver nitrate."[55]

The Crystal Open Laboratories and exhibitions are psychogeophysical investigations, which establish a link between the technological–chemical methods, information technology, and capitalism. The projects summon the narratives of fiction from Ballard to Pynchon but also a different sort of a material history than we inherited from the Marxist legacy. In these practices, (new) materialist critique becomes embedded in geological times of crystallization, applied to an understanding of labor and the specific political economic settings in which material is catalyzed into information technological machines of reproduction of social relations. This refers to the psychogeophysical cartography, not merely of city streets, but of the link between architectures of computing (especially hardware) and the geological strata. Indeed, this is why the *Crystal World* projects need to be recognized for what they are: an investigation of the mineral and substrate materialities as well as the materialities of global media production. In short, there are multiple sorts of materialities in play. In this way, the Marxist thesis of living labor being consumed as well as objectified into dead labor of machines is implicitly rephrased as a process of crystallization but arguing that such machines are not exactly dead. They sustain the living geophysical strata inside them, an archaic trace of a past life that engines the new medium. In this sense, the work and methodology of Kemp, Jordan, and Howse have an interesting relation to fossils and the archaic level.

One can appreciate the bending of the concept of the medium in this operation: from a communicational definition of the term, they hark back to its biological and geological roots, but without neglecting the wider political economy, which is about mobilization of energies and matter. Indeed, the political economic is not just "old" materialism compared to the new science and technological materialism cultural theory nowadays appreciates. Instead, the projects and psychogeophysics are investigating the continuum between cultural techniques and materiality of the earth; of information and its substrates; of the wretched of the earth and their uses and disuses in media technological settings.

In Martin Howse's *Earthcodes* project, the uses and abuses of speculative hardware are taken into a further viscous proximity with the earth. In Braidotti's terms, this would be literally a more geocentric take on digital culture: it approaches the earth as a motherboard and investigates

Figure 7. Jonathan Kemp, *Crystal World v. 2.0*, 2012. Various precipitation products, including sulfates and phosphates, after the continuous cycling for six weeks of weak acid–Grand Union Canal water over an installation of computer junk and rock ores. Courtesy of the artist.

practical possibilities of booting your computer directly from the soil. The experimental hardware configuration allows the operating system to boot from the soil with the custom-made USB device that can be plugged into the ground. The resulting "telluric operating system" is one which in the project acts as a media archaeological excursion to media history as well as a media geological dig reviving "the use of underground flows of electricity or telluric currents which were first exploited as generators of power within the telegraphic communications apparatus of the nineteenth century."[56] The telluric operating system is a twenty-first-century version of the original since the mid-nineteenth-century version discussed "telluric currents" of interest to both the geological discourse and expeditions and the emerging electricity-based technical media. Media acted both as based on electricity and also functioning as measurement devices for existence and demonstration of such Earth circuits and currents.

Telegraphists were the media epistemological pioneers of geophysical investigations.[57]

Back now in the twenty-first-century computer culture, the Earth-boot device is a tactical way of short-circuiting the massive global-level technological use of the earth and geology in corporate computing. The *Earthboot* project stems from a critical realization of the rather vampiric use of materials for proprietary means, packed as part of the hardware (Figure 8). The direct link to the substrate of the soil bypasses not only the usual hardware configurations and boot sequences but also the corporate chain of command—the "arche" in the sense of the command. Of course, this is a rather speculative take but exemplary of a cartography of geology intertwined with media technological capitalism.

The concept of substrate becomes a central part of the computational assemblage. Besides referring to the "complex industrial process to form an electrical logic gate," the concept carries a speculative geophysical connotation that is teased out with a Kittler-influenced[58] reference to Bram Stoker's *Dracula*. Software is a process of abstraction, but we need to consider the substrate in its poetic and yet technical materiality:

> Despite software's abstraction the geological maintains a particular attraction, as earth substrate, that which surrounds us, our material. Substrate equally presents a set of economic, political and economic consequences which contrast with software's lack of coded visibility, its inevitable "encryption." Stories such as Bram Stoker's *Dracula*, itself based on an earlier catalogue of fictions, shift the question of material and substrate to the body. Dracula's viral code is enacted at the interface with his substrate, the freshly dug earth which is transported to London and distributed around the capital; this infection vector.[59]

Viral code refers in this context less to work of software agents than to the substrate.[60] In art historical terms, Howse's contribution to psychogeophysics draws also on Smithson's earth arts and the 1960s discourse of geophysics in the visual arts. The *Earthcodes* project refers directly to Smithson, but the link is rather evident anyway. The entry of metals as well as chemical processes to the art studio highlights both the use of materials of geological and ecological significance and also, importantly, the nontechnological conditions of visual/media arts: for instance, oxidization, hydration, carbonization, and solution, which Smithson coins as "the major processes of rock and mineral disintegration."[61] Smithson's emphasis on this geocentric materiality comes out as a move from industrial mass technologies to what he calls a more fundamental stratum that can affect our sense of artistic materiality: "The breakup or fragmentation of matter makes one aware of the sub-strata of the Earth before it is overly refined by industry into sheet metal, extruded I-beams, aluminum channels, tubes, wire, pipe, col-rolled steel, iron bars, etc."[62] This is a passage, which fulfills the promise hinted by Caillois: rocks, stones, and broadly speaking the geological, are not only objects of aesthesis, they are also the potential catalyzer of chemical and technological alterations. Such a view to geological resources and the geophysical sphere approaches metals as catalysts.[63] Psychogeophysical mapping takes as its object the way in which metals can catalyze not only new chemical reactions but

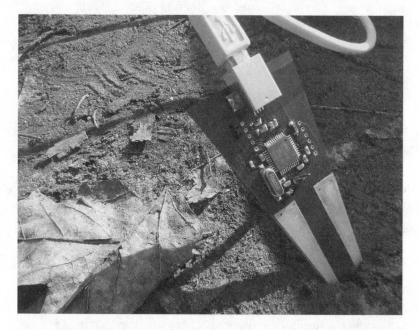

Figure 8. Martin Howse's *Earthboot* rematerializes land art and Smithson's abstract geology in the computer age: it constructs a speculative interface to use earth's electricity to boot an alternative computer operating system. Courtesy of the artist.

also social and economic relations and clusters. It is a cartography of the hardwired power relations by following the metallic and chemical relations in speculative art practices. Instead of a cartography of the city, we are witnessing a cartography of the architecture of the technological that is embedded in the geophysical.

Some of the psychogeophysics manifesto's claims are provocative (but I would claim playful) attacks on the urban focus of the Situationists. It's not that ecological critique was completely absent from the urban focus. It's anyway the case that cities live off and in their geophysical settings—cities are transformative, to quote Wark (discussing Chtcheglov): "[to] lay bare the process by which the city transforms nature into second nature, in the process making nature appear as a resource for the city's consumption."[64] This stance should not be mistaken with a simplistic idea of a sustainable city, Wark notes. Cities erode, disappear, get digested by deserts, and crumble in geophysical events like earthquakes, similarly as a powerful sun flare carrying its electromagnetic pulse would have major consequences both for electronic communications and infrastructure (e.g., electricity). Sometimes we tend to differentiate between the humanistic focus on place as the meaningful terrain of living and the material terrain, which reproduces itself through geology, weather, and climate.[65] Volcanoes don't belong so much to the terrain of our critical theory or cultural geography, but there is a need to theorize the geology especially because any notion of geographic "place" is constantly articulated as much by meaningful acts of signification of inhabitants as it is by the geophysical forces.[66] The urban and nonurban lives are anyway infused with the geophysical, in a parallel manner like our brains, bones, and bodies are infused with the metallic and mineralization processes that in earth durations connect us to histories of hundreds of millions of years of planetary time. But it also means the necessity for a psychogeography or psychogeophysics that is able to talk about erasure of place–space–terrain, and how direct or indirect geoengineering has produced terrains through eradication. From war to engineering, Dresden to Hiroshima, one can in a manner of a hat tip to Paul Virilio talk about the aesthetics of disappearance as pertaining as a geophysical force of technological culture.[67]

The Situationist methods are able to connect to realms of technology and computational culture too. Debord's definitions of the dérive were already ready-made hacker manifestos of sort. "From a dérive point of view cities have psychogeographical contours, with constant currents, fixed points and vortexes that strongly discourage entry into or exit from certain zones."[68] And Wark continues this passage from Debord, commenting on it: "The dérive discovers these contours. The city is an *aesthetic practice* irreducible to the interests of state or market."[69] Replace the city with, for instance, the computer, and you have the beginning of a description and a road map for alternative computing that is keen to find the breaking points, illegitimate uses, and zones that were being discouraged to enter. The technological machine is an aesthetic practice irreducible to the interests of state or market. Add to this mix the geophysical, and one is close to understanding the thinking behind the project(s): how the planetary, geocentric aspects contribute to this technological reality of machines that are bound to geophysics—both as a resource and as an affordance. The underground of deep time (see chapter 2) discovers a reconnection with the experimental art practices that excavate the literal underground, the soil, the substrate, but in touch with technological art practices that speculate with possibilities of bypassing the monopoly relation to the earth that digital industries' corporate capitalism is trying to maintain.

Literary history is filled with fantastic reference points for a geology of media or, more accurately, the geologic impact that cultural studies has to take into account. It ranges from Ovid to Thomas Pynchon's cryptic notes: "Behind the hieroglyphic streets there would either be a transcendent meaning, or only the earth."[70] Pynchon's line (in *The Crying of Lot 49*, from 1966) predates Situationism's similar famous slogan ("beneath the pavement is the beach"), but one is tempted to establish a fabricated link in our psychogeophysical context: Pynchon as a psychogeographic cartographer of technological culture—and in some aspects, even psychogeophysical, like the notes on permafrost in his recent *The Bleeding Edge* (2013) suggest.

The poetic history of geology of media and arts also includes writings on the meticulous arts of mining and metallurgy (not least Georgius Agricola's *De Re Metallica*) alongside stories of copper and alchemy, material histories of media, of astronomy and the planetary dimensions, and of deep times becoming deep space. We were not even able to go to examples such as Trevor Paglen's fantastic photographic research on the interlinkages of the mineral with the orbital, but that will follow briefly in chapter 5.

Pynchon's note toward the end of *Crying of Lot 49* about the hieroglyphic street is a parallel to Caillois's *Writing of Stones.* Stones are pitched by Caillois as a proto-alphabet, a narrative, an invitation to endless speculation, imagination, fabulation, and fleeting meanings that multiply in the seemingly immobile face of the rock. Pynchon's rather dry question is a useful way to orient in the cultural theory landscape as well. Indeed, what if we move from the paranoid interest of knowledge adamantly determined to find meaning, or to fix it to a religious or other transcendent entity to an active and dynamic reality constantly mobilized in relation to bio- and geopolitics of cultural production, but where also *geo* really refers to the ground and the underground? It is in a way the move from biblical time to the deep time and the geological realization of the earth (see chapter 2). Instead of the writings on the stones as hints of a hidden hermeneutic secret of the past or religious revelation, perhaps they are less signs in the semiotic sense than signals—signifying material aspects as part of the mixed semiotics[71] in which geology transforms into media and media reveals their geophysical conditions.

The nonhuman and the unhuman[72] return as tectonics, as earthquakes, as seabeds, layers of waste and synthetic geological formations, which we address in the coming chapters. It also folds as aesthetics of the deepest of times as well as what are the most recurring of times: those of the hieroglyphic inscribed on stones as perhaps a hallucinated meaning, a warning. In the words of Ovid again, "they penetrated to the bowels of earth and dug up wealth, bad cause of all our ills." This is the perfect one-liner for the Anthrobscene age.

The next chapter continues on obscenities of hard work and hardware. It moves from the undergrounds and substrates slightly upward to the surface with dust floating in the indoor and outdoor air. It offers a focus on the microparticles of dust as vectors for critical new materialist analysis. This is an expansion of the psychogeophysical mapping too: to use geophysical case studies, and the entanglement of the nonorganic with contemporary digital capitalism, as a way to understand some political economic implications of new materialism.[73]

4

DUST AND THE EXHAUSTED LIFE

Each particle of dust carries with it a unique vision of matter, movement, collectivity, interaction, affect, differentiation, composition,
and infinite darkness.

—REZA NEGARESTANI, *CYCLONOPEDIA*

I used to live in the north. Even southern Finland had its fair share
of snow some years, which meant the necessity to bring skis to sports
class and, on alternate weeks, skates. Next to the ice skating rink was
something to which one never really paid attention: the snow depot,
growing from the snow gathered by clearing the streets after snowy
nights. The mounds were sometimes rather big even in such a small town
and perfect natural, although temporary, hills for sliding or building a
snow castle.

I never thought of them as much more than that. I never thought of
them, for example, as glaciers—as Christian Neal MilNeil suggests we
should.[1] He pitches city snow dumps as significant geological constellations. We media theorists are primarily thinking of other sorts of waste
dumps as our fields of research—from Walter Benjamin's figure of the
ragpicker to the current interest in e-waste. But snow is a nonhuman
collector; it is an accumulator that by summer leaves this collection in its
wake. What snow demonstrates, acting as a sort of an inscription surface
or more likely as a mushroom sucking it in, is the heavy air that surrounds us. The geological does not stay on the surface:

There is a sediment that hangs in a haze above city streets: a low-dose toxic dust of lead and chromates from tire wear, clouds of carbon soot mixed with hydrocarbon gases and fine particles of nitrates, sulfates, and other metals from exhaust pipes. At every stoplight, worn brake linings leave behind microscopic flakes of copper, zinc, and lead.[2]

The geological is like a membrane, as MilNeil suggests. Might we even talk of a psychogeophysics of dirt, waste, and dust of cities? Such dust from car pollution and other sources leaves a streak on the white snow as it casts a membrane on outer and inner surfaces. Actually, there is no white snow—it rarely stays white for an extended period. The pure white stuff of imaginaries in advertisements and films does not really exist that often. Instead, we have dust, which is itself a curious case of a collective assemblage: dust carries with itself minerals and metals across distances.[3] But it is also a collective assemblage in the sense that it gathers a range of social, political, and media issues as part of its mobilization of materials: "metals and microbes, persistent organic pollutants and pesticides."[4] It's not restricted to specific regions or winds only but is also extra-planetary: tons and tons of cosmic dust remind us that we breathe in the otherworldly, the outer planetary—organic and nonorganic bodies suck in dust and chemicals, a realization we learned in the environmental sciences. Besides dust, our bodies still carry traces of DDT and other chemicals that have not been used for decades but linger as part of the environmental chains linking humans, animals, soil, and earth. And it goes on in other scales too. Ice layers that can be hundreds of thousands of years old record the chemical transformations of our planet. When it comes to corals, we can think of them as recording devices reaching back even millions of years, as indexes of the Anthropocene and, more recently, the residues of the atomic age (measurable in, for instance, carbon-14 concentration in the atmosphere and in corals):

In these rings they have found, for example, that some corals have recorded the atmospheric nuclear weapons tests of the late 1950s and early 1960s. Evidence of the Industrial Revolution is also documented, as is the Little Ice Age of the late seventeenth century. And

daily rings in coral may also document the gradual slowing of the
earth's rotation that astronomers first postulated.[5]

This chapter engages with the microparticles of dust and reads those
in relation to both the earlier themes of the deep time of geophysics of
media culture and its relation to the materialities of human bodies and
labor. Hence this double articulation of the chapter has to do with dust
and exhaustion. The notion of dust transports us to the lungs of miners
and Chinese workers subcontracted to produce digital media components in special economic zones. Health risks entangle with media materialism, dust with speculative realism, which, however, is approached
from a political angle together with Franco "Bifo" Berardi's notes on the
exhausted cognitariat. This chapter looks at this side of the cognitive capitalism, wanting to ground it in more mundane work and material features. Dust narrates the story but in a way that is paying attention to the
nonhuman agency of this narrator. Geology of media can be continued
with dust: not quite of the ground, not quite the atmosphere.

Dust: The Non-thing

There is something poetic about dust. It is the stuff of fairy tales, stories
of deserted places—of attics and dunes, of places from so long ago they
seem to have never existed. Dusty books: the time of the archive that
layers slowly on shelves and manuscripts. Marcel Duchamp's 1920s *Large
Glass* was a compilation of dust. In a way, he allowed dust to do the work:
a temporal, slow compiling by the nonhuman particles as a work of art
installed at the museum, "a purposeful inactivity."[6] Dust can transform,
even if it can itself easily escape any grip. It is amorphous, even metamorphic, in the manner Steven Connor describes.[7] There is also a lot of it.
Nanoparticles are everywhere and form societies unseen and unheard of,
yet they conglomerate on a scale unimaginable to human beings. We are
a minority. They have their say on human things and cover what we leave
behind intentionally or by accident—obsolescent technologies, wrecks,
and monuments—which remind us not only of these things themselves
but of the gradual sedimentation of dust. Dust forms geological strata.
Dust marks the temporality of matter, a processual materiality of piling up,
sedimenting, and—through its own million-year process—transformations

of solids to ephemeral and back. It swarms and overwhelms, exhausts and clouds. "Breathe as deeply as you will, dust will never be depleted."[8]

Even lack of breath has something poetically romantic about it. Lung diseases are after all a sign of the delicate soul and have a long cultural history. Tuberculosis features in a vast range of examples from a Puccini opera to Thomas Mann's *The Magic Mountain* (1924). The pale tuber-culotic body feeds the image of the mythical airiness of lungs, blocked by the disease. It is as if tuberculosis releases the body from matter: "TB is disintegration, febrilization, dematerialization; it is a disease of liquids—the body turning to phlegm and mucus and sputum and, finally, blood—and of air, of the need for better air."[9] But the lung-diseased body is easily exhausted, lacking in air, gasping for it. It is a tired body, and tiredness is one key trajectory we should be following as well: a laboring body.

Indeed, some people already take dust seriously—and not only the likely underpaid cleaning laborer working at a city corporate office at 5:00 a.m. Dust consists of so many things: hair, fibers, dead skin, plant

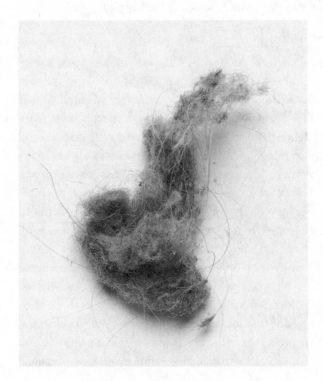

Figure 9. Rachel de Joode, *Dust Portrait*, 2014. Courtesy of the artist.

pollen, and nonorganic stuff like soil minerals. Even dust is metallic, geological. But the other pole is smart. Nanoparticles, smart dust, engineered
tiny things that are able to invade and inhabit organisms as mechanisms
of repair, improvement, and engineering. Smart dust quietly highlights
the world of nonhuman transactions that can facilitate, track, record, and
govern human affairs. We are nowadays fascinated by things minuscule,
mobile, peer networked, and able to calculate, process, and further transmit the data it receives. Dust can be seen in this sense as "the minimum
recognizable entity of material transformation and circulation."[10] But the
archaeology of computational dust goes much deeper into history and
begins with the abacus and the etymological root of the word in *abaq*,
Hebrew for "dust." Ancient dustboards were erasable calculation platforms,
writing surfaces. Babylonians and various scholars in the early Islamic
world used this platform, which consisted of "a board or slab spread with
a fine layer of sand or dust in which designs, letters, or numerals might be
traced and then quickly erased with a swipe of the hand or a rag."[11]

What if we followed dust as a trajectory for theory—theory that is
concerned with materiality and media? What if dust is one way to do
geology of media as "dirt research": a mode of inquiry that crosses institutions and disciplines and forces us to think of questions of design as
enveloped in a complex ecology and geology of economy, environment,
work, and skill. Dirt brings noise, as Ned Rossiter reminds us, and dirt
research can be understood "as a transversal mode of knowledge production [that] necessarily encounters conflict of various kinds: geocultural,
social, political and epistemological."[12] It fits in our emphasis on geology
of media: to track materialities and times of media culture through nonorganic components, entangled in issues of labor, economy, representations, and discourses.

Dust takes us—and our thinking—to different places and opens up
multiple agendas. In this case, dust talks to issues of global labor, media
materialism of digital culture, and illuminates how to approach media
materialism through nonhuman nanoparticles. The argument routes itself
through video games to factories, where gadgets are produced, to theoretical excavations in new materialism and speculative philosophy, to
science fiction and the engineering of everyday realities. Dust fills our
reality as well as our fantasies: the various fiction products set in dust

and dunes, with the obvious ecological example of Frank Herbert's *Dune* (1965).

Material things are often mistaken as modest—their numbers can be mostly counted—yet the immodest countlessness of dust signals something else. Are such "things" immaterial? Are they almost like the air, just a tiny bit heavier? Like gases, they are atmospheric for sure. Dust shares a lot of qualities with air as well as breath—they each force us to rethink boundaries of individuality as well as space. You cannot confine air and breath in a manner that our more stable contours, like skin, suggest. Peter Sloterdijk talks of the processes of inhaling and exhaling in this manner— as deterritorializations of sorts, like when the child blows her breath into a soap bubble, exporting a part of herself, externalization, extension.[13] Dust, too, must be thought as more of an environmental and atmospheric quality through which a different spatial and temporal thinking emerges.

Perhaps, then, dust is not just "matter" but something that troubles our notions of matter. Steven Connor talks of it even as antimatter: "evacuated of air, the gaps between the particles reduced to their minimum— hence its muffling, choking effects."[14] Dust also forces us to think of surfaces—it exposes them:

> At the same time, dust is characterized by a maximum of what might be called internal exposure, in which the ratio of the surface area of particles to their internal mass is extremely high. The availability of such a large surface area for chemical reactions accounts for the effectiveness of powders in forming solutions and suspensions. And, because they have no inside, because they are all a kind of internal exposure, dust-like substances can give contours or clarifying outlines to other things. Thus, dust, itself formless and edgeless, can both dissolve form and disclose it, like the snow that, in the right amount, can give to things a magical new clarity of outline, but passing beyond that point erases every landmark beneath its featureless drifts and dunes.[15]

Games of Hardware and Hardwork

Why dust and games? To talk of nonhumans is to talk not only about things and objects but about long temporal, material, and sometimes even abstract networks—such as networks of labor relations, which are abstract but completely real, and also nonhuman in the way in which dehumanization is at work in contemporary information technology (IT)-related practices. Cultural techniques of IT work are not, however, only techniques of cognitive capitalism, like communication, networking, and creative expression, but the techniques that sustain even the existence of IT—in factories, as well as when discarded electronics are dismantled.

I will focus on two games that address labor, materiality, and IT. The first and better known of the two takes the user to the world of iPhones, but not as we experience them in everyday life. Molleindustria's Phone Story,[16] which is available for Android phones and banned on the iTunes app store, elaborates the production chains and conditions of work from the mineral mines to Apple supplier Foxconn's factories in the "special economic zone" of Shenzhen; plagued by worker suicides, and indexical of the wider health issues having to do with aluminum dust that is a side product of ensuring that our iPads are shiny and properly polished, such places are the murky unconscious of gadget culture.[17] Aluminum itself is one of the primary chemicals and metals of technological modernity: its fetishlike shininess defines Italian futurism as much as post–World War II automobile culture.[18] There is a bitter irony that the residue of the utopian promise is registered in the soft tissue of a globally distributed cheap labor force.

A variety of metal and mineral materialities are essential for a wider picture of digital economy. Some of these are mapped as part of our awareness of the chemical sides of digital culture—entangled with issues of global politics. Good media art examples include *Tantalum Memorial* (2009) (Figure 10) and YoHa's *Aluminium* project (2008), focusing on the residue materiality of the metal. Molleindustria's painfully simple game creates another map of this darker side of media materiality. This map is about nonorganic and organic materialities: mining, suicides, electronic waste, and planned or meticulously scheduled obsolescence form the perverted side of the attractive, entertaining end device.[19] The iDevice is enabled by dubious labor practices, including child labor in the mines of Congo; the appalling working conditions, which lead to a number of suicides, in the Foxconn factories in China; and the planned obsolescence designed into the product, which also contributes to its weighty share of electronic waste problems. To make game play out of such themes is to look at the darker, not-so-immaterial cultural techniques that sustain creative cultures of digitality.

As noted in Nick Dyer-Witheford and Greig de Peuter's *Games of Empire*, Molleindustria games effectively establish procedural critique, a mapping of the algorithmic logic into which you, as the player–subject, are sucked into a systematic production of a limited, repetitive, depressive, and oppressive world without an outside.[20] What if we mobilize such critique in relation to the geopolitics of hardware? What if our mobile-consumer selves have to be understood in connection with the heavier burden of hardware, labor, and work processes? For instance, the outsourcing of production is also an outsourcing of this hardware geology from the Western perspective to far-away places. Outsourcing is historically connected to the emergence of consumer discourses that emphasize the lightness and mobility of digital technology. But it hides the outsourced

Figure 10. The *Tantalum Memorial* installation addresses the entangled circuits of communication, tantalum mining, and the Congolese civil war. Harwood, Wright, Yokokoji, *Tantalum Memorial–Residue*, 2008. Manifesta7 Bolzano/Bozen, Italy, 2008. Raqs Media Collective, "The Rest of Now." Photograph by Wolfgang Trager. Reprinted with permission.

hardness. This harder perspective does not downplay the argument concerning games and immaterial labor—that games as labor involve special "communicative cooperation, use of networked technologies and a blurring of the line between labor and leisure time," to use words from *Games of Empire*—but rather flags that supportive mechanism of labor on which immateriality can exist. This other labor—of factories, production lines, and lung diseases—shows a different notion of immateriality, which takes the near-immateriality of "lungs" and breathing as one central conceptual trajectory that offers a paradoxically different pairing in the context of geology of media.

What if you breathe the heaviest of air? What if you breathe residue of the metals and chemicals of digital culture? Should we speak of the exploitation of the soul through the contamination of the lungs? For Franco "Bifo" Berardi, the Italian philosopher, the soul becomes a way to understand the mobilization of language, creativity, and affect as parts of capitalist exploitation and production. Soul is the new ground for exploitation of cognitive capitalism, but it is a material soul that can also be exhausted:

> For a certain period the conquest of extraterrestrial space seemed to be a new direction of development for capitalist expansion. Subsequently we saw that the direction of development is above all the conquest of internal space, the interior world, the space of the mind, of the soul, the space of time.[21]

This is the world of cognitive capitalism and the cognitariat, which mobilize knowledge, affect, and other intellectual skills as a production force to be exploited—hence the need for careful practices of managing and organizing such skill sets and the cognitive labor force.[22] It is not, however, the case that the immaterial is *without* a material basis. Indeed, in his notes on "Exhaustion/Depression," Bifo argues that there is a relation between the slumping global economic regime and the psychosphere—a conjoining of depressions in a manner that clearly implicitly picks up on Félix Guattari's ecological thought: that we need to think of ecology not only through nature but through subjectivity and social relations. Bifo pays attention to the side effects of a brain-powered cognitive capitalism and its mantras of creativity by pointing out the increase in both various psychopharmacological means of mood management and in mental disorders. He comes to the conclusion that exhaustion and depression are actually the key bodily states through which to understand creative and cognitive capitalism and the world economy—the worn-out soul cannot keep up with its digital machines.

Bifo argues that the expansionist drive of capitalism no longer only reaches out for new natural resources but reaches toward the seemingly infinite creative powers of the human.[23] It is in this manner that I want to continue Bifo's emphasis on exhaustion, but with a slight caveat: that this exhaustion should not be mistakenly read as only about the mental powers of the rather still privileged informational workers, and that digital machines are themselves not understood as infinite or immaterial either. Instead, digital culture is also sustained by the rather exhausting physical work in mining, factory production lines, and other jobs that are not directly counted as part of "cognitive capitalism"—and the machines themselves grow obsolescent and die, their remains leftover media-junk and future fossils (see chapter 5); and ecological resources are exhausted as well, part of the increasing demand for minerals and other materials for advanced technology industries.

But Bifo does also insist on a material notion of the soul. The soul is a matter of breathing, lungs, and entanglements across scales. Indeed, we need to understand how the air and atmosphere of digital culture is one heavy with metals and chemicals, and the ground of digital culture is opened up for mining operations, such as minerals. The materiality of minerals and metals, from silicon to coltan, is entangled with the materiality of the lungs. In other words, this is the materiality of the nonorganic at the hardware end of things and a materiality of hardwork that connects to the labor sustaining the hardware.

The second game I want to discuss—iMine—does not differ much in terms of its content. Also available on various platforms, iMine focuses on the difficult life of the coltan miner in the Democratic Republic of the Congo. The game is rather simple, and to put it mildly, is rather boringly depressing in its repetitious content, with action limited to tiring, repetitive gestures on the phone or the keyboard to mine for tantalum. The game play is different; whereas in Phone Story, the user just touches a screen, in iMine, the user has to thrust the phone. But more conceptually, and in terms of the narrative, the game touches on what is described by the game developers/artists as "persistence of hardware":

> All the "magic" that today's technology offer [*sic*], ubiquitous com-
> puting and networked communities, depends on the reliability of
> hardware and physical power and communications infrastructure.
> This means that though the experience of electronically augmented
> daily life has changed significantly over the past few decades, the
> physical conditions which support these new realms of experience
> has not. Hardware still has to be made, under precise often difficult
> conditions. And hardware is made from materials which all started
> out, at one point, in the earth. The closer we get to the origin of the
> materials of digital technology, the more difficult the conditions
> often are.[24]

What both games seem to convey is the goalless, helpless situation of digging and working for hardly any reward. The miner in iMine is mapped as part of the more abstract flow of mineral prices on the global market in relation to valuations of tin, tantalum, tungsten, and gold. The game articulates the repetitious processes of mining as part of the abstract valuations that offer a financial basis for the trade of minerals and fights against some of the misperceptions of past decades of media theory that believed that telematics could free us from repetitious and boring work and release our playful cognitive capacities and transform "the redundant into the information."[25] Instead, both games remind us of points important for any material theory of media: like labor, IT is material. This materiality is made of components—mineral and chemical—and will some day end up somewhere. It won't just disappear; both ends of this simple chain include labor and organic bodies, each of which are the registering surfaces for effects and affects of media.

Media work in and through bodies, or, more widely, through materials and things. Hence we turn to a different focus concerning what Friedrich Kittler's material media theory flagged as *Aufschreibesysteme*, or "discourse networks," which refers to systems of inscription and a more genealogical account of the term that recalls the axis of Nietzsche–Kafka–Foucault to which Kittler belongs: social instructions are carved into the flesh by meticulous drilling, which is not only metaphorical but can also act through the disciplinary power of (media) machines. Bodies are made docile and behave in certain patterns of gesture and memory.[26]

The term *Aufschreibesysteme* originates from a curious case from the late nineteenth and early twentieth centuries—that of Daniel Paul Schreber, a prestigious German high court judge who was eventually diagnosed with paranoid schizophrenia and subsequently spent much of his time in treatment and in hospitals, becoming a widely discussed case study for Freud and many others. This was partly because of his book *Memoirs of My Nervous Illness* (1903).[27] In the peculiar but rather appealing piece of autobiographical prose, Schreber talks of bodies and inscription surfaces for the celestial scribes who write down everything about him, which for Kittler becomes a way to understand the new effects of technical media.[28] The body becomes passivized into a victim as "divine nerve rays invade and retreat, destroy organs and extract brain fiber, lay down lines of communication and transmit information."[29] Such hallucinatory case studies as Schreber's also produce the body as the locus of research and as epistemic objects too: for Freud psychic, for Kittler technological.

Kittler elaborates the idea further in relation to technology and argues that the focus on "bodies" remains insufficient when it comes down to the world of technical media. Indeed, such a stance is important in transporting the cultural theoretical vocabulary to take nonhumans seriously; so far this move has been often in terms of technologies, scientific elements, or what pejoratively has been called a technodeterminist approach (the media theoretical equivalent to "strangling cute puppies,"[30] as media theorist Geoffrey Winthrop-Young so aptly and with definite black humor calls it).

And yet perhaps we can extend that approach back to bodies—only not the model of the body adopted from Schreber's story, which inspired Kittler to write about technical media. What if we replace Schreber's tortured body with the focus on underpaid (and mistreated) workers' bodies at the hardware end of digital electronic media production as the model for inscription systems—sick, vulnerable, sacrificial bodies on the systematic production lines of products where the polished brand has its direct link to production processes and cheap labor? These bodies are epistemic objects as well, in the sense that they register the materiality of

IT production—and discarding—in lungs, brains, nervous systems, and more. They are indeed inscription surfaces for the "persistence of hardware," a conceptual turn Sean Cubitt also called for.

One way to make sense of this is to look at it through a chart I have devised—what I call a syndrome per metal or chemical chart. So, instead of celestial scribes that influence through, as well as inscribe upon, Schreber's body, this chart shows how other sorts of materials are inscribed on bodies of IT hardware laborers who open up the devices for valuable materials, such as gold:

Lead. Damages the central and peripheral nervous systems, blood systems, kidney, and reproductive system.

Cadmium. Accumulates, for instance, in the kidney.

Mercury. Affects the brain and kidneys, as the fetus in pregnant women.

Hexavalent chromium/chromium VI. Passes through cell membranes, producing various toxic effects in contaminated cells.

Barium. Causes brain swelling, muscle weakness, and damage to the heart, liver, and spleen.[31]

Such a list could be continued, but the preceding is enough to make the point about the materiality of media technologies and their material entanglement with our brains and spleens. It also points to the chemical, metal, and mineral materiality of both hardware and *hardwork,* and ways in which we can map those genealogical traces through labor. This is not merely an issue that has recently popped up with digital media and the global processes of mining and distribution of labor to cheaper conditions. A lot of hazardous chemicals were effects from mining and the use of coal and copper, lead from gasoline keeping transport media running, or the sulfur dioxide air we breathe and cough that characterizes the atmosphere of modernity, especially in urban areas and across borders as acid rain.[32]

Besides machines, chemicals facilitate the birth of the modern media age. Richard Maxwell and Toby Miller point this out brilliantly. Well supported by the range of research and statistics they are able to mobilize, they discuss the material effects that early print technologies had on the body and the environment. Besides the toxic by-products of the

nineteenth-century innovation of processing of fiber for making paper—
the effects of which I witnessed when I lived on a river next to a paper
mill in Finland—that directly contribute to massive water pollution and
deforestation,[33] consider, for instance, ink. Quite a banal, gray factor when
considering media studies topics that are keener to talk about the semiotics of what the ink stands for, ink is, however, worth considering for its
crucial material role in the emergence of print media. As Maxwell and
Miller write, "the ink was composed of lampblack, turpentine, and boiled
linseed oil—the first was harmful to the lungs and mucous membranes;
the second to the nervous system, liver, and kidneys; and the third irri-
tated the skin. For most of the nineteenth century, turpentine extraction
and distillation in the southern United States depended on slave labor;
after the Civil War, forced labor became the norm."[34]

This mapping of an alternative "Schreber" can be carried over to
more technical media, like the telegraph, too. The effects of media's materiality as chemistry and as toxicity are evident in considering what was
necessary to sustain such seemingly immaterial communication. Indeed,
just as with our digital communications, which have been consistently
branded with a breath of lightness in marketing discourses and even theoretical writings since the 1980s, illusions of telegraphic immateriality
are inscribed directly on the bodies of workers. Telegraphic communication was naturally based in electricity and, more specifically, the, in media
historiography, often neglected innovation of the battery. Again, to quote
Maxwell and Miller, early batteries were prime examples of "chemical
energy storage" consisting of sulfuric and nitric acid: "Liquid battery acid
helped produce the chemical reaction that generated the electricity, and
as the components (zinc, copper, and other materials, including mercury)
dissolved, toxic gases (nitric oxide in the case of the early Grove cell used
in U.S. telegraphy) were produced."[35]

Take a deep breath, inhale: damage to your lungs and mucous membranes and skin irritation. The air you breathe is metallic.

The Residue Elements

Modern media technologies elaborate what we could call "mixed materialities," similar to the manner of how Félix Guattari talks of mixed semiotics. This idea acknowledges that there are various materialities at work,

from practices of labor to production chains and on to the chemicals and components that compose the technology: these are semiotechnological arrangements. Indeed, speaking of "new materialism"—a term recently suggested to counter the overemphasis on meaning, representation, and signification—reminds that we are facing a variety of materialisms. We are dealing with multiple materialities and contested meanings of what materiality is: post–Fordist Marxism offers alternatives to German media theory. Actor-network theory offers a different set of interests to those of the feminist materialism of, for instance, Deleuzian scholars such as Braidotti and Grosz. Affect theory addresses topics of embodiment in new material ways. Cultural studies have, since the early days of Raymond Williams, been talking of materialism in relation to practices of cultural production. Speculative realism is one latecomer to these discussions as well.[36] So-called German media theory has been instrumental in reframing the materiality of media technologies (see chapter 1): the brilliant studies of the likes of Kittler and, more recently, Claus Pias, Wolfgang Ernst, Bernhard Siegert, Markus Krajewski, and others, have shown how we need a meticulous understanding of histories and practices of science and technology to understand technical media. However, modern media is about chemistry too—it is about components such as zinc and lead and about systematic health hazards that are directly connected to production mechanisms and conditions of labor.

A lot of the discussion goes under the name of new materialism, but perhaps we should consider historical materialism of the Marxist sort as a parallel stream to that. In a critical fashion, Manuel Delanda has rather aptly pointed out the anthropocentricity in Marx's theory of value: "only human labor was a source of value, not steam engines, coal, industrial organization, et cetera."[37] Yet instead of a full-fledged dismissal, this actually prompts the necessity to reconsider a postanthropocentric and a more, in the context of this book, geocentric and nonorganic (from chemicals and metals to technology/media) appropriation of the issues of labor, value, capitalism, and depletion of resources.

Marx was very aware of the relation between the soil (advances in agriculture) and capital. Indeed, we too should be aware of the relation of the *bios* to capital, which extends to what Jason W. Moore has called "peak appropriation," described as "the long history of enclosure and exhaustion of coal seams, oil fields, aquifers, and peasantries across the space and time of historical capitalism. In this light, the chief problem is not 'peak everything' but peak *appropriation.* Capital's problem today is not depletion in the abstract but the contracting opportunities to appropriate nature cheaply (with less and less labor)."[38] But of course, there is work, and then there is hard work: work that does not correspond to the idealized notions of capitalism of the brain (cognitive capitalism) but cheap, repetitive, and physically exhausting labor. It is this connection between labor and the biosphere of which we should also be aware. Labor consists of work and of working "the biosphere where the time-scale may be 1 million years";[39] processes of photosynthesis, fossil fuels, and the now-increasing centrality of rare earth minerals as memories of geological durations but mined as an essential part of advanced technological information culture—all these are part and parcel of the entanglement of materiality of work and the long-term duration of the materiality of the earth. For sure, such perspectives are usually only revealed in the critical breaking points of the normal processes of production to which twentieth-century philosophers— from Heidegger to Gilles Deleuze to Bruno Latour—continuously referred: only once things fail, *then* you start to see their complexity. In our case, that failure might come on such a scale that it is planetary: the depletion of resources, from fossil fuels (oil as the obvious case, and the discourse of peak oil[40]) to the already mentioned rare earth minerals. To this list let us add clean water, air, and soil.

Gary Genosko has referred to the Empedoclean four elements of earth, water, air, and fire as ways to molecularize also the contemporary realities of material reality where the elements and their new variations take a double role: empirical and metaphysical. In his reading, relying on Negarestani, Genosko moves further from an environmental or aesthetic understanding of the elements[41] toward a more molecular insight: how to map the constitution of contemporary issues, including polluted air, blood-stained mineral mining, new forms of contamination, and other mixing of elements into a new planetary machinic phylum resurfacing from the inherited four:

> Wrapped around these elements is the planetary phylum, a great tellurian cable bunch with its own products: EARTH: electronics;

WATER: liquidities like bottled water, which throws forward diagrammatic intensities in the explosion of plastic debris; AIR: gases (greenhouse) and; FIRE: artificial plasmas and lasers.[42]

This new mix of things is a way to investigate the elements of the media technological but also the wider mix of things in which contemporary culture takes place and takes form as part of environmental, political, and economic issues. In terms of dust, as mentioned earlier, it can be seen as a collective assemblage of materials as well as issues. It covers a lot of the globe (deserts) and a lot of our obsolescent media but also participates in processes of production of electronic high tech. The YoHa art project *Coal Fired Computers* (2010) articulated the entanglement of fossil fuels, miners' lungs, bronchitis, and emphysema with computer culture (Figure 11). Coal is one of the most significant energy sources, powering cloud computing data centers, but also an essential part of computer production itself—as the exhibit points out, "81% of the energy used in a computer's life cycle is expended in the manufacturing process, now taking place in countries with high levels of coal consumption."[43] Besides the

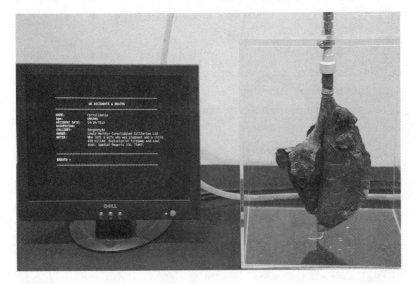

Figure 11. A close-up from the YoHa installation *Coal Fired Computers*, 2010. Arnolfini, Bristol, United Kingdom, 2010. "Coal Fired Computer and Tantalum Memorial." Photograph by Jamie Woodley. Reprinted with permission.

environmental impact, such a production process is a direct health hazard to the lungs that register the geologically heavy air. It's about the breathlessness: "Breathless from the strained vigilance, breathless from the oppressiveness of the stuffy night-air," writes Hermann Broch in *The Death of Virgil*.[44] The underground culture of mines and mining is essential for an evaluation of not only industrialization but also the elemental Anthrobscene in computer culture. The breathless state of the organic inscription surface persists, registering the geophysical traces as well as the dust of mines.

Coal dust is not the only type of dust relevant to this mining perspective to digital culture. Silicon dust has been identified as another significant danger to miners.[45] In terms of the older (visual) medium of film stock production, Eastman Kodak's Park Plant in Rochester, New York, was, besides being a heavy polluter of the region and a massive consumer of freshwater, also a place of acid vapors and dust.[46] The silver of the silver screen was at the less glamorous production end of things and produced serious health effects among workers. In addition, as Maxwell and Miller elaborate, the other essential material in the early years of cellulose nitrate film was cotton. Cotton, too, with its dusty media material trail, registered in the old media workers' bodies another health hazard, this one named *byssinosis*: brown lung syndrome.

Dust covers insides of lungs, and it covers our abandoned electronic devices. Planned obsolescence ensures that this happens with a quick turnaround. Dust is also supposed to be kept out from devices defined by refined electronics and their manufacture: the detailed and laboratory-conditioned fabrication processes of computer technology demand a specific dust-freeness. As Jennifer Gabrys writes, "electronics are rendered functionless if they are contaminated with even a speck of dust during manufacture. . . . Dust threatens the functioning of these machines, yet dust returns as a definitive mark of the materiality and temporality of electronics."[47]

There is something that feels so obsolete about coal and other dust. Mines are a central part of this picture of cognitive capitalism and IT too, as Harwood reminds us, even if they are displaced to locations such as India and China. Such centrality of metals and minerals was true already of the earlier media age, with its need for silver and copper, for instance.

As for the "new" media? Even "clean" digital media come with a residue dust: coal-fired computing that supports the existence of such glossy products.[48] Media are polished, also literally.

Aluminum dust is one of the excess "products" from the manufacture of computerized technology, such as from the process of polishing iPad cases. The minuscule dust particles already mentioned carry with them a double danger: they are highly inflammable and, more importantly, they can cause a variety of lung diseases among workers.

YoHa's *Coal Fired Computers* provides a good way of understanding the underground mining perspective to computational culture, and their *Aluminium* project from 2008 is a parallel one that relates to the metal–chemical composition of technology.[49] The project picks up on the imaginary of the aluminum defined by "beauty, incorruptibility, lightness and abundance, the metal of the future," mixed together with political realities (futurism and fascism in the Italy of the earlier part of the twentieth century) and materiality. Aluminum carries and assembles both realms of imagined meanings and the long trail of material residue, which becomes a method for the location-based installation at an Italian aluminum factory of the 1930s, investigating it from a media ecological perspective. This included both local elements, for instance, the power grid energizing the factory and the mythology of aluminum as the symbolically national metal of Italy of the time, alongside the accelerated industrialization throughout the 1930s and the rather longer and more abstract connections linking aluminum to contemporary concerns of material and technological culture.

The collaboration with the Raqs Media Collective rested on key terms and methodologies such as the notion of "residue":

The extraction of value from any material, place, thing, or person, involves a process of refinement. During this process, the object in question will undergo a change in state, separating into at least two substances: an extract and a residue. With respect to residue: it may be said it is that which never finds its way into the manifest narrative of how something (an object, a person, a state, or a state of being) is produced, or comes into existence. It is the accumulation of all that is left behind, when value is extracted. . . . There are no histories of residue, no atlases of abandonment, no memoirs of what a person was but could not be.[50]

The artistic methodology of refinement connects especially to the residue. It refers to the alternative narratives of materials, labor, and imaginaries surrounding the leftovers, resonating with a certain media archaeological spirit of lost paths and losers in (media/political) history,[51] but in this case, it also relates to the metallic geology of media culture. The residue is evident in the theoretical methodology of tracking dust, which connects new sorts of contexts, stories, and nondiscursive realities. This refinement does not lead only to the highly functional high-tech and scientific material components that quietly constitute the everyday life. It also resurfaces as the residue that is registered on two "surfaces" deemed expendable and disposable: human labor and the environment, which both bear the chemical effects of hardware.

Health risks are just one of the indicators of cost-saving practices at the production end of digital culture, but dust can, in this sense, act as a good trajectory to understand the significance of the nearly imperceptible nonhuman element. This narrativization through residue links up with the realization of taking dust as one element in the constitution of contemporary biopolitical and geopolitical reality. It shares some insights from Negarestani's idea of the singularity of dust too:

> Each particle of dust carries with it a unique vision of matter, movement, collectivity, interaction, affect, differentiation, composition and infinite darkness—a crystallized data-base or a plot ready to combine and react, to be narrated on and through something. There is no line of narration more concrete than a stream of dust particles.[52]

Such narratives are less linguistic and symbolic chains. The dust itself carries an affective force that is material and assembles collectivities around it. Dust does not stay outside us but is a narrative that *enters* us: dust has access in every breath inhaled, and it entangles with our tissue. Indeed, such a material agent of transformation as dust—whether smart or just irritating to the lung—is itself a reminder that there is an <u>excess</u> to the symbolic narratives.[53]

A Political Economy of Dust and Labor

So-called new materialism has great philosophical potential to assist in analyzing dust's materiality across scales and artistic methods.[54] It is able to offer a cartography of residue. New materialism is also a potentially vibrant methodology in that it helps to understand agency of nonhuman particles and the fabrics of materiality in which they function. My media studies–biased proposition goes something like this: new materialism is not only about intensities of bodies and their capacities—such as voice or dance, movement and relationality, fleshiness, ontological monism, and alternative epistemologies of generative matter—and active meaning making of objects themselves nonreducible to linguistic signification. I do not wish to dismiss any such perspectives; I rather want to point out the specificity and agency in *mediatic* matter too. New materialism is already present in the way technical media transmit and process "culture," and it engages in its own version of the continuum of natureculture (to use Donna Haraway's term) or, in this case, medianatures (see chapter 1).

The dust particle from a polished iPad is a residue of the admittedly beautiful fetishistic surface; the dust particle is what registers the global-ized wage labor relation on the soft organic tissue of the Chinese worker. Of course—to paraphrase Ned Rossiter—perhaps dust is simply a good indication of the "fantastic power of the commodity-form to abstract itself from the experience of labor and life."[55] The clean surface of the electronic commodity only betrays "the toxic conditions of production and their effects on worker's health and the environment."[56] Indeed, if we want to stick by such terms as the "nonhuman" and the "nonhuman turn," and also insist on using new materialisms irreducible to the vocabulary of atoms, or even forces of production, perhaps we still can think of the political economy of new materialism too—where new materialism can contribute to perspectives on work, waste, and wasting human bodies as part of work. We need to attend to the material soul, made of lungs and breath—and the shortness and time management of breath. The soul is not just an immaterial, quasi-mystical entity of immaterial inhaling and exhaling; it is constantly produced across the body—this is what Foucault argues. It is produced as emblematic of incorporeal materialism and, as such, of what can attach to lungs too. The soul is at work, and the work leaves its stain on the lung in the heavy air of computer-industrial capitalism.

In short, I am trying to work through some themes that are clearly part of the agenda of media materialism by showing how they gesture toward a politically significant materialism. This relates to geology of media through a tracking of the residues and materialities that tie planetary durations, chemical compositions, and media technologies into such assemblages, which move in different ways than traditional political, aesthetic, or media vocabularies.

As Harwood from YoHa articulates in relation to the activity of matter, materials have their own ability to "recursively unfold possibilities, transforming the flesh, the social, political and economic. Essentially what a material makes possible and what it shuts down when it's ripped from the earth and it's [sic] context and contaminates human ecologies."[57] This is where activity of the material, nonhuman, and nonorganic articulates itself: as a reality entangled with human concerns. Harwood, while articulating the idea behind the *Coal Fired Computers* project, makes a point relevant to the previously discussed contexts of materiality, minerals, and geopolitics:

> The materials also come into existence as a force when the political, geographical and economic situations are right for them to do so. Aluminium "needs" Italian Fascism to "need" a national metal, it "needs" Italy to lack coal, iron and have bauxite instead. Coal for a long time in the UK was dug from deep cast mines and the shafts required pumping out which creates the steam engine which in turn requires more coal and more labor. Tantalum "requires" political unrest in the Congo, kids playing Sony games.[58]

We could add various as absurd-sounding but as real "needs" produced alongside commodity and digital culture production. It is as if the electronic culture "needs" the increasingly growing e-waste mountains with their garbage collectors who are after the valuable materials inside the machines. Or we could say that digital culture needs the underbelly of underpaid workers displaced from the center of consumption to the global south (so to speak), endangering their health in poor working conditions, removed from corporate responsibility by way of subcontractor arrangements. Or we could even argue that the digital capitalism demands the exploitation of nature through its unsustainable exploitation and depletion of resources that range from energy (oil) to materials (copper and others). This should not be mistaken as a deterministic attitude that would forget the contingency of modes of production; it just flags how the other, darker sides of production are attached to labor and global economy.

An afterlife of the machines (see the Appendix) presents one further "materiality" in our investigative tracking of the nonhuman dimensions of media culture—and a focus on media materiality before media devices becomes another track for the cartography of residue and refinement.

Hence focusing on the materiality of components and the waste of electronic media suggests the extremely long and uneven networks of spatial distribution—and labor distribution—of media cultures. It oddly emphasizes the broadening of the markets on a global scale. In some disturbing accounts, such as one by the media rating company Nielsen, the fact that "more Africans have access to mobile phones than to clean drinking water"[59] is seen as a rather unproblematic statistic that cries out loud for the importance of business opportunities in the technologically revolutionizing African continent. Sometimes dust also equals lack of water. There is in any case a weird feedback loop between the race for resources of modern technological society, which started with colonialism and continued throughout the twentieth and twenty-first centuries: the search for minerals, metals, and oil across the globe, including Africa, only to return in the refined form of consumer products and the continent reterritorialized as a business opportunity. In this context of refinement, we need constantly to ask, what is the residue—both environmental and human?

Imagine materiality as a multifarious complexity: it is expressed in the perspective of minerals that are sedimented for millions of years before being mined by cheap labor in African countries for use in IT factories. After the short use-period for which an iPhone is destined, the device becomes part of the materiality of e-waste, leaking environmental hazards into nature through river dumping or incineration. In the latter, the burning produces toxic vapors that attach to the nervous systems of underpaid laborers in China, India, and Ghana. Manuel Delanda wrote of the thousand years of nonlinear history as a proposition to engage with the long durations of rocks, minerals, biomatter, and language.[60] As suggested in this book, we need to turn that into a million, a billion, years of nonlinear history—in the way Negarestani suggests in his work of theory-fiction—concerning petroleum, dust, and other material agencies. We need to think like new materialists, archaeologists-cum-geologists excavating how the *stratified* participates in the contemporary biopolitical sphere. This is a media geology of minerals, of chemicals, of soil as the resource for the active mobilization of those things constitutive of contemporary media consumer cultures; in short, it is about energy and the energetic regime that not only seems to have succeeded the industrial regime of the nineteenth and twentieth centuries but also the postindustrial regime: abandoned paper factories in Finland, after their production has moved to cheaper locations, are being reused as server farms partly because of their proximity to water, which acts as a cooling mechanism—renewable energy. The digital is a regime of energies: human energy and the energy needed for technological machines.

To conclude, it is in this context of the materiality of labor and dust that we need to talk not only of the soul at work but of the lungs at work. This chapter serves as a reminder of the alternative materialities of technical media culture that tie together issues of political importance and the murky sides of hardware. Bifo's reference to the "cognitariat"—the class of cognitive, creative, IT-supported smart labor—as the "semiotic labor flow" includes a wider materiality than any loose reference to a virtual class. For him, the cognitariat involves "the body, sexuality, mortal physicality, the unconscious." This description resonates with Matteo Pasquinelli's call to include both material and darker, libidinal energies in our accounts concerning media cultures and creativity discourses.[61] It is precisely because of this call that any extended understanding of the cultural techniques and technologies of the cognitariat needs to be able to take into account not just souls but where the breath comes from. This includes both the mental labor that is increasingly invested in high-tech communicative work processes that consume mental energies and the lungs violated by dust. It also includes chemicals, minerals, and hardware as sociotechnical conditions for the existence of IT culture. In Bifo's words, "life, intelligence, joy, breathing—humanity is going to be sacrificed in order to pay the metaphysical debt."[62]

    The lack of breath, whether from dust particles or from the increase in anxiety disorders and panic attacks, is indicative of the tie between immaterial labor and the material exhaustion of bodies of nature. Le Corbusier's modern fantasy of rationalized, filtered, and optimized "exact air" in *The Radiant City* has proven to be a short-term dream. With a different focus, Peter Sloterdijk identifies the beginning of the twentieth century with a specific event of breathlessness, in the early phases of World War I: "April 22, 1915, when a specially formed German 'gas regiment' launched the first, large-scale operation against French-Canadian troops in the northern Ypres Salient using chlorine gas as their means of combat."[63] Lack of breath, or "atmo-terrorism" (as Sloterdijk calls it), escorts the technological twentieth century into the twenty-first century, where we continuously face the same danger: not only from state terrorism but from (in)corporate(d) terrorism across industrial and postindustrial production—the twenty-first century as the century of dust, depletion of water resources, desertification leading to reduced crop lands. These issues expose the residues in our modes of production. This is geophysical terrorism.

5
FOSSIL FUTURES

As rocks of the Miocene or Eocene in places bear the imprint of monstrous creatures from those ages, so today arcades dot the metropolitan landscape like caves containing the fossil remains of a vanished monster: the consumer of the pre-imperial era of capitalism, the last dinosaur of Europe. On the walls of these caverns their immemorial flora, the commodity, luxuriates and enters, like cancerous tissue, into the most irregular combinations.

—WALTER BENJAMIN, *THE ARCADES PROJECT*

Waste like dinosaurs must return to dust or rust.

—ROBERT SMITHSON

Fossil Production,
Silicon Valley to Shenzhen

This chapter follows the path of geology outward to space. It also moves from deep times to future times by speculating on the idea of future fossils, as a future temporality turned back to the current moment. The fossil is in this sense a question about the contemporary that expands across multiple times. We are forced to investigate the persistence of the fossil as a material monument that signals a radical challenge to prevailing notions of time. This happened in the early modern times, with fossils presented as material evidence that was incapable of fitting into the scheme of biblical time and also challenging views of nature of earlier scientific heroes such as Linnaeus, who, with his taxonomic mission, was happy to be referred to as the Second Adam. Outside the world of adams and eves, in which ways could the future fossils of media waste, the "anthropocenic (re-)fossilizations" (see chapter 3) be also such uneven temporalities that force a consideration of how complex the time of the contemporary Anthropocene, in its obscenity, is?

If the current fossils from paleontological evidence to the fossil fuel layers are the things that mobilize the desires of contemporary imagination, how about the fossils we are producing now? What is the layer of dead matter residue that we are producing as future fossils? The earth is itself not a stable entity but constantly in a state of process. The body of the earth is a compilation machine, an assembly line, which offers a natural history of the changes over past decades of intensive industrial involvement in our planet. "Things like trash, construction debris, coal ash, dredged sediments, petroleum contamination, green lawns, decomposing bodies, and rock ballast not only alter the formation of soil but themselves form soil bodies, and in this respect are taxonomically indistinguishable from soil."[1]

The soil bodies are paradoxically unnatural natural formations, which will assemble the current afterglow of the industrial world and digital culture into the synthetic geological future. The synthetic future of soil is enveloped in an environmental context, but it also is related to the fact of soil becoming a tradable entity, entering into circulation of not only the earth but also the monetary reality.[2]

Elements become isolated, analyzed, synthesized, and enter into circulation as deterritorialized bits of information that can be traded in complex, global ways. From soil to minerals to chemicals, their scientific framing and engineering is also a prelude to their status as commodities. The four elements persist and yet mutate into hybrid objects telling the tale of scientific, high-tech engineered capitalism.[3] We have shifted from alchemy to chemistry. The periodic table is one of the most important reference points in the history of technological capitalism. The insides of computers are folded with their outsides in material ways; the abstract topologies of information are entwined with geophysical realities. The silicon of the contemporary computer world is one minor indicator of the other geophysical memories we will leave behind for the future archaeologists of media and environmental catastrophe. Let's start with some site-specific examples.

First up, a bit obviously, is Silicon Valley. Its brand and impact on digital economy are for sure beyond doubt, as is the aftereffect of the chemical leaks affecting the groundwater and releasing, for example, tricholoroethene. That was already a shock discovered in the 1980s: that the purified industries of computing were secretly just as dirty as the industrial ancestors that at least indicated danger with their smoke stacks.[4] Now the Superfund sites of Silicon Valley remind of this toxic legacy: instead of the promises of brain-fueled computer capitalism, one is still left with the residue of chemicals, toxins, and the materiality of electronic culture. In the early 1980s, the digital industries were featured as the "oil business of the eighties."[5] Like oil has had its dirty sides, from environmental pollution to dirty wars, so does the manufacturing industry of computation get its hands dirty. This includes labor rights violations and dubious practices where proper laws don't exist, historically moving from Silicon Valley to various locations in Asia. But this dirt also includes chemicals as the geological legacy of digital culture.[6] Computer culture never really left the fossil (fuel) age anyway; the previous chapter spoke of *Coal Fired Computers* (YoHa), and in more factual terms, we can remind that "to produce a two-gram memory microchip, 1.3 kilograms of fossil fuels and materials are required."[7]

So despite "the digital" carrying continuously the immaterial connotations of information, it is and always has been grounded and also territorialized.[8]

From prune and orchids to silicon, Silicon Valley changed gradually over the decades since the 1950s. By the 1980s, it had become a symbol of a new economy. By 2013, it had become a global brand but not always celebrated. Only recently, we witnessed the corporate commuter busses attacked for their symbolic role signaling of the toxic impact it had on the local areas. From "Fuck Off Google" to more elaborated articulations of the issue, Silicon Valley was not the solution but the problem. "While you guys live fat as hogs with your free 24/7 buffets, everyone else is scraping the bottom of their wallets, barely existing in this expensive world that you and your chums have helped create,"[9] as one of the fliers of the protestors attacked. But perhaps the map on which Silicon Valley finally appeared was not only about the pollution of social and economic conditions of living. Perhaps there was another map that is invisible to the eye, the underground, which registers another toxicity of digital culture?

The underbelly of Silicon Valley is one of toxic capitalism. Of course, it is not merely a feature of that one specific territory but is also moved to other places of production of the global digital economy. Indeed, consider Shenzhen and Huaqiangbei, "the electronics component mecca,"[10] as echoes of the Silicon Valley legacy, what has been branded "environmental racism and environmental injustice" by Pellow and Sun-Hee Park.[11]

In a certain way, we can consider this legacy in relation to both space and time: the material production of a massive amount of electronics and the logistics of their shipments back and forth, as functional, cheaply produced hardware and to other directions as disused and sometimes broken obsolete media. The legacy points to the future fossil record for a robot media archaeologist interested in the paleontology of scrapped electronics, but it also forces us to consider what is our current relation to hardware at the moment. This is where death—but also living deads—features as part of current enthusiasm for discardability.

In the midst of the wider excitement for a global digital economy of software, some business correspondents, such as Jay Goldberg, have realized that hardware is dirt cheap and even "dead."[12] His claim is less related to the Bruce Sterling–initiated proposal for a "Handbook of Deadmedia," "a naturalist's field guide for the communications palaeontologist,"[13] than it is to observing a business opportunity.

Goldberg's dead media business sense is focusing on the world of super cheap tablet computers he first encounters in China, then in the United States for forty dollars. For this particular story, it triggers a specific realization regarding business models and hardware—the latter becomes discardable, opening a whole new world of opportunities:

> When I show this tablet to people in the industry, they have universally shared my shock. And then they always ask "Who made it?" My stock answer is "Who cares?" But the truth of it is that I do not know. There was no brand on the box or on the device. I have combed some of the internal documentation and cannot find an answer. This is how far the Shenzhen electronics complex has evolved. The hardware maker literally does not matter. Contract manufacturers can download a reference design from the chip

maker and build to suit customer orders. If I had 20,000 friends and an easy way to import these into the US, I would put my own name on it and hand them out as business cards or Chanukah gifts.[14]

The reduced price of the tablets means widespread availability even for niche uses: from waitresses to mechanics, elderly people to kids, tablets could become the necessary accessory in such visions that are astonished when realizing the business prospects. The visceral reaction by Goldberg is followed by rational calculations of what it might mean in the context of digital economy business models:

> Once my heart started beating again, the first thing I thought was, "I thought the screen alone would cost more than $45." My next thought was, "This is really bad news for anyone who makes computing hardware. . . .
>
> No one can make money selling hardware anymore. The only way to make money with hardware is to sell something else and get consumers to pay for the whole device and experience.[15]

Even hardware gets drawn as part of the discourse of *experience* economy and the immaterial connotations it carries. Hardware seems to be immaterialized. Goldberg misses the point that hardware does *not* die, not even in the Sterling sense of unused dead media that become a sedimented layer of fossils left for quirky media archaeological digging. Instead, media technologies from monitors to game cartridges are abandoned, forgotten, stashed away, but retain their toxic materiality that surpasses the usual time scales we are used to in media studies. Such abandoned media devices are less about the time of use, or practices of users, and more the time and practices of disuse. It certainly would be interesting to write a history of cultural techniques of technological disuse.

Besides moving on from use to disuse, progress to failure, I want to remind of the chemical durations of metal materiality. Think of this idea as the media technological equivalent of the half-life of nuclear material, calculated in hundreds and thousands of years of hazard; in media technological contexts, it refers to the dangerous materials inside screen and computing technologies that are a risk to scrap workers as well as nature, such as the soil.

A utopia of cheap hardware produced in places of cheap labor indicates the creation of a new future layer of zombie media. Hence we can start to perceive these clusters as producing not only new sorts of gadgets of consumption, implied new business models, or just economic opportunities but also a layer of fossils of electronics. It means that a list of things produced equals another list of zombie media future fossils, an immense quantity of electronic culture that is indicative of new senses of futurity as well.

> Oscilloscopes and multimeters, connectors of every shape and variety, LCDs and LEDs, motors, wheels and buttons, resistors, capacitors, miles of USB cables and row upon row of copper tape, soldering paste and every manner of specialized glue. Hundreds of stalls each with hundreds of components organized and displayed for browsing. You may never have seen a reel of PCB components for loading into pick-and-place machines. At Huaqiangbei you'll see thousands upon thousands of them.[16]

The visual image of immense piles of electronic rubble that the list provokes is one indication of an attempt to cognitively grasp the scale of production of digital culture. From visual arts such as Pieter Hugo's photography of bleak landscapes (see his "Permanent Error" work) to United Nations reports, there are various overlapping and reinforcing ways in which different institutions are trying to make sense of the contemporary conditions of technological waste. Often the images of solitary e-waste workers in non-Western locations, standing next to the piles of dead or zombie media, correspond to the tropes favored by the written journalistic descriptions: counting the mass of electronic waste per year (last year around fifty tons globally) or eventually as "a 15,000-mile line of 40-tonne lorries"[17] full of phones, computers, monitors, electronic gadgets of all sorts. The United Nations action-step initiative is in this context a rather significant and comprehensive attempt to tackle the e-waste problem from policy, design, and, for instance, reuse and recycling practices perspectives so as to be able to address the dual issue of waste and critical material depletion.[18]

This chapter's perspective is, however, on fossils. These bodies of dying media technology are not merely disappearing as part of the soil but constitute a defining mix in terms of their chemicals, hardware elements, metals, and more: something of a different sort of a dying body than the organic layer that condensates as part of the earth. This layer, we can speculate, will persist as an odd reminder of electronic culture and its entanglement with nature. This chapter is a discussion of different art projects and theoretical debates concerning (media) fossils, a sense of digital futurity and the temporal scales of digitality. Similarly as the modern scientific interest in fossils in the zoologist Georges Cuvier's early-nineteenth-century work tied them with the history of earth catastrophes,[19] our chapter and its artistic examples speculate on the future environmental catastrophe we are producing now in terms of the environmental.

Professor Ichthyosaurus's Lesson

Fossils have been for a while part of the media and culture debates in conferences, festivals, and book pages. The deep time perspective on the earth and its media (see chapter 2) stems from the interest in paleontology. Sterling's media paleontology of dead media used similar ideas. The Atari games dump is the widely circulated story of thousands of E.T. and other game cartridges buried in early 1980s in Alamogordo in New Mexico, turning in 2013 and 2014 into a literal excavation and exhumation of dead media, even if enthusiasts first had to wait for testing of the landfill for hazardous chemicals such as methyl mercury, malathion, and DDT (see Figure 5). In April 2014, through concrete unearthing of media from the earth, plenty of examples of discarded materials were discovered.

Jennifer Gabrys's "natural history of electronics" is perhaps the most elaborated use of the notion of the fossil in the context of digital culture. She picks up on Benjamin's methodological focus on dead and decaying objects as a way to understand the material imaginary of commodity culture. Indeed, as Gabrys points out, Benjamin's natural history of commodities and capitalism was a paradoxical unnatural natural history, which focused on the material effects of the itself historically contingent modes of production and circulation.[20]

In this context, for Gabrys too,

electronic fossils are in many ways indicative of the economies and ecologies of transience that course through these technologies.

Electronics are not only "matter," unfolding through minerals, chemicals, bodies, soil, water, environments, and temporalities. They also provide traces of the economic, cultural, and political contexts in which they circulate.[21]

Fossils have been at the center of the new modern worldview at least since the nineteenth century: both geologists like Charles Lyell and biologists like Charles Darwin focused on the fossil as an object of analysis that opened up a book of fragments. The fossil was the buried temporal object that was a gateway to past times as a monument in the present. These are signals of the historicity of the planet condensed in the present and show the earth as a library as well as "a recording medium."[22] The fossil enthusiasm of the nineteenth century was visible in how geology mobilized the earth as a secret treasury of the past, with volcanoes as one source of disruption that sometimes fold the visible surface with the hidden depths of the planet. Lyell's *Principles of Geology* (1830) preempts with its early geological scientific touch what Pink Floyd did poetically later with sound technologies in Pompeii ("Live in Pompeii," 1971–72): in the shadow of Vesuvius and the wake of its magma to depict Pompeii as a place of frozen time and frozen bodies, but as ways to understand the overlapping temporalities where the past exists in the present as monument.[23] The magma is in such geological imagination the original time-based art process, which imprints us images as fossils.[24] In later parlance of the information age, we can say that fossils are the *data* that geology processes.[25]

But the important thing and indication of the multitemporality of the fossil layer is really brought to light only in contemporary paleontology, which rethinks fossils through punctuated equilibrium. For Darwin in *Origin of Species* some decades later, following Lyell, the fossil record is like a book with only fragments left: it is only a fragmented part of a totality that cannot be discovered, and the only things scientists—and the contemporary living world—are left with are traces. However, for our contemporary scientists, such as Stephen Jay Gould and Niles Eldredge, the fossil layers' seeming deficiencies, random jumps, and nonlinear nature are exactly the striking fact that demonstrates the essential: the archaic and the current are entangled through such fossil monuments. Instead of a uniform, slow, gradual evolution of the planet, from its geological record to its life, we must consider the possibility of both as *punctuated equilibrium*:[26] abrupt changes and relative stasis, or in other words, coexisting different temporal orders of change, both as real.

Gould's critical recap of the arguments of early geologists is useful in conceptualizing the nature of contemporary media fossils. In a way, the early geologists did a dress rehearsal for the Anthropocene discussions now, some two hundred years later. Despite shortcomings corrected by more accurate recent theories of geological time and change, even early pioneers like Lyell were imagining possible pasts and futures without humans. This comes out strikingly well in a popular satirical image targeting Lyell's idea of a cyclicality of the geological. De la Bèche's image shows a future Professor Ichthyosaurus giving lessons about the past fossil humans as exotic of a memory as the *sauruses* discovered by paleontologists in the midst of the nineteenth-century fossil frenzy (Figure 12)![27] Revisualize this into an image of the future professor showing fossil remains of not only humans but also their technological extensions. Who is her audience though?

The mid- and late-nineteenth-century geological imagination was constantly talking about the future. A fascination with archaeology, geology, and ruins was complemented with an imaginary of future ruins. Besides the enthusiasm for the archaeological excavations of antiquity, one was painting future perspectives of the contemporary imagined as a forthcoming excavation site of similar importance: Joseph Michael Gandy was invited to paint the Bank of England with a bird's-eye view of how it would look after hundreds of years of decay, abandoned to the mercy of natural forces. The piece was first exhibited in 1830. About a hundred years later, a similar fantasy of ruins as a sign of great civilizations was adopted in the architecture of the Third Reich in Nazi Germany. It was meant as a demand to build in such a way that leaves only honorable lasting ruins for future archaeologists: a theory of the value of ruins, as it was coined by Albert Speer.[28]

Fiction such as H. G. Wells's *The Time Machine* (1895) created the Morlocks, far-future inhabitants of the underworld, machine operators of a slightly human sort. Evolutionary ideas from Darwin to Thomas Huxley had a penetrating impact on imagining the future of the planet and human species on and underground of the earth. Besides evolutionary

Figure 12. Professor Ichthyosaurus lecturing to an animal audience on fossilized human remains. Lithograph by Sir Henry de la Bèche, 1830, after his drawing. Wellcome Library, London.

remnants and underground life, "the . . . nineteenth century was haunted by that prospect of future burial."[29] Also in Antonio Stoppani's pre-Anthropocene account from 1873, something of a similar idea was employed. Besides predicting that new "anthropozoic" era that mankind had entered, he suggested to speculate "that a strange intelligence should come to study the Earth in a day when human progeny, such as populated ancient worlds, has disappeared completely."[30] Instead of the past cyclical formations returning in new guises, the future holds an alien visitor who finds traces of the earth molded by modern science. Future geology becomes a narration of "history of human intelligence," meaning science and technology growing on top of nature, animals, and plants. It represents a novel geological periodization projected and then retrojected from the future back onto our world. Professor Ichthyosaurus's and Stoppani's alien intelligences are representatives of this new geology of non-humankind that starts in the nineteenth century, not just the twenty-first-century Anthropocene debate.

With Lyell and the birth of geology, we access the periodization of the earth's deep time into specific layers and their fossil remains. From the Paleocene to the Eocene, Oligocene, Miocene, Pliocene, and Pleistocene to the most recent Holocene before the discussed Anthropocene (or, as I prefer, the Anthrobscene): even if such present seemingly stable "layers" of uniform process, they are more like singular points indicating events; they are assemblages of specific fossil materials as well as accelerated by sometimes catastrophic changes.[31] Stratification is not necessarily a smooth, slow process but multitemporal, speeding up, slowing down.

We need to address how fossils, whether of humans, dinosaurs, or indeed electronics, infuse with the archaic levels of the earth in terms of their electronic waste load and represent a "third nature" overlapped and entangled with the first and the second. These various natures of course refer to how McKenzie Wark has developed the Marxist conceptualization: the second nature is the sphere of consumer goods production characterized by wage labor relations in a capitalist society as well as the different modes of alienation that the exploitation of first nature brings about; the third nature is the logistical vector of information through which production of second nature takes a new informational pace.[32] But as we see from the existence of media fossils, the spheres of two and three are as entangled with "first nature" as they are with each other. They are historically codetermining in a way that defies any clear-cut differences between the modern era of industralization and the postmodern era of information.[33] In addition, the material residue of the third nature is visible in the hardware and waste it leaves behind, despite its ability to reach abstract informational levels; the abstract comes with its underground of energy costs and environmental burden that we are registering with various scientific and artistic means. If Benjamin already pitched the world of emerging consumer culture through the concept of "fossils,"[34] we can now ask what sort of fossil layer is defined by the technical media condition. Instead of the sudden apocalypse brought about by Vesuvius, our future fossils layers are piling up slowly but steadily as an emblem of an apocalypse in slow motion.

Telofossils

Media artist Grégory Chatonsky's *Telofossils* (2013), a collaboration with sculptor Dominique Sirois and sound artist Christophe Charles, picks up on this context of technologies, obsolescence, and fossils. The exhibition at the Museum of Contemporary Art in Taipei, Taiwan, focuses on the slow, poetic level of decay that characterizes technopolitical society and nature. The "future archaeologist" perspective that Chatonsky summons with immersive affective moods created in the exhibition's installations is akin to Manuel Delanda's figure of the future robot historian that gazes back at our current world emphasizing not the human agency of innovators but the agency of the increasingly automated and intelligent machine (as part of the military constellation).[35] The future archaeologist in Chatonsky's installations and immersive narrative is a displacement of the human from a temporal perspective (the future) and from the Outside (alien species):

> *Telofossils* is a speculative fiction about this Earth without us. If another species arrives on Earth in thousands of years, what will it find? It will uncover from the ground billions of unknown objects with no apparent use, fossilized. It will certainly wonder why there are so many of them. A plastic bag can last hundreds of years when I only have 2,500 weeks left to live. This disproportion between the human life expectancy and the one of our technical artifacts gives a new dimension to our time. It will be a material trace for our memories. Making this absence and this disappearance visible is the goal of *Telofossils,* an impossible project.[36]

The long-term perspective that starts from banalities of everyday consumer materials, like the plastic of the shopping bag, is an echo of Benjamin's style of narrating culture through its relations with the natural, but it is also embedded in the contemporary political context. In a mix of spatial narrative through escorting the exhibition viewer–participant through the rooms and spaces, Chatonsky creates affective states surrounded by signs, audiovisuals, and technologies of modernity. The mood management signals of affective atmospheres of the post-9/11 catastrophe that brands the past ten years of everyday life in consumer-surveillance societies. For Chatonsky, this mix is a necessary way to make sense of the multitemporality of the looming catastrophe: the notion of the fossil addresses the slow stratification of a synthetic layer of technological rubbish. It refers to the aura of the accident[37] that surrounds the technological of past decades and hundreds of years and transposes it to the future. After the accident that was predetermined as part of the unsustainable technological modes of innovation, we can realize also why Chatonsky's work is about "telo" instead of just "tele" fossils; the "telofossil" hints more of the implicit "telos" of the processes of fossilization with a dose of mourning and sadness. Every technological invention is an invention of specific accidents that accompany it, reminded Virilio. Perhaps this is the true insight of Chatonsky's piece—to unfold speculative teleological hidden task of technologies as one to record our slow passing away; like technical media for the first time were able to record the dead and allow them to speak from the afterlife, they also in the digital form are the projection technologies of this telos: a projection toward the future as the canvas for the past fossils.

Indeed, for Chatonsky, the double role of technology becomes understood through future as a fossil: in his words, "they participate to the exhaustion of our planet but they also constitute traces of our existences."[38] The material contribution of technologies to the environmental damage to the planet is matched by their role as carriers of a memory of the past. They are in this sense "monuments" like briefly mentioned earlier concerning fossils. By their material duration, they insist on living after their use period (see again the Appendix to this book). And they also carry with them the potential to trace the existence of the world that was around them, including human cultures. It is recorded in the storage devices of technical media microtemporalities of hard drives (summoned in one installation piece in Chatonsky's exhibition through a broken hard drive) as much as it is in the chemical composition of man-made artifacts (Figure 13).

Telofossils is a project about time, and it is pitched as an archaeological and archival investigation of the future. The ways in which media archaeology has offered new insights into media cultural temporality cannot be ignored. Erkki Huhtamo's way of arguing for the cyclical and recurring nature of media culture through its narratives and topoi can be related with Zielinski's deep times (chapter 2) and Wolfgang Ernst's microtemporal investigations (see chapter 1). Also Kittler's insistency to see media history through its material contexts that depict the human agent only as an aftereffect might need to be radicalized to a media geological history of technology: that Man is the aftereffect of the geological durations, mineral excavations, metal affects (Delanda), that catalyze technological reactions and social events.

An archaeology of the future has a double function in Chatonsky's work. On one hand, it reminds of the ways in which memory is always a remediated material event: memory is always a monument and inscription, whether that happens on the random-access principles of magnetic storage media like hard drives or in the still experimental modes of storage in biological material like bacteria. The future memories might be embedded in the archaic materiality of the organic, such as bacteria and cells. And for certain, the fossilized remains of the past from some three hundred to four hundred million years ago still burn to make data circulate in contemporary network computing and big data mining, despite the warnings from Greenpeace: the Internet companies "are powering the twenty-first-century data centers that are the engine of

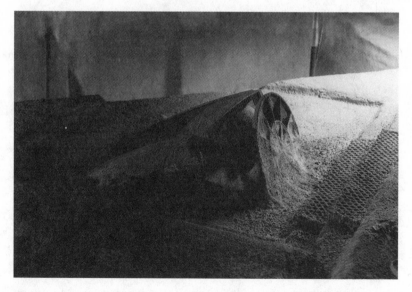

Figure 13. A close-up from Grégory Chatonsky and Dominique Sirois's installation *Telofossils*, 2012. Courtesy of Xpo Gallery.

the Internet economy with nineteenth- and twentieth-century coal and nuclear power,"[39] demonstrating the complex temporal layers of digital technology itself. New media, archaic power.

On the other hand, Chatonsky's interest in memories has to do with the future and what we can imagine. It is about archaeologies of the future, partly in the sense that Fredric Jameson talks about the link between imaginaries and modes of social production. Also imagination, and imagination of futures in the plural, is tied to the current economic and political contexts. Jameson writes in *Archaeologies of the Future*, lamenting on this impossibility to think outside capitalism, "What is crippling is not the presence of an enemy but rather the universal belief, not only that this tendency is irreversible, but that the historic alternatives to capitalism have been proven unviable and impossible, and that no other socioeconomic system is conceivable, let alone practically available."[40] Chatonsky's way of writing the future fossil layer through the present concerns in technologically fueled crisis of political credibility—visible in the various measures of surveillance, control, and (in)security of the post-9/11 planet—marks it as a work that is, despite the aspects of affective mourning, actually still keen to investigate how to imagine alternative futurities. Hence the fossils of the future are the ones we live among, and in this speculative fiction, the extrapolation of current technopolitics is returned to us via memories of the future. This link of present and the forthcoming is implicitly there in any kind of an apocalyptic future scenario. The question is, why are we imagining now such postextinction futures, worlds that are mediated and *in medias res*—a mediated technological future?

The notion of telofossils as employed by this imagined future is one sort of a continuation of "paleofutures." It refers to a transposition of the speculative and the archaeological fragment to the future and a variation of the imagined future-theme. It parallels with the imaginary media discourse as much as it comes close to design fictions as one speculative methodology of creative practice. Bruce Sterling's interest in it as "the reserve of historical ideas, visions and projections of the future"[41] is one clear indication of a field of relevant research, and it would not be far-fetched to claim that Chatonsky's fabulation of the future archaeologist is one way to extend design fictions. Paleofuturism is most clearly articulated in the blog *Paleofuture* by Matt Novak:[42] it maintains a discourse of past futures that are the fossils of the contemporary—a perspective on the speculative nature of scientific and technological discourse in the twentieth century that fuses the times of future and deep time so as to create the weird mixed temporality that brands technological culture. The emphasis on the current and the new in contemporary media culture becomes one of the objects of critique: Zielinski's notes against "psychopathia medialis"[43] of standardization and the political critique by Jameson are important ways to understand what in this chapter and in this book amount to the environmental geology of media—the fossils of paleofuturism are the aftereffects of the increasing piles of waste, and the melancholic postapocalyptic scenario painted by Chatonsky likens the future of the present not to a progress-inspired myth of cybernetic control of nature through technology but to a massive accident that happened because of technology. Virilio, the primary theorist of the accident, spoke also of gray ecology, which comes with the accelerating tendencies of modern technical media: a reframing of relations and disappearance of distances that have a fundamental effect on our aesthetic–ethical stance in the world.[44] However, gray is also the color of the covers of hardware and surroundings of the metallic parts as well as plastics, which create a further surface of the planet. It is another layer that becomes at the same time an historical and geological index of advanced technological culture. This gray ecology is the ecology of media technical fossils—telofossils.

The notion of the fossil is a hint at a future grounded in dysfunctional technology: indeed, similarly as in new insights in technology and repair studies, we need to be able to rethink the modernist fantasies (also visible in the historical maps of past imaginary futures in paleofuturism) of technology as clean, smooth, and progressing and replace such with the primacy of the accident. Scholars such as Steven Jackson and Lisa Parks have outlined this in brilliant ways. Following Jackson, we need to be also thinking of future fossils as "exercise[s] in broken world thinking,"[45] which is branded by the post-9/11 scenarios articulated by Chatonsky's art and design practice. If furthermore read in parallel with Jackson's words, it means that "we take erosion, breakdown, and decay, rather than novelty, growth, and progress, as our starting points in thinking through the nature, use, and effects of information technology and new media." Hence a truly paleofuturistic take on fossilization of mediatic technology starts from this scenario: things broken down, abandoned, and decaying as part of the future fossils of medianatures (cf. chapter 1).

Outer Space Fossils

I won't go into the issues of repair culture, as articulated by Parks, although it is an important step in acknowledging the geopolitical and postcolonial stakes in this fresh perspective to broken technologies. Instead of Eurocentric myths, it suggests a different take on media history and archaeology through its Others and the dysfunctional.[46] A focus on repair is what dislocates the place of technology from the Western emphasis on a wider set of cultural techniques, including repair, for instance, in Ghana and Namibia. It also illuminates bigger questions about infrastructures. Technology is itself an increasingly efficient vessel for establishing neocolonial structures of corporate presence in African countries; from infrastructure to end users, Africa is the next continent of consumers for the global corporations. This parallels the other work of technological development and resources: the corporate rush to the energy and mineral reserves also in Africa.

Fossils present a temporal perspective to current digital culture, and they can be used to speculate on geographical dislocations of where we find media practices. The speculation of media fossil futures can be matched with a different sort of experimental idea that exhibits "a displaced fossil record."[47] Trevor Paglen's *The Last Pictures* project (2012) mobilizes a concrete satellite-enabled art project but also speculates with the multiplicity of temporalities that constitute a set of very important questions in regard to memory, media, and fossils.

In short, Paglen—known for his politically engaged photographic work that fuses art, technology, and visual culture—collaborated with a set of material scientists to create what the project calls an ultra-archival disc (see Figure 14). Its lifetime is designed to surpass what we usually consider human archival time of some thousands of years and instead promises a life of billions of years for the one hundred photographs that are etched onto the silicon wafer.[48] It is not a digital artifact in the usual sense of binary coding of images on silicon, but it brings to mind questions of technological memory and sustainability of the cultural heritage.

Figure 14. Trevor Paglen's project included the development of a special ultra-archival disc. Courtesy of the artist; Metro Pictures, New York; Altman Siegel, San Francisco; Galerie Thomas Zander, Cologne.

Paglen's project can be seen as a reference to the 1977 Voyager Golden Record, which on a phonograph record sent audiovisual material to space. As Ryan Bishop has wonderfully argued, the Golden Record already constituted an interplanetary media archaeological act in sending the disc with a stylus to outer space, which, if one day would accidentally happen to crash back to earth would constitute a piece of dead media returning from its galactic trip.[49] Whereas Bishop tracks the media historical connections of the Golden Record to the analog sound technologies of the vocoder, revealing links with Laurie Anderson and, of course, Wendy Carlos, we should also focus on the vessel itself. The medium is the message, but in this case, we can scale up from the obvious medium of the phonograph and even the constant data traffic between the vessel and the Deep Space Network to the spaceship itself. Voyager I as a piece of technology will become space junk by 2025, when it runs out of energy and slowly drifts outside the heliopause as a silent reminder of what happens when technology stops working and media stop mediating.

Moving from Voyager to EchoStar XVI, Paglen's satellite project has various angles through which we could approach it. I am focusing less on the images and more on the material–temporal aspects. The speculative billions of years of future time reminds of the material waste aspects that such an archival fantasy has. In a way, the existence of an archive meant for a nonhuman future is itself a meditation on the paradoxical task of cultural heritage to outlast humans as well as the material and techno-logical support of the archive itself. In this case, the specially made disc transported to geostationary orbit with the EchoStar XVI turns our attention from the object to its support. The system of satellites is one of rocket-fueled technological mediation that guarantees that we have media entertainment on a global scale—but is also crucial to the military-surveillance complex, extending its reach to a scale that makes the earth a geographical, geopolitical, and geophysical target:

> Since 1963, more than eight hundred spacecraft have been launched into geosynchronous orbit, forming a man-made ring of satellites around the Earth. These satellites are destined to become the longest-lasting artifacts of human civilization, quietly floating through space long after every trace of humanity has disappeared from the planet.[50]

The material memory of the earth continues outside its surface. The extension of technology to space is a sort of return of the various mate-rials and minerals to a geosynchronous orbit. Besides the orbit of func-tioning satellites, Paglen turns our attention to the circular temporality of the orbit slightly higher to that. The junk orbit is one of future media fossils, which as a project fuses a deep time interest with the technologi-cal realities of contemporary geopolitics. The EchoStar XVI itself is an important media relay for the fifteen years it will continue transmitting images—an approximate ten trillion—but it becomes a different sort of media object when it is moved to the graveyard orbit of zombie media "so far from earth that the derelict spacecraft will never decay."[51]

It is this slightly higher orbit that sustains a new geological layer of technological rubbish, media fossils that have a geological duration, but not only on earth's surface or underground. The escape velocity[52] exports geological earth in the form of technological artifacts thousands of miles above the surface, first as a media relay that extends the electromagnetic communication sphere, second as a fossil sphere of dead and zombie media technologies, which in Paglen's project are matched with the time of the solar system. Imagining the orbit and, for example, lunar space as a cemetery illustrates one aspect of how our junk becomes an odd memorial and part of human cultural heritage outside the earth.[53] But the space, space rocks, or the moon are not only cemeteries—not of dead media objects nor of other human remains. In addition, they are like the earth itself, increasingly imagined (and imaged) as a resource. In a way, this is not a new phenomenon but more of a rediscovery of earlier interest in space as the next frontier of the sort that escorted the enthusiasm for a scientific calculation and mapping of the earth into a resource. The Cold War space race fueled by geopolitical aims, but also mapping the material constitution of the moon, meant that despite that it was rendered free from military activity (with the 1967 Treaty on Principles Governing the Activities of States in the Exploration and Use of Outer Space, including the Moon and Other Celestial Bodies), the idea of being able to stake a territorial claim might have enormous benefit for the military sector. Similarly as the globe, for instance, around the north pole, is intensively territorialized as a continuation of the Cold War,[54] it is no wonder that an interest in the outerplanetary resources is again resurfacing.

Richard Seymour suggests that "the outer space really is the final frontier for capitalism,"[55] referring both to China's recent moon mission and to Rosa Luxemburg's famous theoretization that capitalism works by folding its outsides as its resource. The interest in space might be because of the energy promises in helium-3, but to be honest, the moon is not the only rock of interest to the technologically advanced geopolitics of our times. Also asteroids are important. For instance, platinum, iridium, palladium, and gold are believed be to found in abundant quantities in such space rocks, but even more important might be water, silicon, and, for instance, nickel.[56] Indeed, companies are able to bypass the 1967 legislation because of their status as private mining corporations, such as Deep Space Industries or the earlier founded Planetary Resources Inc. (behind the venture, among other investors, also are Google's Larry Page and Eric

Schmidt). The focus on asteroids shifts from the narrativization of the end of life as we know it—scenarios of apocalyptic proportion of past years of Hollywood audiovisuals—and concentrates more on the resource basis for future technological competition. The interest in geology that has mapped the earth as a resource leading to the recent years of digital culture devices, hungry for minerals, metals, and energy, is being replicated now outside our planetary scale. In the midst of the satellites, relaying massive network transmissions of entertainment and military content, we have the future plans of geological surveys and mining expanded much beyond the underground of the earth, from the deep time of the media of mining its underground to the space of geological objects, within reach exactly because of the development of advanced (space) technologies.

The Last Pictures establishes an aesthetic framework to understand this wider context of geology of media reaching outside the globe. In many ways, we are increasingly conscious of the mediasphere as significantly defined by the orbital.[57] But discussing the orbital in terms of geology— both fossils from the dying technological waste and the resources from asteroids—is what opens a new horizon for a media materialist analysis. Paglen makes explicit this link with the geological sphere and the influence of the Anthropocene reaching out thousands of miles high above earth itself. His photography has a relation to the resourcing of the geophysical sphere as part of the geopolitical (military) missions of past decades and how scientific visual worlds demonstrate the intertwining of aesthetics with power.

As Brooke Belisle points out, already Paglen's earlier work, a photographic diptych *Artifacts* (2010) (see Figure 1), works through relating geological formations and astronomical space.[58] It offers a photographic argument concerning the nineteenth-century temporalization of geology (deep time) and the ongoing spatialization of space (deep space) in a way that entangles also the extraterrestrial into a geological discourse. Belisle is able to show the geological connotations of Paglen's interests: the outer space and satellite orbits as the future fossils of human-made space debris and the focus on the earth's topology from geological sciences to geo-engineering of canals and other formations that tied industrialization, colonialism, and capitalist globalizing logistics to the opening up of deep time. This supports the argument in this book concerning the deep time of the media, of which some of Paglen's visual themes are good examples. From the geological strata of Canyon de Chelly in Arizona to the night sky of strata of light, as traces from satellites, *Artifacts* paves the way for the Anthropocene that is further investigated in *The Last Pictures.* The historical genealogy of photography shows the close links the new visual medium had with the mapping of the geophysical; U.S. Geological and Geographical Surveys were closely linked with the media of visualization since the nineteenth century, as Belisle brings out in the context of Paglen's practice. The geological ground was dug through, mined but also made flat and into an information surface with the aid of the new technical medium of photography connected to various other techniques, such as air balloons and aerial photography.

But besides the aerial, the militarized technological imaginary has as much been haunted with the necessity of trying to see the underground. As Ryan Bishop skillfully shows, this penetration of the underground

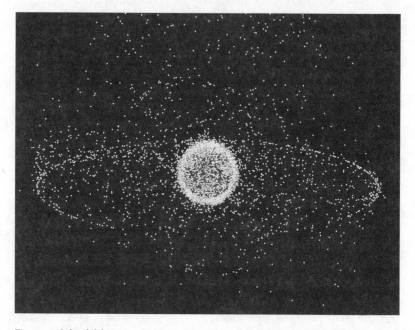

Figure 15. Orbital debris visualizations give a sense of the vast quantity of objects that form an external geotechnological layer circulating the earth. This refers to the layer of living dead, obsolete technological objects in circulation in the geosynchronous region (around 35,785 kilometers altitude). Image from NASA Orbital Debris Program Office.

layer is as important a step in techniques of visualization as the surveys that produced the flatness of the ground. Perhaps we could say that the geological discoveries of the nineteenth century, not least Lyell's *Principles of Geology* in the 1830s, prescribed the fantasy of the earth of deep time and deep space, paralleled in the outer space that is seen as a sort of geological frontier.[59] In both cases, the military–corporate enthusiasm was the perfect engine for the aesthetic and epistemological mapping, demonstrating again the medianatures double link: the media technologies giving us the real and imagined visions of the geophysical reality available for mining are the ones of future technological fossils of debris and waste.

Media Temporealities: The Media-Arche-Fossil

This chapter has continued the earlier focus on temporality of the geology of media. The time of fossils is one of tear and wear, of decay and rust, which characterize our notions of memory as much as they do the physical temporality of materials. Indeed, the so-called geological turn is at least as much about time as it is about materiality of space. The different temporal scales of debris raise questions that are fundamental for any analytic framework we use to make sense of the technologically stretched as part of deep times, deep spaces. The slowness of the geological strata and the earth's different spheres are paralleled by the distances of asteroids' travels. Even interstellar objects are able to enter the fantasy framework of contemporary capitalist mining as much as the underground persists as the military–corporate sector imagining not only a total reach over human communications but a transparency of the earth itself with new visualization and sonification techniques. The underground is of importance because of its relation to the infrastructures that sustain the operational readiness of any (military) organization on the ground. The "underground . . . is the final frontier," as the Geospatial corporation puts it,[60] offering a different emphasis on what Seymour argues is the final frontier. Perhaps both are correct; perhaps it is more generally just the geological and the geophysical—the abstract geology deterritorialized from first nature—that is the final frontier.

However, the seemingly spatial axis of the earth opens up also a temporal axis. Trevor Paglen's interest is as much in the slowness of earth's duration as it is in our contribution to what will play out as (from our human perspective) a slow impact over thousands of years: the climate change, nuclear waste stored underground, and technological debris. But slowness and acceleration become entangled in complex ways. For Paglen, not just the surface of the planet but time itself is uneven. We reshape the planet through temporal modification. Capital and military interests are the prime movers, continues Paglen:

> Mostly, we think about this in terms of speeding up time (increasing capitalist turnover times, labor productivity, financial transactions in the case of capital, and things like GPS targeting and hypersonic cruise missiles in the case of militarism). But in addition to the industrial annihilation of space with time that we see, the nineteenth century and early twentieth century marks the advent of the so-called "Anthropocene Age," a moment in earth's history when humans begin moving more sediment than traditional geomorphic processes (erosion, glaciation, etc. . .). In the Anthropocene, things like real-estate markets become geomorphic agents, because fluc-tuations in housing prices, for example, determine how huge amounts of sediment gets [sic] moved across the planet. My point is that human societies are both speeding up and slowing down at the same time. One consequence of these "anthropogeomorphic" pro-cesses is that the effects of our activities are played out over longer and longer time periods: one example is climate change: we are setting earth processes in motion that are going to play out over a hundreds, of [sic] not thousands of years.[61]

Paglen's ideas resonate with contemporary analyses of capitalism and time and could be seen as a relevant comment on recent acceleration-ism discussions. They connect to psychogeography but entangle with geophysics (see chapter 2): urban realities such as housing prices have an effect where building materials, production, energy needs, get logistically addressed.

The preceding quotation is also related to a media archaeology of visualization technologies. After Galileo's seventeenth-century telescopic opening of space around our globe, William Herschel's astronomical observations gave us a sense of geological deep times expanded into deep space in the nineteenth century. The longer histories of space as an object constituted by visual technologies demonstrate what Paglen calls time's unevenness. Even Herschel's telescope-enhanced views to space framed it in terms of time and as an emblem of the duration of the universe: the millions of years of light traveling across space. "A telescope with the power of penetrating into space has also, as it may be called, a power of penetrating into time past."[62] The geological and astronomical interests of knowledge and media of perception conjoin in John Durham Peters's apt term *paleoscopes*: telescopes gaze into space as well as time.

But media don't just observe, they actively guide the way the world spins. What Paglen emphasizes with the unevenness of time (as a productive force, even if not with necessarily positive outcomes when it comes to the survival of a significant amount of the planet's life) is that also capitalism is able to accelerate such processes with its own logic, whether abstract housing price fluctuations or the massive shifts of geological material because of differing reasons tied to exchange value processes that otherwise might hide the actual environmental–ecological relations involved in the process of abstraction.

The notion of fossil relates to contemporary discussions of the nonhuman in philosophy and the so-called noncorrelationist philosophy. In Quentin Meillassoux's take, the notions of the "arche-fossil" and the ancestral become mobilized as a philosophical thought-experiment with strong ontological impact. Turning toward the fossil is part of Meillassoux's task of finding an alternative to the Kantian critical thought that is interested in the correlated—in other words, the world only as it is given to us in the relation to our critical faculties of thought. The scientifically proved and exactly dated existence of fossils that predate the human being as a species is also a question of where the thinking of such things that predate thinking stands. The *arche-fossil* and *fossil-matter* terms become ways to indicate "the existence of an ancestral reality or event, one that is anterior to terrestrial life."[63] Indeed, for Meillassoux, this notion refers to the "material support on the basis of which the experiments that yield estimates of ancestral phenomena proceed,"[64] whether it is an isotope or light emission from deep space. The arche-fossil becomes a way to realize the existence of a reality outside thought that does not indeed necessarily correlate with what thought is: the faculties of the human. This existence of a rift between the human and the nonhuman is an important influence on things that are not only manifested to us but "intrawordly occurrences,"[65] to use Meillassoux's term.

It's, however, not a new discovery that the nonhuman exists and that the flaws in so-called correlationist thought need to be addressed. Already the likes of Donna Haraway, Michel Serres, and the new materialists Rosi Braidotti and Manuel Delanda have written about related things since the 1980s and 1990s. With Braidotti, this was also connected to arguments in the emerging science and technology studies field as well as feminist theory. In a way, the legacy of new materialism reminds that perhaps it is not merely the human as "thinking being" we should be thinking about but the various other modalities of which the human consists; the multiple temporalities that are being coordinated in ways that make time uneven but constantly modified; the fossil as both a material support, as Meillassoux argues, and a deeply challenging entity that is definitely irreducible to how it manifests to us. And yet the ways in which we have thought and acted in the world have had a definite impact on the future fossils that are material supports for something else. The discussions of fossils in this chapter, and in relation to the soil and dust earlier, remind that such nonhuman things are compilations of heterogeneous transformations as part of temporally formed sediments. The soil is part of the gradual formation of deeper layers of the planet.

The various ideas circulating around the concept of the Anthropocene also in art practices, such as Chatonsky's and Paglen's, actually remind that their view of media and technology acknowledges the human impact. The human-made becomes a manifestation of the infraworldly, irreducible to thinking. But the practices remain carefully aware of the multiple scales that are constantly coordinated in this assembly. Hence the focus on trash, media waste, and, in general, the industrial impact on the planet is tightly related to the philosophical ideas concerning fossils as much as they are to a necessity to account for the role of media and technology. The significant political questions we are now facing must be somehow temporally synchronized with the longer-term durations to realize the connections political economy and, for instance, exchange relations, technological modes of production, and the immaterialization of labor have with geophysical realities, fossil-matter, and what I will call the *media-arche-fossils*. This notion refers to the media technological stratum, which is irreducible to the human and yet partly supports and conditions it along-side various aspects of the earth and its outer space geological layers. It refers back to the notion of medianatures I used earlier. In other words, perhaps instead of dismissing relations and mediations, we need carefully to refine what we mean by media and communication in the noncorrelationist as well as new materialist contexts of contemporary media culture.[66]

Notions of temporality must escape any human-obsessed vocabulary and enter into a closer proximity with the fossil. The deep time even in its historical form is a mode of scientific temporality that allows imagination of planetary time without humans. It presents epochs that stratify dynamics of the earth (see chapter 2) but also in later geological research reminding that the periods are formed of dynamic, even catastrophic events: a punctuated equilibrium.

If history has been the discourse concerning narratives of men and their lives, then fossils set the scene for a different challenge: a world without humans, and narrativizing a future-present in which media and residues of waste might be the only monuments we left behind. In some ways, this is acknowledged by Tim Morton: also on the level of design, we must necessarily think of the other-times than that of humans—from thousands to hundreds of thousands of years and, for instance, accounting for things such as "Plutonium 239, which remains dangerously radioactive for 24,100 years."[67]

In the humanities and social sciences, we are engaging with this challenge, which comes under different names: the Anthropocene, the nonhuman, media materialism, the posthuman, and so forth. Discussions of microtemporality (see chapter 1) are trying to present a technical media temporality different to narrative writing of media history (from the human perspective and for the humans[68]); discussions of archives are turning toward the constitutive role of data centers as the infrastructural support for memory;[69] furthermore, data centers are themselves also geophysically determined organizations, reliant on energy and efficient cooling systems. The geological is one way to account for the ecological relations in how they address change across scales: the slow duration of deep times but also the accelerated microtemporalities that govern the algorithmic world of communication and trading reliant on as much as *about* the planet and its resources. Acceleration, deceleration.

AFTERWORD
SO-CALLED NATURE

Geology of media deals with the weird intersections of earth materials and entangled times. It includes several events that reveal this combination of the planetary ancient and the technologically advanced. The futuristic changes place with the obsolete in ways that are at times too close to notice. The design culture of the new hides the archaic materials of the planet.

The explosive event of industrialization was dependent on new forms of energy; coal, oil, and gas became main drives replacing the reliance on wind, water, plants, trees, and animals as energy sources.[1] After dirty aesthetics of coal that painted the surface and the sky black, through other fossil fuels we accessed the deep time of the earth: over three-million-year-old deposits of plants and animals from the predinosaur era; age-old photosynthesis that the planet stored to enable for instance capitalism to expand in its current scientific technological form. The scientific studies on deep time were paralleled with this practical tapping into the underground where mining engineers were discovering in the depths both coal and valuable metals such as gold, silver, and copper.

Computers are a crystallization of past two hundred to three hundred years of scientific and technological development, geological insights, and geophysical affordances. They are dependant on precious metals, and even early-nineteenth-century networks needed copper for conducting the signal traffic of globalizing media culture. During the past decades, optical fiber has made its entry as the glassy backbone of global infrastructures. Rare earth minerals already useful in earlier eras become essential in new technological contexts, when the computer turned visually attractive: graphical user interfaces, advanced screen technologies, and digital design culture geared for the consumer pleasure on massive scales, to gather through interactive participation data on digital habits—material for the data-mining industry.

The use of certain key minerals enables the miniaturization of the computational worlds; they become mobile, ubiquitous, pervasive, and embedded into the natural environment.[2]

The coal that fired first Western Europe then gradually other bits of the world into industrialism is still very much present in the information culture. "Dig more coal, the PCs are coming"[3] alerted an article in *Forbes* magazine, referring already in 1999 to the energy-intensive processes of computers. Increasing bandwidth, more efficient processors, data-heavy digital design practices, and the sheer increase in the number of computational events tell the story of the upward curve in absolute numbers of energy consumption of the supposedly immaterial matrix of computation. The microchipped world burns in intensity like millions of tiny suns: "On its surface, where bits are incarnated as electrons, a chip runs at enormously high power densities—up to one-tenth those at the surface of the sun."[4]

In Roger Caillois's little book on stones, he hints of a passage from the earth to inscription: "Already present in the archives of geology, available for operations then inconceivable, was the model of what would later be an alphabet."[5] In a later media technological perspective, we can adjust this prophetic statement relating to the mystical "readability" of the earth as a sign into something more technical: the archives of geology give, not a model, but the material for what would later be media and technology. Already Lyell and Darwin imagined the earth as a library and a recording machine, continued in the elemental imagination of Charles Babbage, who pitched even the "air as one vast library, on whose pages are for ever written all that man has ever said or woman whispered."[6]

The readability of the earth is still a continuing trope. The earth is constantly read as if it were a script needing to be interpreted, a trace of hermeneutics persistent in the age of advanced technology. Yet this refers less to the long traditions of animistic nature and a world of meaning inside its seemingly silent bowels than to the military operations that constantly, to use Ryan Bishop's words, "convert geography (geo-graphy, writing on the earth's surface) into geology, a logos of the earth."[7] Besides the military, there are different contexts, too—including the arts. In their piece *Medium Earth*,[8] the Otolith Group speaks of the earthquake-sensitive group of people who channel the "subconscious" tremors of the earth like the figure of a nineteenth medium who was channeling the dead. "It listens to its deserts, translates the writing of its stones, and deciphers the calligraphies of its expansion cracks."[9] This sort of mapping the earth as our geophysical underground is one of sensitive bodies but also the technical and audiovisual culture in which the earth is circuited as part of mediatized expression.

To return to where we started: notions of materiality of media must take into account this geophysical reality as both the source and the target of our technical media. Lewis Mumford spoke of paleotechnics but restricted that to the earlier phase of industrialization, which was based in mining. But mining and the appropriation of the geophysical have never stopped: they are still part and parcel of the advanced media technological culture through which environmental sensing, smart dust, and new protocols allow the world to be filled with IP addresses that map the "natural" effectively as part of media.

This book is less a critique of theorists such as Friedrich Kittler or others than it is a call for a further materialization of media not only as media but as that bit which it consists of: the list of the geophysical elements that give us digital culture. It is not a world devoid of war, but in a rather pessimistic way, we can say that the Cold War culture of surveillance, paranoia, and national and intra/extranational state interests is only intensified with the scarcity of energy and material resources necessary to maintain those technological national regimes as economic and security units. Media materiality is not contained in the machines, even if the machines themselves contain a planet. The machines are more like vectors across the geopolitics of labor, resources, planetary excavations, energy production, natural processes from photosynthesis to mineralization, chemicals, and the aftereffects of electronic waste. Where exactly in this mix do you find the materiality of media? Kittler spoke about the "so-called Man" as a constructed object of media technological culture: the human being made visible in the intersection of scientific mapping of its modes of sensation and the technological mobilization of its regimes of sensation. The human being was understood as a second-order creation wired into the circuit. Yet we need to extend and ask if it is as important to map the existence of "so-called Nature":[10] the existence of the environmental as we see it through our technoscientific sensorium and gradually disappearing from view, from existence, in the midst of the Anthrobscene.

APPENDIX
ZOMBIE MEDIA
CIRCUIT BENDING
MEDIA ARCHAEOLOGY
INTO AN ART METHOD

Garnet Hertz and Jussi Parikka

"Zombie Media" was cowritten with the artist–writer Garnet Hertz and is added here as an appendix to the book. The text supplements several of the themes discussed in the book and reaches out to the important fields of critical design, do-it-yourself (DIY) culture, and discussions such as (planned) obsolescence and electronic waste. We continue from Bruce Sterling's ideas of dead media and media paleontology but by claiming that media do not die; media persists as electronic waste, toxic residue, and its own sort of fossil layer of disused gadgets and electronics. The text refers to the field of media archaeology as well. Media archaeology is not the main focus of this book otherwise, despite references, for instance, to Siegfried Zielinski's use of the concept "deep time" and to the context of media materialism of Friedrich Kittler. "Zombie Media" does, however, express the link both to materiality of the residue and to some practice-theory developments as well.

Obsolescence Returns

In the United States, about 400 million units of consumer electronics are discarded every year. Electronic waste, like obsolete cellular telephones, computers, monitors, and televisions, composes the fastest growing and most toxic portion of waste in American society. As a result of rapid technological change, low initial cost, and planned obsolescence, the federal Environmental Protection Agency (EPA) estimates that two-thirds of all discarded consumer electronics still work—approximately 250 million functioning computers, televisions, VCRs, and cell phones are discarded each year in the United States.[1]

Digital culture is embedded in a large pile of network wires, lines, routers, switches, and other very material things that, as Jonathan Sterne acutely and bluntly states, "will be trashed."[2] Far from being accidental, discarding and obsolescence are in fact internal to contemporary media technologies. As Sterne argues, the logic of new media does not only mean the replacement of old media by new media but that digital culture is loaded with the assumption and expectation of a short-term forthcoming obsolescence. There is always a better laptop or mobile phone on the horizon: new media always become old.

This text is an investigation into planned obsolescence, media culture, and temporalities of media objects; we approach this under the umbrella of media archaeology and aim to extend the media archaeological interest of knowledge into an art methodology, following the work of scholars such as Erkki Huhtamo[3] and others who have given the impetus to think about the complex materiality of media as technology—from Friedrich Kittler to Wolfgang Ernst and Sean Cubitt. Hence media archaeology not only becomes a method for excavation of the repressed, the forgotten, or the past but extends itself into an artistic method close to DIY culture, circuit bending, hardware hacking, and other exercises that intervene the political economy of information technology. Media in their various layers embody memory: not only human memory but the memory of things, of objects, of chemicals, and of circuits.

Planned Obsolescence

Planned obsolescence is a concept first put forward by Bernard London in 1932, as a proposed solution to the Great Depression. In London's mind, the economic downturn was prolonged by consumers who continued to use and reuse devices long after they were purchased. His proposal outlined that every product should be labeled with an expiration

date and that the government should charge tax on products that were
used past their determined life-span: "I propose that when a person continues to posses and use old clothing, automobiles and buildings, after
they have passed their obsolescence date, as determined at the time
they were created, he should be taxed for such continued use of what is
legally 'dead.'"[4]

Although London's proposal was never implemented as a government initiative, the planning of obsolescence was adopted by product
designers and commercial industry: artificially decreasing the life-span of
consumer commodities—like new fashions that make old clothing appear
outdated—increasing the speed of obsolescence, and stimulating the need
to purchase. Industrial designers like Brooks Stevens popularized the
dynamic of planned obsolescence in 1954 as instilling a "desire to own
something a little newer, a little better, a little sooner than is necessary."[5]
Retailing experts like Victor Lebow further clarified this mandate in 1955:
"These commodities and services must be offered to the consumer with
a special urgency. We require not only 'forced draft' consumption, but
'expensive' consumption as well. We need things consumed, burned up,
worn out, replaced, and discarded at an ever increasing pace."[6]

In reference to contemporary consumer products, planned obsolescence takes many forms. It is not only an ideology, or a discourse; more
accurately, it takes place on a micropolitical level of design: difficult-to-
replace batteries in personal MP3 audio players, proprietary cables and
chargers that are only manufactured for a short period of time, discontin-
ued customer support, or plastic enclosures that are glued shut and break
if opened.[7] In other words, the technological objects are designed as a
"black box"[8] that is engineered not to be fixed and has no user-serviceable
parts inside.

Repurposing Obsolescence in Contemporary Art

Despite a planned obsolescence, the probing, exploring, and manipulating of consumer electronics outside of their standard life-span is a key
tactic in contemporary art practice. Reuse of consumer commodities
emerges within various art methods of the early avant-garde in the early
twentieth century, from Pablo Picasso and Georges Braque's work with
found newspapers in 1912 to Marcel Duchamp's *Bicycle Wheel* of 1913 or

his inverted Bedfordshire urinal "fountain" of 1917. Such practices have been widely addressed in media art historical writing already.[9] The mass production of commodities has shifted significantly in the century since Braque, Picasso, and Duchamp's readymade work in the 1910s: since a significant "readymade" portion of commodities in American society is electronic, artists have moved to working with and exploring electronics, computers, televisions, and household gadgets. Early artistic repurposers of consumer electronics include Nam June Paik, who worked with electrically rewiring televisions as early as 1963 to display abstract, minimalist shapes. Although many artists using electronics have focused on exploring the potentials of new media forms, others have approached using electronic commodities in the spirit of assemblage, bricolage, readymade, or collage: as an everyday and standing reserve, or *bestand*, of available raw materials.[10] Instead of using electronics to explore or develop cutting-edge technologies, this approach uses "trailing-edge" everyday and obsolete technologies as its key resource.

Bending Circuits: The Incantor

Reed Ghazala, a Cincinnati-based American artist born in the 1950s, is a pivotal figure in the development of what is termed "circuit bending": the creative short-circuiting of consumer electronics primarily for the purpose of generating novel sound or visual output.[11] The technique of circuit bending takes found objects like battery-powered children's toys and inexpensive synthesizers and modifies them into DIY musical instruments and homemade audio generators.

Likely the most recognizable example of circuit bending is Ghazala's Incantor series of devices, highly customized Speak & Spell, Speak & Read, and Speak & Math children's toys that he has built since 1978. The methodology of bending the toy involves dismantling the electronic device and adding components like switches, knobs, and sensors to allow the circuit to be altered and shifted by the user. Ghazala's Incantor devices completely reconfigure the synthesized human voice circuitry within the toy to spew out a noisy, glitchy tangle of sound that stutters, loops, screams, and beats.

The process of circuit bending typically involves going to a second-hand store or garage sale to obtain an inexpensive battery-powered device, taking the back cover of the device off, and probing the mechanism's circuit board. Any two points on the circuit board are connected by using a "jumper" wire that temporarily short-circuits and rewires the device. The battery-powered device is powered on during this process, and the speaker of the system is listened to for unusual sound effects that result from probing. If an interesting result is found, the connections are marked for modification, and switches, buttons, or other devices can be inserted between these points to enable or disable the effect.

Circuit Bending Formerly New Media

Circuit bending is an electronic DIY movement focused on manipulating circuits and changing the taken-for-granted function of the technology without formal training or approval. This approach is characteristic of post–World War II electronic culture, especially post-1970s electronic amateurism, hobbyism, or DIY tinkering that was typified in organizations like the Homebrew Computer Club.[12] In Certeau's terms, "these 'ways of operating' constitute the innumerable practices by means of which users reappropriate the space organized by techniques of sociocultural production."[13] Circuit bending is a way of operating that reminds us that users consistently reappropriate, customize, and manipulate consumer products in unexpected ways, even when the inner workings of devices are intentionally engineered as an expert territory. Ghazala's Incantor is useful as a tool to remind us of sociotechnical issues in contemporary society, including planned obsolescence, the black boxing of technology, and the interior accessibility of everyday consumer products.

As a way of operating, circuit bending is an aspect of digital culture that does not easily fit under the term *new media*—the customized, trashy, and folksy methodologies of circuit bending recall historical practices of reuse and serve as a useful counterpoint to envisioning digital culture only in terms of a glossy, high-tech "Californian Ideology."[14] We find Ghazala's explorations similar in spirit to media archaeology and propose a stronger articulation of media archaeology as an art methodology—and furthermore not only an art methodology that addresses the past but one that expands into a wider set of questions concerning dead media, or what we shall call zombie media: the living dead of media history,[15] and the living dead of discarded waste that is not only of inspirational value to artists but signals death in the concrete sense of the real death of nature through its toxic chemicals and heavy metals. In short, what gets bent is not only the false image of linear history but the circuits and archive that form the contemporary media landscape. For us, *media* is approached through the concrete artifacts, design solutions, and various technological layers that range from hardware to software processes, each of which in its own way participates in the circulation of time and memory. The medium is an archive in the Foucauldian sense as a condition of knowledge, but also as a condition of perceptions, sensations, memory, and time. In this text, a special emphasis is placed on hardware even if we do not wish to claim that it is the only aspect about media and obsolescence we should consider.

Media Archaeology as Bending Circuitry

The political economy of consumer capitalism is a media archaeological problem as well. Media archaeology has been successful in setting itself as a methodology of lost ideas, unusual machines, and reemerging desires and discourses searching for elements of difference in relation to mainstream technological excitement and hype, but not always connecting such ideas to political economy or ecology.

With wide implications for the media archaeological methodology, the archive is increasingly being rethought not as a spatial place of history but as a contemporary technological circuit that redistributes temporality. This is how Wolfgang Ernst suggests that theorists and artists rethink media archaeology, not only as an excavation of the past, but as an intensive gaze on the microtemporal modulations that take place in computerized circuits of technology.[16] This alternative sense of technological temporality is closer to engineering diagrams and circuits than the historian's hermeneutic interpretation of documents. Drawing directly from Foucault, media archaeology is for Ernst monumental, not narrative; it is keen on excavating solely on the basis that something exists, and its object-oriented mode of media materialism is happy to proceed on the basis of an existence of a circuit. Hence Ernst is not interested in alternative media histories in a similar way as, for example, Huhtamo or Siegfried Zielinski, or even in imaginary media that challenges mainstream discourses of media technology,[17] but in concrete devices through which we can understand the nature of temporality in contemporary electronic and digital culture. For Ernst, just like for so many media archaeological artists, such as DeMarinis, Gebhard Sengmüller, or a more recent wave of young artists such as the Institute for Algorhythmics, interested in concrete sonic archaeologies of contemporary media, media archaeology starts from the media assemblage—a concrete device that is operational.

Circuits are what define modernity and our IT-oriented condition. Circuits inside radios, computers, televisions, are only one face of circuitry. The circuits that can be opened up from their plastic enclosures are only relays to wider, more abstract circuits in terms of cables and lines, of electromagnetic radiation and wireless transmission. The air is heavy with "disembodied" information technology, and culture is permeated with circuits of political economy. Hence it would be an important project to write a media archaeology of circuits. The circuit, not the past, is where media archaeology starts if we want to develop a more concrete design-oriented version of how we can think about recycling and remediating[18] as art methods.

Yet there is a special challenge for work that takes as its object a concrete opening up of technologies. The inner workings of consumer electronics and information technologies are increasingly concealed as a result of the development of newer generations of technologies, a feature that is characteristic of recent decades of technological culture. So what does a media archaeology of consumer objects look like when we do not go back in time to media history but rather inside a device?

Once developed and deployed widely, technical components are understood by users as objects that serve a particular function: an electronic toy makes a sound when a button is pressed, a telephone makes a telephone call, and a computer printer outputs a document when requested. The inner workings of the device are unknown to the user, with the circuitry of the device like a mysterious "black box" that is largely irrelevant to using it. It is only an object with a particular input that results in a specific output; its mechanism is invisible. From a design perspective, the technology is intentionally created to render the mechanism invisible and usable as a single punctualized object.

Punctualization refers to a concept in actor-network theory to describe when components are brought together into a single complex system that can be used as a single object. We refer to the disassembly of these single objects as "depunctualization"—which shows a circuit of dependencies that ties the owner to the corporation that manufactured the device[19] (see Figure 16).

Black boxing, or the development of technological objects to a point where they are simply used and not understood as technical objects, is a requirement of infrastructure and technological development. A computer system, for example, is almost incomprehensible if thought of in terms of its millions of transistors, circuits, mathematical calculations, and technical components. Black boxes are the punctualized building blocks from which new technologies and infrastructures are built.[20]

A black box, however, is a system that is not technically understood or accessed, and as a result, these technologies are often completely unusable

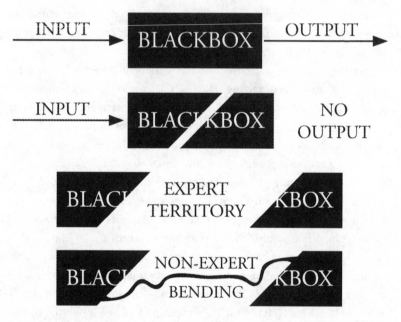

Figure 16. A black-boxed system processes input into output without the user's knowledge of the interior functionality of the system. When a black-boxed system is broken, output stops. At this point, the black box becomes depunctualized. The interior of a black-boxed system is expert territory and tends not to be user serviceable. Despite being expert territory, portions of the non-user-serviceable interior of the black box system can be manipulated and bent by nonexperts. We propose that both computer hardware and historical archives can be bent. Image by Garnet Hertz.

when they become obsolete or broken. Once the input–output or desired functionality of the device stops working, it is often unfixable and inaccessible for modification for most individuals. Unlike a household lamp, which can be fitted with replacement lightbulbs, many consumer electronic devices have no user-serviceable parts, and the technology is discarded after it breaks. The depunctualization, or breaking apart the device into its components, is difficult because of the highly specialized engineering and manufacturing processes used in the design of the artifact: contemporary electronic devices are intentionally built to be discarded, and their obsolescence is clearly planned.

Within the framework of media archaeology, it is important to note that there is not only one box. Instead, one box hides a multitude of other black boxes that have been working in interaction, in various roles, in differing durations. As Bruno Latour notes, its often when things break down that a seemingly inert system opens up to reveal that objects contain more objects, and actually those numerous objects are composed of relations, histories, and contingencies.

Consider Latour's methodological exercise as an art methodology for media archaeology:

> Look around the room. . . . Consider how many black boxes there are in the room. Open the black boxes; examine the assemblies inside. Each of the parts inside the black box is itself a black box full of parts. If any part were to break, how many humans would immediately materialize around each. How far back in time, away in space, should we retrace our steps to follow all those silent entities that contribute peacefully to your reading this chapter at your desk? Return each of these entities to step 1; imagine the time when each was disinterested and going its own way, without being bent, enrolled, enlisted, mobilized, folded in any of the others' plots. From which forest should we take our wood. In which quarry should we let the stones quietly rest.[21]

For the arts, objects are never inert but consist of various temporalities, relations, and potentials that can be brought together and broken apart. Things break apart every day anyhow—especially high technology—and end up as seemingly inert objects, dead media, discarded technology.

Yet dead media creep back as dangerous toxins into the soil, or then as zombie media recycled into new assemblies. According to Ernst, media archaeology is less "about dead media, but on media undead. There is an untimeliness of media which is incorporated here."[22] Hence there is a distinct difference to the dead media project of Bruce Sterling that in a different kind of way addressed media forgotten and obsolescent. Zombie media is interested in media not only out of use but resurrected to new uses, contexts, and adaptations.

Archivist / Circuit Bender

For the figure of the artist, technical media has meant nods both toward engineering and the archive, as Huhtamo has noted: "the role of the artist-engineer, which rose into prominence in the 1960s (although its two sides rarely met in one person), has at least partly been supplanted by that of the artist-archaeologist."[23] Yet methodologies of reuse, hardware hacking, and circuit bending are becoming increasingly central in this context as well. Bending or repurposing the archive of media history strongly relates to the pioneering works of artists such as Paul DeMarinis, Zoe Beloff, or Gebhard Sengmüller—where a variety of old media technologies have been modified and repurposed to create pseudo-historical objects from a speculative future.

Referring to DeMarinis's various sound-based projects, such as *The Edison Effect* (1989–93) and *Gray Matter* (1995), Huhtamo has suggested that the notion of the artist-archaeologist can be thought of as a t(h)ink-erer.[24] In the age of consumer electronics, the artist can also be thought of as an archaeological circuit bender and hacker, which links media archaeology with the political agenda of contemporary media production. The black boxes of the historical archive and consumer electronics are cracked open, bent, and modified.

Media Archaeological Time: Time of the Living Dead

We want to bring these various components now together: planned obsolescence, the material nature of information, and electronic waste. Planned obsolescence was introduced as the logic of consumer technology cycles, which is embedded in a culture of material information technologies that in themselves should be increasingly understood through chemicals, toxic components, and the residue they leave behind after their media function has been so to speak "consumed." The realization that information technology is never ephemeral and therefore can never completely die has both ecological and media archaeological importance. As a material assemblage, information technology also has its duration that is not restricted to its human-centered use value: media cultural objects and information technology have an intimate connection with the soil, the air, and nature as a concrete, temporal reality. Just like nature affords the building of information technology—how, for example, gutta-percha was an essential substance for insulating nineteenth-century telegraphic lines or how columbite tantalite is an essential mineral for a range of contemporary high-tech devices—those devices return to nature.[25]

In short, information technology involves multiple ecologies that travel across political economy and natural ecology.[26] This Guattarian take on media ecology is connected to an ecosophical stance: an awareness of overlapping ecologies feeding into interrelations between the social, mental, somatic, nonorganic, and animal. Indeed, following Sean Cubitt's lead, we argue that archaeologies of screen and information technology media should increasingly not look only at the past but inside the screen to reveal a whole different take on future-oriented avant-garde: "The digital realm is an avant-garde to the extent that it is driven by perpetual innovation and perpetual destruction. The built-in obsolescence of digital culture, the endless trashing of last year's model, the spendthrift throwing away of batteries and mobile phones and monitors and mice . . . and all the heavy metals, all the toxins, sent off to some god-forsaken Chinese recycling village . . . that is the digital avant-garde."[27] Our proposed alternative archaeology of tinkering, remixing, and collage would not start from Duchamp and others but from opening up the technological gadget, the screen, and the system.

Media archaeological methods have carved out complex, overlapping, multiscalar temporalities of the human world in terms of media cultural histories, but in the midst of an ecological crisis, a more thorough nonhuman view is needed. In this context, bending media archaeology into an artistic methodology can be seen as a way to tap into the ecosophic potential of such practices as circuit bending, hardware hacking, and other ways of reusing and reintroducing dead media into a new cycle of life for such objects. Assembled into new constructions, such materials and ideas become zombies that carry with them histories but are also reminders of the nonhuman temporalities involved in technical media. Technical media process and work at subphenomenological speeds and frequencies[28] but also tap in to the temporalities of nature—thousands, even millions, of years of nonlinear and nonhuman history.[29]

As a conclusion, communications have moved beyond the new media phase, through the consumer commodity phase, and much of it is already obsolete and in an "archaeology phase." The practice of amateurism and hobbyist DIY characterizes not only early adoption of technologies but also the obsolescence phase. Chronologically, digital media have moved from a speculative opportunity in the 1990s to become widely adopted as a consumer commodity in the 2000s and have now become archaeological. As a result, studying topics like reuse, remixing, and sampling has become more important than discussions of technical potentials. Furthermore, if temporality is increasingly circulated, modulated, and stored in technical media devices—the diagrammatics and concrete circuits that tap into the microtemporality that is below the threshold of conscious

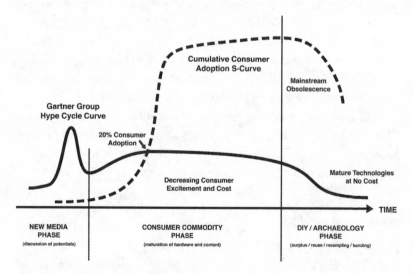

Figure 17. Phases of media positioned in reference to political economy: new media and media archaeology are overlaid on Gartner Group's hype cycle and adoption curve diagrams, graphic representations of the economic maturity, adoption, and business application of specific technologies. Diagram by Garnet Hertz.

human perception—we need to develop similar circuit bending, art, and activist practices as an analytical and creative methodology: hence the turn to archives in a wider sense that also encompasses circuits, switches, chips, and other high-tech processes. Such epistemo-archaeological tasks are not only of artistic interest but tap into the ecosophical sphere in understanding and reinventing relations between the various ecologies across subjectivity, nature, and technology.

Although death of media may be useful as a tactic to oppose dialogue that only focuses on the newness of media, we believe that media never die: they decay, rot, reform, remix, and get historicized, reinterpreted, and collected. They either stay as a residue in the soil and as toxic living dead media or are reappropriated through artistic tinkering methodologies.

NOTES

Preface

1   Charles Lyell, *Principles of Geology* (London: John Murray, 1830), 1. Online facsimile at http://www.esp.org/books/lyell/principles/facsimile/.

2   Michael T. Klare, *The Race for What's Left: The Global Scramble for the World's Last Resources* (New York: Metropolitan Books, 2012), 29.

3   Ibid.

4   Karl Marx and Friedrich Engels, *The Communist Manifesto* (London: Pluto Press, 2008), 40.

5   Bruno Latour, *An Inquiry into Modes of Existence: An Anthropology of the Moderns*, trans. Catherine Porter (Cambridge, Mass.: Harvard University Press, 2013), 10.

6   "As we have seen, man has reacted upon organized and inorganic nature, and thereby modified, if not determined, the material structure of his earthly home. The measure of that reaction manifestly constitutes a very important element in the appreciation of the relations between mind and matter, as well as in the discussion of many purely physical problems." George Perkins Marsh, *Man and Nature: Physical Geography as Modified by Human Action* (New York: Charles Scribner, 1865), 8.

7   Paul N. Edwards, *A Vast Machine: Computer Models, Climate Data, and the Politics of Global Warming* (Cambridge, Mass.: MIT Press, 2010).

8   Antonio Stoppani, "First Period of the Anthropozoic Era," trans. Valeria Federighi, ed. Etienne Turpin and Valeria Federighi, in *Making the Geologic Now: Responses to the Material Conditions of Contemporary Life*, ed. Elizabeth Ellsworth and Jamie Kruse (New York: Punctum, 2013), 38.

1. Materiality

1 Sean Cubitt, *The Practice of Light: A Genealogy of Visual Technologies from Prints to Pixels* (Cambridge, Mass.: MIT Press, 2014), 2. To quote Cubitt in full: "Mediation is the ground of relationship, the relationship that precedes and constructs subjects and objects. Media matter, both in the sense of giving material specificity to our descriptions of such abstract concepts as society and environment, and in the sense of the active verb: mediation comes into being as matter, its mattering constitutes the knowable, experienceable world, making possible all sensing and being sensed, knowing and being known."

2 As Geoffrey Winthrop-Young aptly notes, the term *German media theory* is an outsider construct. See Winthrop-Young, "Krautrock, Heidegger, Bogeyman: Kittler in the Anglosphere," *Thesis Eleven* 107, no. 1 (2011): 6–20.

3 Friedrich Kittler, *Discourse Networks 1800/1900*, trans. Michael Metteer with Chris Cullens (Stanford, Calif.: Stanford University Press, 1990).

4 John Durham Peters, "Space, Time and Communication Theory," *Canadian Journal of Communication* 28, no. 4 (2003), http://www.cjc-online.ca/index .php/journal/article/view/1389/1467. See also Sean Cubitt, *Digital Aesthetics* (London: Sage, 1998). Cubitt's recent book, an utterly important one, *The Practice of Light*, focuses especially on the modulations of light becoming media.

5 Douglas Kahn, *Earth Sound Earth Signal: Energies and Earth Magnitude in the Arts* (Berkeley: University of California Press, 2013), 23. See also Sean Cubitt, "Current Screens," in *Imagery in the 21st Century*, ed. Oliver Grau with Thomas Veigl, 21–35 (Cambridge, Mass.: MIT Press, 2011).

6 Klare, *Race for What's Left*, 152.

7 Robert Smithson, "A Sedimentation of the Mind: Earth Projects" (1968), in *Robert Smithson: The Collected Writings*, ed. Jack Flam (Berkeley: University of California Press, 1996), 101.

8 See also Kahn, *Earth Sound Earth Signal*.

9 The current mission of the agency is described as follows: "The [U.S. Geological Survey] serves the Nation by providing reliable scientific information to describe and understand the Earth; minimize loss of life and property from natural disasters; manage water, biological, energy, and mineral resources; and enhance and protect our quality of life." http://www.usgs.gov/.

10 James Risen, "U.S. Identifies Vast Mineral Riches in Afghanistan," *New York Times*, June 13, 2010. For a short history of the U.S. Geological Survey, see

Mary C. Rabbitt, "The United States Geological Survey 1879–1989," U.S. Geological Survey Circular 1050, http://pubs.usgs.gov/circ/c1050/index.htm.

11 Siegfried Zielinski, *Deep Time of the Media*, trans. Gloria Custance (Cambridge, Mass.: MIT Press, 2006).

12 See also Timothy Morton, *Hyperobjects: Philosophy and Ecology after the End of the World* (Minneapolis: University of Minnesota Press, 2013).

13 On media archaeology, see Erkki Huhtamo and Jussi Parikka, eds., *Media Archaeology: Approaches, Applications, and Implications* (Berkeley: University of California Press, 2011). Jussi Parikka, *What Is Media Archaeology?* (Cambridge: Polity, 2012). In addition, the cultural techniques approach, pioneered by the likes of Bernhard Siegert, flags media analysis in relation to technologies of knowledge and discourse operators. Siegert, "Cultural Techniques: Or the End of the Intellectual Post War Era in German Media Theory," trans. Geoffrey-Winthrop Young, *Theory, Culture, and Society* 30, no. 6 (2013): 50.

14 Wolfgang Ernst, "From Media History to Zeitkritik," trans. Guido Schenkel, *Theory, Culture, and Society* 30, no. 6 (2013): 134–35.

15 Wolfgang Ernst, *Digital Memory and the Archive*, ed. Jussi Parikka (Minneapolis: University of Minnesota Press, 2013), 71.

16 Kittler argues that since Aristotle, there has been an ontological neglect of "media." For Aristotle, it was not part of the ontological sphere (reserved for things), which excluded "medium": *tòmetaxú* "is relegated to his theory of sensorial perception *(aisthesis).*" Friedrich Kittler, "Toward an Ontology of Media," *Theory, Culture, and Society* 26, nos. 2–3 (2009): 24.

17 Trevor Paglen, "The Last Pictures," *Journal of Visual Culture* 12, no. 3 (2013): 508–14.

18 Kahn, *Earth Sound Earth Signal*, 107, 146.

19 Friedrich Kittler, "Lightning and Series—Event and Thunder," *Theory, Culture, and Society* 23, nos. 7–8 (2006): 69.

20 "We no longer needed electronic music studios; we already had them in our brains." Oliveros, as quoted in Kahn, *Earth Sound Earth Signal*, 175.

21 Elizabeth Grosz, *Chaos, Territory, Art: Deleuze and the Framing of the Earth* (New York: University of Columbia Press, 2008).

22 Kahn, *Earth Sound Earth Signal*, 177.

23 Theodore Ziolkowski, *German Romanticism and Its Institutions* (Princeton, N.J.: Princeton University Press, 1990), 28–29.

24 Fortey, as quoted in Ian W. D. Dalel, "Vestiges of a Beginning and the Prospect of an End," in *James Hutton—Present and Future*, ed. G. Y. Craig and J. H. Hull (London: Geological Society Special Publications, 1999), 150.

25 Dalel, "Vestiges of a Beginning," 122–23.

26 John Shimkus, "Mining Helium-3 Will Transform the Dark Side of the Moon," May 9, 2011, http://www.energydigital.com/global_mining/mining-helium -3-will-transform-dark-side-of-the-moon.

27 "Russia will begin Moon colonization in 2030—a draft space program," May 9, 2013, http://rt.com/news/157800-russia-moon-colonization-plan/.

28 Cubitt, *Digital Aesthetics*, 45–49.

29 Bruce Clarke, "Gaia Matters," *Electronic Book Review*, November 30, 2006, http://www.electronicbookreview.com/thread/criticalecologies/looped.

30 Martin Heidegger, *The Question Concerning Technology and Other Essays*, trans. William Lovitt (New York: Garland, 1977), 17.

31 Samih Al Rawashdeh and Bassam Saleh et Mufeed Hamzah, "The Use of Remote Sensing Technology in Geological Investigation and Mineral Detection in El Azraq-Jordan," *Cybergeo–European Journal of Geography*, October 23, 2006, http://cybergeo.revues.org/2856.

32 Eyal Weizman, Heather Davis, and Etienne Turpin, "Matters of Calculation: Eyal Weizman in Conversation with Heather Davis and Etienne Turpin," in *Architecture in the Anthropocene: Encounters among Design, Deep Time, Science, and Philosophy*, ed. Etienne Turpin (Ann Arbor, Mich.: Open Humanities Press, 2013), 64.

33 See Edwards, *Vast Machine*.

34 Kahn, *Earth Sound Earth Signal*, 157.

35 For Kittler, the phonograph and in general the technical media of sound recording tap into the Lacanian Real. See Friedrich Kittler, *Gramophone, Film, Typewriter*, trans. Geoffrey Winthrop-Young and Michael Wutz (Stanford, Calif.: Stanford University Press, 1999).

36 Donna Haraway draws from the work of ethnographer Marilyn Strathern in this formulation that resonates with the emphasis on cross-species connections across a range of micropractices, interfaces, relationality: "Marilyn Strathern, drawing on decades of study of Papua New Guinean histories and politics, as well as on her investigation of English kin reckoning habits, taught us why conceiving of 'nature' and 'culture' as either polar opposites or universal categories is foolish. An ethnographer of relational categories, she showed how to think in other topologies. Instead of opposites, we get the whole sketchpad of the modern geometrician's fevered brain with which to draw relationality. Strathern thinks in terms of 'partial connections'; i.e., patterns within which the players are neither wholes nor parts. I call these the relations of significant otherness. To think of Strathern as an ethnographer of naturecultures; she will not mind if I invite her into the kennel for a

cross-species conversation." Haraway, *The Companion Species Manifesto: Dogs, People, and Significant Otherness* (Chicago: Prickly Paradigm Press, 2003), 9. On "medianatures," see also Jussi Parikka, "Media Zoology and Waste Management: Animal Energies and Medianatures," *Necsus–European Journal of Media Studies,* no. 4 (2013), http://www.necsus-ejms.org/.

37 Haraway, *Companion Species Manifesto,* 12.

38 Rick Dolphjin and Iris van der Tuin, *New Materialism: Interviews and Cartographies* (Ann Arbor, Mich.: Open Humanities Press, 2012), 90. Of course, one can argue, to quote Scott McQuire, that "defining the technological activates the border between nature and culture." McQuire, "Technology," *Theory, Culture, and Society* 23, nos. 2–3 (2006): 252. And at the same time, technology also is based on the crossing of the border between the two.

39 Sean Cubitt, interviewed by Simon Mills, *Framed,* http://www.ada.net.nz/library/framed-sean-cubitt/.

40 See Colin Dickey, "Review of *Why Hell Stinks of Sulfur: Mythology and Geology of the Underworld,*" *Los Angeles Review of Books,* July 14, 2013, https://lareviewofbooks.org/.

41 See Rosalind Williams, *Notes on the Underground: Essays on Technology, Society, and the Imagination,* new ed. (Cambridge, Mass.: MIT Press, 2008).

42 Tarde's short novel was originally published in 1904 as *Fragment d'histoire future* (Fragment of a history of future).

43 Williams, *Notes on the Underground,* 81.

44 Lewis Mumford, *Technics and Civilization* (1934; reprint, Chicago: University of Chicago Press, 2010), 228–29.

45 Paul J. Crutzen, "Geology of Mankind: The Anthropocene," *Nature* 415, no. 3 (2002): 23.

46 The International Commission on Stratigraphy should reach a decision on the formal acceptance of the designation by 2016.

47 The "obscenity" of the Anthropocene can be read as an ethical qualification of the term to underline the role of corporations and nation-states in a systemic exploitation of work and natural resources. The Anthrobscene is executed through engineered, scientific, and, for example, legislative means. But it has also implicit connotations to the ontological shift that Jean Baudrillard writes as the *ob-scene.* Even if the link to Baudrillard is not the engine for this concept, there is an element of obscene exposure and exploitative visuality that produces nature as a resource. On Baudrillard, see Paul Taylor, "Baudrillard's Resistance to the Ob-Scene as the Mis-en-Scene (Or, Refusing to Think Like a Lap-Dancer's Client)," *International Journal of Baudrillard Studies* 5, no. 2 (2008), http://www.ubishops.ca/baudrillardstudies/vol-5_2/

v5–2-taylor.html. In *The Geology of Media,* however, this implosion happens on the level of the material ob-scene: the myths of immateriality support the engineered depletion of crucial resources, energy crisis, and the corporate mobilization of the earth as part of the circuit of medianatures. The *pornographic* is evident primarily in the manner in which nature–ecology is viewed as a corporate resource, exposed down to its molecular intensities. The obscene is both a mode of exploitation and an epistemological framework. However, I want to underline that there should be no nostalgic longing for a connection of the earth in the mythological or Heideggerian sense but rather in a different sense of ecosophic relation across the spheres of economic, social, and environmental engineering and production.

48 Will Steffen, Paul J. Crutzen, and John R. McNeill, "The Anthropocene: Are Humans Now Overwhelming the Great Forces of Nature?," *Ambio* 36, no. 8 (2007): 615.

49 See Mumford, *Technics and Civilization,* 232–33.

50 Steffen et al., "The Anthropocene," 616.

51 Crutzen, "Geology of Mankind," 23.

52 John McNeill, *Something New under the Sun: An Environmental History of the Twentieth-Century World* (New York: W. W. Norton, 2000), 52.

53 Steffen et al., "The Anthropocene," 616.

54 McNeill, *Something New under the Sun.*

55 Dipesh Chakrabarty, "The Climate of History: Four Theses," *Critical Inquiry* 35 (Winter 2009): 206–7.

56 Ibid., 219.

57 In the manner Félix Guattari uses and introduces the terms alongside "mixed semiotics" of material intensities and signifying structures entangled. For an elaboration, see Gary Genosko, *Félix Guattari: An Aberrant Introduction* (London: Continuum, 2002), 169–71.

58 A crisis demands a temporal framework that is able to premediate futures, even changing them: modeling climate change, for instance, is based on the hope that if we take such predictions seriously, we might be able to stop them from becoming true, to paraphrase Wendy Hui Kyong Chun. Chun, "Crisis, Crisis, Crisis, or Sovereignty and Networks," *Theory, Culture, and Society* 28, no. 6 (2011): 107.

59 See Mieke Bal, *Travelling Concepts in the Humanities* (Toronto: Toronto University Press, 2002).

60 See also Rosi Braidotti, *The Posthuman* (Cambridge: Polity, 2013).

61 Gilles Deleuze and Félix Guattari, *A Thousand Plateaus,* trans. Brian Massumi (Minneapolis: University of Minnesota Press, 1987), especially chapter 3.

Eric Alliez, *The Signature of the World: What Is Deleuze and Guattari's Philosophy?*, trans. Eliot Ross Albert and Alberto Toscano (New York: Continuum, 2004), 25.

62 Gilles Deleuze and Félix Guattari, *What Is Philosophy?*, trans. Hugh Tomlinson and Graham Burchell (London: Verso, 2009), 85.

63 See Matthew Fuller, *Media Ecologies: Materialist Energies in Art and Technoculture* (Cambridge, Mass.: MIT Press, 2005). See also Michael Goddard and Jussi Parikka, eds., "Unnatural Ecologies," special issue, *Fibreculture*, no. 17 (2011), http://seventeen.fibreculturejournal.org/.

64 Asko Nivala, "The Chemical Age: Presenting History with Metaphors," in *They Do Things Differently There: Essays on Cultural History*, ed. Bruce Johnson and Harri Kiiskinen, 81–108 (Turku: Turku, 2011).

65 Theodore Ziolkowski, *German Romanticism and Its Institutions* (Princeton, N.J.: Princeton University Press, 1990). See chapter 2 on mining in that book.

66 Ben Woodard, *On an Ungrounded Earth: Towards a New Geophilosophy* (New York: Punctum Books, 2013). Iain Hamilton Grant, *Philosophies of Nature after Schelling* (London: Continuum, 2006). Reza Negarestani, "Undercover Softness: An Introduction to the Architecture and Politics of Decay," *COLLAPSE VI: Geo/Philosophy*, January 2010, 382.

67 Iain Hamilton Grant, "Mining Conditions," in *The Speculative Turn: Continental Materialism and Realism*, ed. Levi Bryant, Nick Srnicek, and Graham Harman (Melbourne: re.press, 2010), 44.

68 This ungrounding and constituent exhumation is picked up by Reza Negarestani too: "If archeologists, cultists, worms and crawling entities almost always undertake an act of exhumation (surfaces, tombs, cosmic comers, dreams, etc.), it is because exhumation is equal to ungrounding, incapacitating surfaces ability to operate according to topologies of the whole, or on a mereotopological level. In exhumation, the distribution of surfaces is thoroughly undermined and the movements associated with them are derailed; the edge no longer belongs to the periphery, anterior surfaces come after all other surfaces, layers of strata are displaced and perforated, peripheries and the last protecting surfaces become the very conductors of invasion. Exhumation is defined as a collapse and trauma introduced to the solid part by vermiculate activities; it is the body of solidity replaced by the full body of trauma. As in disinterment—scarring the hot and cold surfaces of a grave—exhumation proliferates surfaces through each other. Exhumation transmutes architectures into excessive scarring processes, fibroses of tissues, membranes and surfaces of the solid body." Negarestani, *Cyclonopedia: Complicity with Anonymous Materials* (Melbourne: re.press, 2008), 51–52. It would

be interesting to extend and develop Zielinski's methodology of deep time and variantology of media in connection with such notes by geophilosophers from Woodard to Grant to Negarestani.

69 Jane Bennett, *Vibrant Matter: A Political Ecology of Things* (Durham, N.C.: Duke University Press, 2010). Manuel Delanda, *Deleuze: History and Science* (New York: Atropos Press, 2010). Dolphjin and van der Tuin, *New Materialism*.

70 Deleuze and Guattari, *A Thousand Plateaus*, 372. "*There are itinerant, ambulant sciences that consist in following a flow in a vectorial field across which singularities are scattered like so many 'accidents.'*"

71 Bennett, *Vibrant Matter*, 58–60.

72 Ibid., 60.

73 Andrew Blum, *Tubes: A Journey to the Center of the Internet* (New York: HarperCollins, 2012), 258.

74 Ibid., 260.

75 Ibid.

76 Ibid., 259.

77 Mumford, *Technics and Civilization*, 229.

78 Ibid., 231.

79 And also increasingly an artistic and curatorial mapping. A good example is *The Oil Show* exhibition at HKMW, Dortmund (November 12, 2011, to February 19, 2012), curated by Inke Arns. See also Mumford, *Technics and Civilization*, 232–33.

80 For a good journalistic mapping of the issues of resources and geopolitics, see Klare, *Race for What's Left*.

81 Sean Cubitt's work-in-progress book project *Ecomediations* addresses these issues in detail. See also Cubitt, "Electric Light and Energy," *Theory, Culture, and Society* 30, nos. 7–8 (2013): 309–23.

2. An Alternative Deep Time of the Media

1 Seb Franklin, "Cloud Control, or the Network as a Medium," *Cultural Politics* 8, no. 3 (2012): 443–64.

2 See Ippolita, *The Dark Side of Google*, trans. Patrice Riemens (Amsterdam: Institute of Network Cultures), 2013, http://networkcultures.org/wpmu/portal/publication/no-13-the-dark-side-of-google-ippolita/.

3 "What the N.S.A. Wants in Brazil," *The New Yorker*, July 24, 2013, http://www.newyorker.com/online/blogs/newsdesk/2013/07/why-the-nsa-really-cares-about-brazil.html.

4 Williams, *Notes on the Underground*, 72.

5   On sea cables and infrastructural (in)visibility, see Nicole Starosielski, "'Warning: Do Not Dig': Negotiating the Visibility of Critical Infrastructures," *Journal of Visual Culture* 11, no. 1 (2012): 38–57. See also Ryan Bishop, "Project
'Transparent Earth' and the Autoscope of Aerial Targeting: The Visual Geopolitics of the Underground," *Theory, Culture, and Society* 28, nos. 7–8
(2011): 270–86. Williams, *Notes on the Underground*.

6   Kahn, *Earth Sound Earth Signal*.

7   Arthur Conan Doyle, "When the World Screamed," 1928, http://www.clas
sic-literature.co.uk/scottish-authors/arthur-conan-doyle/when-the-world
-screamed/ebook-page-10.asp.

8   Ibid. The idea of a living earth was part of an imaginary of the earth and
technology, but one has to note that far until the late nineteenth century, the
nature of the earth's interior was much debated. As Williams argues, the
likes of prominent geologists such as Archibald Geikie listed various possibilities of what lies under the crust; the theories of the Hollow Earth might
have been discarded a long time ago, but whether there is a liquid substra-
tum under the crust was still left as a possibility. Williams, *Notes on the
Underground*, 14.

9   Doyle, "When the World Screamed."

10 Ibid. The allusion to rape is made even more obvious when considering
the long-term mythological articulation of the earth with the female. The
gendered interior of the earth is one of valuable richness. Steven Connor,
Dumbstruck: A Cultural History of Ventriloquism (Oxford: Oxford University Press, 2000), 52.

11 Doyle, "When the World Screamed."

12 Novalis, as quoted in Ziolkowski, *German Romanticism and Its Institutions*,
31.

13 Williams, *Notes on the Underground*, 11. As I won't deal with literature and
geology in a systematic way in this short book, I want to point readers interested in the narrativization of geology in the nineteenth century to Adelene
Buckland, *Novel Science: Fiction and the Invention of Nineteenth Century
Geology* (Chicago: University of Chicago Press, 2013).

14 Williams, *Notes on the Underground*, 90–91.

15 Richard Maxwell and Toby Miller, *Greening the Media* (Oxford: Oxford University Press, 2012), 55.

16 Fritz Leiber, "The Black Gondolier," in *The Black Gondolier and Other Stories* (n.p., 2002). Negarestani, *Cyclonopedia*. Eugene Thacker, "Black Infinity,
or, Oil Discovers Humans," in *Leper Creativity*, 173–80 (New York: Punctum,
2012).

17 Brett Neilson, "Fracking," in *Depletion Design,* ed. Carolin Wiedemann and Soenke Zehle (Amsterdam: Institute of Network Cultures and xm:lab, 2012), 85.

18 Kola superdeep borehole, http://en.wikipedia.org/wiki/Kola_Superdeep_ Borehole. Larry Gedney, "The World's Deepest Hole," *Alaska Science Forum,* July 15, 1985, http://www2.gi.alaska.edu/ScienceForum/ASF7/725.html. The drilling operation proved some geophysical theories from the 1920s inaccurate and discovered other oddities in old ages of depth: "The Kola well has now penetrated about halfway through the crust of the Baltic continental shield, exposing rocks 2.7 billion years old at the bottom (for comparison, the Vishnu schist at the bottom of the Grand Canyon dates to about 2 billion years—the earth itself is about 4.6 billion years old). To scientists, one of the more fascinating findings to emerge from this well is that the change in seismic velocities was not found at a boundary marking Jeffreys' hypothetical transition from granite to basalt; it was at the bottom of a layer of metamorphic rock (rock which has been intensively reworked by heat and pressure) that extended from about 3 to about 6 miles beneath the surface. This rock had been thoroughly fractured and was saturated with water, and free water should not be found at these depths! This could only mean that water which had originally been a part of the chemical composition of the rock minerals themselves (as contrasted with ground water) had been forced out of the crystals and prevented from rising by an overlying cap of impermeable rock. This has never been observed anywhere else."

19 Maxwell and Miller, *Greening the Media,* 93.

20 T. E. Graedel, E. M. Harper, N. T. Nassar, and Barbara K. Reck, "On the Materials Basis of Modern Society," *PNAS,* October 2013, Early Edition, 1.

21 Ibid. See also Akshat Raksi, "The Metals in Your Smartphone May Be Irreplaceable," *Ars Technica,* December 5, 2013, http://arstechnica.com/science/ 2013/12/the-metals-in-your-smartphone-may-be-irreplaceable/.

22 Brett Milligan, "Space-Time Vertigo," in *Making the Geologic Now: Responses to the Material Conditions of Contemporary Life,* ed. Elizabeth Ellsworth and Jamie Kruse (New York: Punctum, 2013), 124.

23 Manuel Delanda, *A Thousand Years of Nonlinear History* (New York: Swerve/ MIT Press, 2000). Delanda's argument for a geological approach to human history stems from an understanding of self-organization as the general drive on how matter and energy are distributed. In this way, he is able to argue provocatively that "human societies are very much like lava flows" (55), referring to the certain nonlinear patterns of organization. In addition, he does a good job illuminating the historical character in which there is an

extensive continuum between geological formations and what we tend to call human history, for instance, of urbanity. Indeed, the processes of mineralization some five hundred million years ago give rise to the endoskeleton and materiality of the bone affecting the processes crucial for the birth of humans (and a range of other specific types of bony organic life), as well as later affording a range of other processes. Indeed, Delanda talks of the exoskeleton of urban cities as being afforded by this same process and tracks how metals play their part in the formation of urban centralization and clustering. We could in this vein argue that the processes of mineralization extend to the current computer age too, in terms of how the sedimented but deterritorializing layers of geological time are affording a further exoskeleton—an argument that has its implicit resonances with the way in which, for instance, Bernard Stiegler has pitched the various externalizations of human memory, leaning on Husserl and Simondon.

24 Deleuze and Guattari, *A Thousand Plateaus*, 40. They are adamant in emphasizing that this is not about substance and form (the hylomorphic model persistent in philosophy), the dualism usually haunting the linguistically modeled idea of meaning. Instead, they want to introduce a geologically driven idea of the materiality of signification, including asignifying elements. The double nature of the articulation is expressed as follows: "The first articulation chooses or deducts, from unstable particle-flows, metastable molecular or quasi-molecular units *(substances)* upon which it imposes a statistical order of connections and successions *(forms)*. The second articulation establishes functional, compact, stable structures *(forms)*, and constructs the molar compounds in which these structures are simultaneously actualized *(substances)*. In a geological stratum, for example, the first articulation is the process of 'sedimentation,' which deposits units of cyclic sediment according to a statistical order: flysch, with its succession of sandstone and schist. The second articulation is the 'folding' that sets up a stable functional structure and effects the passage from sediment to sedimentary rock" (40–41). A good and necessary philosophical reading of the geological is Ben Woodard's *On an Ungrounded Earth*. It offers a critique and expansion of the Deleuze–Guattari perspective.

25 In short, in *A Thousand Plateaus*, Deleuze and Guattari pitch the idea of a geology of morals (a reference to Nietzsche) as illuminating an idea of stratification as a double articulation. The previous endnote clarified this aspect. Such a process is not, however, restricted to geology, but it allows Deleuze and Guattari to talk of a geology of morals. In my further development, geology of media is besides a philosophical figure and a nod toward *A Thousand*

Plateaus, an emerging perspective of the careful selection and sedimentation of certain material elements necessary for the consolidation of functional media technologies. Such technologies express continua between
nature and culture, or what I have called *medianatures,* which often signal
themselves through ecological implications or, to be frank, problems—energy
production, waste, and so forth. For Delanda, the Deleuze and Guattari geological model provides a new materialism of stratification that as an abstract
machine runs across various materialities: "sedimentary rocks, species and
social classes (and other institutionalized hierarchies) are all historical constructions, the product of definite structure-generating processes that take
as their starting point a heterogeneous collection of raw materials (pebbles,
genes, roles), homogenize them through a sorting operation, and then con-
solidate the resulting uniform groupings into a more permanent state."
Delanda, *A Thousand Years of Nonlinear History,* 62. Furthermore, the link
between Smithson's in other places in this book mentioned "abstract geology" and Deleuze and Guattari's thought (including Bateson) is an interesting theme to elaborate, but it is out of my reach in this short book.

26 Sebastian Anthony, "MIT Creates Tiny, 22nm Transistor without Silicon,"
Extremetech, December 11, 2012, http://www.extremetech.com/extreme/143
024-mit-creates-tiny-22nm-transistor-without-silicon.

27 See Wiedemann and Zehle, eds., *Depletion Design* (Amsterdam: Institute of
Network Cultures and xm:lab, 2012).

28 Jussi Parikka, "Dust and Exhaustion: The Labor of Media Materialism,"
Ctheory, October 2, 2013, http://www.ctheory.net/articles.aspx?id=726.

29 Ippolita and Tiziana Mancinelli, "The Facebook Aquarium: Freedom in a
Profile," in *Unlike Us Reader: Social Media Monopolies and Their Alterna-
tives,* ed. Geert Lovink and Miriam Rasch (Amsterdam: Institute of Network
Cultures, 2013), 164.

30 Zielinski, *Deep Time of the Media,* 3.

31 Stephen Jay Gould, *Time's Arrow, Time's Cycle: Myth and Metaphor in the
Discovery of Geological Time* (Cambridge, Mass.: Harvard University Press,
1987), 86–91.

32 James Hutton, *Theory of the Earth,* e-version on Project Gutenberg, (1792)
2004, http://www.gutenberg.org/files/12861/12861-h/12861-h.htm.

33 Jack Repchek, *The Man Who Invented Time: James Hutton and the Discovery of Earth's Antiquity* (New York: Basic Books, 2009), 8.

34 Charles Lyell, *Principles of Geology* (London: John Murray, 1830), 1–4. Online
facsimile at http://www.esp.org/books/lyell/principles/facsimile/.

35 Gould, *Time's Arrow, Time's Cycle,* 167, 150–55.

36 Elizabeth Grosz, *Becoming Undone: Darwinian Reflections on Life, Politics, and Art* (Durham, N.C.: Duke University Press, 2011).

37 See Repchek, *Man Who Invented Time*. Repchek's account posits Hutton as an important discoverer, but some of this discourse focusing on the originality of Hutton neglects earlier geological research that is not always pertaining to a Christian worldview of limited biblical proportions. Furthermore, the invention of modern time in historiography follows slightly differing paths, opening up the idea of an open, radically different future. See Reinhart Koselleck, *Futures Past: On the Semantics of Historical Time*, trans. Keith Tribe (New York: Columbia University Press, 2004), 240–43.

38 Gould, *Time's Arrow, Time's Cycle*.

39 Martin J. S. Rudwick, *Bursting the Limits of Time: The Reconstruction of Geohistory in the Age of Revolution* (Chicago: University of Chicago Press, 2005), 160. Hutton's world does not allow for the accidental but remains in the natural theological view of an orderly universe.

40 Gould, *Time's Arrow, Time's Cycle*, 87.

41 Simon Schaffer, "Babbage's Intelligence," http://www.imaginaryfutures.net/2007/04/16/babbages-intelligence-by-simon-schaffer/.

42 Rudwick, *Bursting the Limits of Time*, 161.

43 Ibid., 159–62.

44 Zielinski, *Deep Time of the Media*, 5.

45 Stephen Jay Gould, *Punctuated Equilibrium* (Cambridge, Mass.: Harvard University Press, 2007), 10.

46 Niles Eldredge and Stephen Jay Gould, "Punctuated Equilibria: An Alternative to Phyletic Gradualism," in *Models in Paleobiology*, ed. T. J. M. Schopf (San Francisco: Freeman Cooper, 1972), 82–115.

47 Peters, "Space, Time, and Communication Theory."

48 Fredric Jameson, *Archaeologies of the Future* (London: Verso, 2005).

49 See Alexander R. Galloway, Eugene Thacker, and McKenzie Wark, *Excommunication: Three Inquiries in Media and Mediation* (Chicago: Chicago University Press, 2013), 139.

50 Zielinski has continued these discussions in the Variantology book series as well as in the recently translated *[. . . After the Media]*, trans. Gloria Custance (Minneapolis, Minn.: Univocal, 2013).

51 The figures as to exactly how much network computing and data centers consume varies a lot, as does the dependence on carbon emission–heavy energy. Peter W. Huber, "Dig More Coal, the PCs Are Coming," *Forbes*, May 31, 1999. Duncan Clark and Mike Berners-Lee, "What's the Carbon Footprint

of . . . the Internet?," *The Guardian*, August 12, 2010, http://www.theguard ian.com/. Seán O' Halloran, "The Internet Power Drain," *Business Spectator*, September 6, 2012, http://www.businessspectator.com.au/article/2012/9/6/ technology/internet-power-drain.

52 Amy Catania Kulper, "Architecture's Lapidarium," in *Architecture in the Anthropocene: Encounters among Design, Deep Time, Science, and Philosophy*, ed. Etienne Turpin (Ann Arbor, Mich.: Open Humanities Press, 2013), 100. Lewis Mumford's technological reading of mines is also important; it underlines them as the site of crystallization of a specific early phase of modern technology. "*The mine is nothing less in fact than the concrete model of the conceptual world which was built up by the physicists of the seventeenth century.*" Quoted in Williams, *Notes on the Underground*, 22.

53 Recent media and cultural theory has, in most interesting ways, picked up the notion of temporality again. In media archaeology, such a desire has resonated with a non-narrative- and non-human-based understanding of temporalities—for instance, microtemporality (Wolfgang Ernst). For Ernst, microtemporalities define the ontological basis of how media as reality production works in speeds inaccessible by the human senses. See Wolfgang Ernst, *Chronopoetik: Zeitweisen und Zeitgaben technischer Medien* (Berlin: Kadmos, 2013). See also Ernst, "From Media History to Zeitkritik," trans. Guido Schenkel, *Theory, Culture, and Society* 30, no. 6 (2013): 132–46. Similarly Mark Hansen's recent work has flagged the need to embed media theoretical vocabulary in a different regime of sensation than the conscious perception. In Hansen's Whitehead-inspired perspective, the limitations of phenomenology are explicated so as to find a sufficiently developed approach that helps to address the current ubiquitous digital media culture and the speeds at which it folds as part of the human, without being accessible through human senses. See Mark B. N. Hansen, *Feed Forward: On the Future of the Twenty-First Century Media* (Chicago: University of Chicago Press, 2014). At the other scale, the duration of climatic and geological time scales has to be addressed. Besides this book on geology, see, for instance, Claire Colebrook on extinction and the weird temporalities of nature and knowledge of nature. Colebrook, "Framing the End of Species," in *Extinction: Living Books about Life* (Ann Arbor, Mich.: Open Humanities Press, 2011), http://www.livingbooksaboutlife.org/books/Extinction/Introduction.

54 Peters, "Space, Time, and Communication Theory."

55 Fuller, *Media Ecologies*, 174.

56 Sean Cubitt, Robert Hassan, and Ingrid Volkmer, "Does Cloud Computing Have a Silver Lining?," *Media, Culture, and Society* 33 (2011): 149–58.

57 Paul Feigelfeld, "From the Anthropocene to the Neo-Cybernetic Underground: An Conversation with Erich Hörl," *Modern Weekly*, Fall/Winter 2013, online English version at http://www.60pages.com/from-the-anthropocene-to-the-neo-cybernetic-underground-a-conversation-with-erich-horl-2/.

58 Ibid.

59 Benjamin Bratton, *The Stack* (Cambridge, Mass.: MIT Press, forthcoming); Michael Nest, *Coltan* (Cambridge: Polity, 2011).

60 Rob Holmes, "A Preliminary Atlas of Gizmo Landscapes," *Mammolith*, April 1, 2010, http://m.ammoth.us/blog/2010/04/a-preliminary-atlas-of-gizmo-landscapes/.

61 For a specific focus on scrap metals, technology, and China, see Adam Minter, "How China Profits from Our Junk," *The Atlantic*, November 1, 2013, http://www.theatlantic.com/china/archive/2013/11/how-china-profits-from-our-junk/281044/. On the life cycle of metals as part of technological society, see Graedel et al., "On the Materials Basis of Modern Society."

62 Ibid.

63 Garnet Hertz and Jussi Parikka, "Zombie Media: Circuit Bending Media Archaeology into an Art Method," *Leonardo* 45, no. 5 (2012): 424–30.

64 U.S. Environmental Protection Agency, "Statistics on the Management of Used and End-of-Life Electronics," 2009, http://www.epa.gov/osw/conserve/materials/ecycling/manage.htm.

65 McKenzie Wark, "Escape from the Dual Empire," *Rhizomes* 6 (Spring 2003), http://www.rhizomes.net/issue6/wark.htm.

66 Klare, *Race for What's Left*, 12.

67 "Chevron Announces Discovery in the Deepest Well Drilled in the U.S. Gulf of Mexico," press release, December 20, 2005, http://investor.chevron.com/. Currently the deepest wells are located on the Al Shaheen Oil Field, offshore in the middle of the Persian Gulf (12,290 meters) and offshore the Sakhalin Island, on the Okhotsk Sea, reaching the depth of 12,376 meters. The latter project was executed by Exxon Neftegas Ltd.

68 Heidegger, *Question Concerning Technology*, 16.

69 European Union Critical Raw Materials Analysis, by the European Commission Raw Materials Supply Group, July 30, 2010, executive summary by Swiss Metal Assets, October 1, 2011, http://www.swissmetalassets.com.

70 Clemens Winkler, "Germanium, Ge, ein neues, nichtmetallisches Element," *Berichte der deutschen chemischen Gesellschaft* 19 (1886): 210–11.

71 See Ryan Bishop, "Project 'Transparent Earth' and the Autoscopy of Aerial Targeting: The Visual Geopolitics of the Underground," *Theory, Culture, and Society* 28, nos. 7–8 (2011): 270–86.

72 Williams, *Notes on the Underground.*

73 One could speculate that such theory is definitely *"low* theory," to refer to McKenzie Wark's notion in *Telesthesia: Communication, Culture, and Class* (Cambridge: Polity, 2012), 12.

74 Jonathan Sterne has also raised the need for a deep time perspective, without using those terms: "if the span of media history in human history amounts to approximately 40,000 years, we have yet to really seriously reconsider the first 39,400 years." Jonathan Sterne, "The Times of Communication History," presented at Connections: The Future of Media Studies, University of Virginia, April 4, 2009.

75 Friedrich Kittler, "Of States and Their Terrorists," *Cultural Politics* 8, no. 3 (2012): 388. See also the University of Brighton project "Traces of Nitrate: Mining History and Photography between Britain and Chile," funded by the AHRC. Online at http://arts.brighton.ac.uk/projects/traces-of-nitrate.

76 Kittler, "Of States and Their Terrorists," 394.

77 Chris Taylor, "Fertilising Earthworks," in Ellsworth and Kruse, *Making the Geologic Now,* 130.

78 Sean Cubitt, "Integral Waste," presented at the transmediale 2014 Afterglow festival, Berlin, February 1, 2014.

79 Geoffrey Winthrop-Young, "Hunting a Whale of a State: Kittler and His Terrorists," *Cultural Politics* 8, no. 3 (2012): 406. He continues with a reference to Pynchon's words about World War II in *Gravity's Rainbow* (New York: Viking, 1973), perhaps a relevant guideline to the wider issue of media, materiality, ideology, and wars: "This War was never political at all, the politics was all theatre, all just to keep the people distracted . . . secretly, it was being dictated instead by the needs of technology. . . . The real crises were crises of allocation and priority, not among firms—it was only staged to look that way—but among the different Technologies, Plastics, Electronics, Aircraft, and their needs which are understood only by the ruling elite." Ibid., 407.

80 iMine game, http://i-mine.org/. See also Parikka, "Dust and Exhaustion."

81 William Jerome Harrison, *History of Photography* (New York: Scovill Manufacturing Company, 1887). What makes Harrison even more interesting for our purposes is his career in geology. See Adam Bobbette, "Episodes from the History of Scalelessness: William Jerome Harrison and Geological Photography," in Turpin, *Architecture in the Anthropocene,* 45–58.

82 Thank you to Kelly Egan for sharing the autoethnographic account of her artistic practice with films and chemicals.

83 Jane Bennett uses this conceptual figure, borrowed from Deleuze and Guattari, as well. See Bennett, *Vibrant Matter,* 58–60.

84 Thomas Pynchon, *Against the Day* (London: Vintage Books, 2007), 72.

85 See Paul Caplan, "JPEG: The Quadruple Object," PhD thesis, Birkbeck College, University of London, 2013.

86 Homer H. Dubs, "The Beginnings of Alchemy," *Isis* 38, nos. 1–2 (1947): 73.

87 "When the effluvia from the cow lands ascend to the dark heavens, the dark heavens in six hundred years' give birth to black whetstones, black whetstones in six hundred years give birth to black quicksilver, black quicksilver in six hundred years gives birth to black metal (iron), and black metal in a thousand years gives birth to a black dragon. Where the black dragon enters into [permanent] hibernation, it gives birth to the Black Springs." Quoted in ibid., 72–73.

88 William Newman, "Technology and Alchemic Debate in the Late Middle Ages," *Isis* 80, no. 3 (1989): 426.

89 Vincent of Beauvais's *Speculum doctrinale,* quoted in Newman, "Technology and Alchemic Debate," 430.

90 Pynchon, *Against the Day,* 88.

91 Cubitt et al., "Does Cloud Computing Have a Silver Lining?" See also Michael Riordan and Lillian Hoddeson, *Crystal Fire: The Invention of the Transistor and the Birth of the Information Age* (New York: W. W. Norton, 1997).

3. Psychogeophysics of Technology

1 Rachel Armstrong, "Why Synthetic Soil Holds the Key to a Sustainable Future," *Guardian Professional,* January 17, 2014, http://www.theguardian.com/.

2 Rudwick, *Bursting the Limits of Time,* 162.

3 Delanda, *Deleuze: History and Science,* 78.

4 See Chun, "Crisis, Crisis, Crisis." Edwards, *Vast Machine.* In more general terms, one could relate this to the discourse of cultural techniques too and to consider media technologies as cultural techniques: "namely, to relate the concept of media/mediums historically to ontological and aesthetic operations that process distinctions (and the blurring of distinctions) which are basic to the sense production of any specific culture." From this anthropological definition by Bernhard Siegert, one can move on to a more ecological sense in which media technologies operate. The quotation is from Siegert, "The Map Is the Territory," *Radical Philosophy* 169 (September/October 2011): 14. This connection is not fully explored in this book and is left more as a hint of an alternative route that can be picked up in the future in more detail and consistency.

5 Afterglow was the transmediale 2014 festival theme.

6　McKenzie Wark, *The Beach beneath the Street: Everyday Life and the Glorious Times of the Situationist International* (London: Verso, 2011). Wark, *The Spectacle of Disintegration: Situationist Passages out of the 20th Century* (London: Verso, 2013).

7　The London Psychogeophysics Summit, "What Is Psychogeophysics?," *Mute*, August 4, 2010, http://www.metamute.org/.

8　Indeed, for Friedrich Kittler and others, this marked a radical epistemic threshold from the psychological subject to the physiological object of measurement: physiology instead of the interior experience, scientific measurability of reaction thresholds and speeds instead of "feeling." See Kittler, *Gramophone, Film, Typewriter*, 188. Cf. Sybille Krämer, "The Cultural Techniques of Time-Axis Manipulation: Friedrich Kittler's Conception of Media," *Theory, Culture, and Society* 23, nos. 7–8 (2006): 93–109. On Helmholtz, see also Henning Schmidgen, *Helmholtz Curves: Tracing Lost Time*, trans. Nils F. Schott (New York: Fordham University Press, 2014).

9　This claim can be best understood through A. N. Whitehead's philosophy. See Steven Shaviro, *Without Criteria: Kant, Whitehead, Deleuze, and Aesthetics* (Cambridge, Mass.: MIT Press, 2009).

10　Quoted in Ziolkowski, *German Romanticism and Its Institutions*, 33.

11　John Durham Peters, "Space, Time, and Communication Theory."

12　Marina Warner, "The Writing of Stones," *Cabinet*, no. 29 (Spring 2008), http://cabinetmagazine.org/issues/29/warner.php.

13　Roger Caillois, *The Writing of Stones*, trans. Barbara Bray (Charlottesville: University Press of Virginia, 1985), 4–6.

14　This is a variation on the Deleuze and Guattari idea of metallurgy (as a minor science), found in *A Thousand Plateaus* and in a vital materialist way mobilized by Jane Bennett: "The desire of the craftsperson to see what a metal can do, rather than the desire of the scientist to know what a metal is, enabled the former to discern a life in metal and thus, eventually, to collaborate more productively with it." Bennett, *Vibrant Matter*, 60.

15　Bennett, *Vibrant Matter*, 115.

16　Matthew Fuller, "Art for Animals," *Journal of Visual Art Practice* 9, no. 1 (2010): 17–33.

17　Rosi Braidotti, *The Posthuman* (Cambridge: Polity, 2013), 81.

18　Morton, *Hyperobjects*.

19　See the introduction to Jussi Parikka, ed., *Medianatures: The Materiality of Information Technology and Electronic Waste* (Ann Arbor, Mich.: Open Humanities Press, 2011). Online at http://www.livingbooksaboutlife.org/.

20　Workshop description of the London Geophysics Summit, August 2–7,

2010, http://turbulence.org/blog/2010/06/21/the-london-psychogeophysics
-summit-london/.

21 Of course, in philosophical discourse as well as in mythology, the invisible
underground (or caves, the preempting of the much later German romanti-
cist focus on mines) has a long history. This relates to the differentiation of
the senses and the rational mind, the work of perception versus the operations of reason. It also has a topology that comes out in Plato's differentiation
that is besides philosophical, also related to the grounds and undergrounds
that can be only reached by the mind, not the body: "The visible is accessible
to the senses, while the invisible can only be grasped by the reasoning of
the mind. By referring to the invisible as το αιδες, Plato sets up the identifi-
cation of the invisible world proper to the soul with the traditional mythic
idea of the realm of Hades, Αιδου. This connection of Hades and the unseen
is part of the mythic tradition at least as early as Homer, and Plato refers to
it in the Cratylus as well, where he makes the etymology of Hades not from
αειδες (not-visible) but rather from ειδεναι (to know) (404b, cp. 403a)." Rad-
cliffe Guest Edmonds, *Myths of the Underworld Journey: Plato, Aristophanes,
and the "Orphic" Gold Tablets* (Cambridge: Cambridge University Press,
2004), 179.

22 Guy Debord, "Introduction to the Critique of Urban Geography," trans. Ken
Knabb, in *Critical Geographies: A Collection of Readings*, ed. Harald Bauder
and Salvatore Engel-Di Mauro (Kelowna: Praxis (e)press, 2008), 23. Originally: "Introduction à une critique de la géographie urbaine," *Les Lèvres
Nues*, no. 6 (September 1955).

23 Wark, *Beach beneath the Streets*, 28.

24 The term and the collective work behind it have many layers. The text in
Mute magazine is primarily by Wilfred Hou Je Bek, even if the concept was
most probably coined by Oswald Berthold and Martin Howse. The term
became more defined in the research group and project *Topology of a Future
City* for the transmediale 2010 festival, even if one can justifiably say that
some of the work of people involved and active in the research and projects,
including Jonathan Kemp, goes back to the 2008 xxxxx-Peenemünde-
project (with its strong Pynchon–Kittler connotations). More information
on the history and layers of the term are on the wikipage http://www.psycho
geophysics.org/wiki/doku.php?id=wikipedia. Thanks also to Jonathan Kemp,
whom J. P. interviewed via e-mail about the term and its history in January
2014.

25 The London Psychogeophysics Summit, "What Is Psychogeophysics?"

26 Ibid.

27 Robert Smithson, "A Sedimentation of the Mind: Earth Projects," in *Robert Smithson: The Collected Writings,* ed. Jack Flam (1968; repr. Berkeley: University of California Press, 1996), 100–113. See Etienne Turpin, "Robert Smithson's Abstract Geology: Revisiting the Premonitory Politics of the Triassic," in *Making the Geologic Now: Responses to the Material Conditions of Contemporary Life,* ed. Elizabeth Ellsworth and Jamie Kruse (New York: Punctum, 2013), 174.

28 The London Psychogeophysics Summit, "What Is Psychogeophysics?"

29 Gary Genosko, "The New Fundamental Elements of a Contested Planet," talk at the Earth, Air, Water: Matter and Meaning in Rituals conference, Victoria College, University of Toronto, June 2013.

30 See, e.g., Cary Wolfe, *What Is Posthumanism?* (Minneapolis: University of Minnesota Press, 2009). Kari Weil, *Thinking Animals: Why Animal Studies Now?* (New York: Columbia University Press, 2012). Nicole Shukin, *Animal Capital: Rendering Life in Biocapital Times* (Minneapolis: University of Minnesota Press, 2009). Matthew Calarco, *Zoographies: The Question of the Animal from Heidegger to Derrida* (New York: Columbia University Press, 2008). See also Dominic Pettman, *Human Error: Species-Being and Media Machines* (Minneapolis: University of Minnesota Press, 2011).

31 Ellsworth and Kruse, *Making the Geologic Now.*

32 Ziolkowski, *German Romanticism and Its Institutions,* 18–22. There is unfortunately no space to go into the Kantian questions of the beautiful and the sublime. Partly this has resurfaced in the recent Whitehead-based aesthetic discourse of philosophy, especially in Shaviro, *Without Criteria.* The themes of what we might now call "geopoetics" might be seen as part of Kant's focus on the sublime, as much as it uses notions referring to the natural—from mountains to the sea. But for Kant, this aspect of the sublime actually points inward, toward the mind: "This also shows that true sublimity must be sought only in the mind of the judging person, not in the natural object the judging of which prompts this mental attunement. Indeed, who would want to call sublime such things as shapeless mountain masses piled on one another in wild disarray, with their pyramids of ice, or the gloomy raging sea? But the mind feels elevated in its own judgment of itself when it contemplates these without concern for their form and abandons itself to the imagination and to a reason that has come to be connected with it— though quite without a determinate purpose, and merely expanding it—and finds all the might of the imagination still inadequate to reason's ideas." Immanuel Kant, *Critique of Judgment,* trans. Werner S. Pluhar (1790; reprint, Indianapolis, Ind.: Hackett, 1987), §26, "On Estimating the Magnitude of

Natural Things, as We Must for the Idea of the Sublime," 257. Hence, in this context, consider Shaviro's argument concerning the beautiful and the Whitehead perspective to the inorganic as perhaps hinting at some aspects relevant to our geocentric argument.

33 Williams, *Notes on the Underground*, 17.

34 Tate Britain's exhibition *Ruin Lust* in London (March 4–May 18, 2014) was a well-curated collection of this modern imaginary of the ruins in visual arts.

35 Kenneth White, as quoted in Matt Baker and John Gordon, "Unconformities, Schisms and Sutures: Geology and the Art of Mythology in Scotland," in Ellsworth and Kruse, *Making the Geologic Now*, 163–69. For some notes on the emergence of the concept by White in the 1970s and its theoretical influences from Heidegger to Deleuze and Guattari and onward to some more cosmological dimensions, see Kenneth White, "Elements of Geopoetics," *Edinburgh Review 88* (1992): 163–78. See also the Scottish Centre for Geopoetics, http://www.geopoetics.org.uk/.

36 Richard Grusin, *Culture, Technology, and the Creation of America's National Parks* (Cambridge: Cambridge University Press, 2004).

37 Ibid., 131. Clarence E. Dutton, *Tertiary History of the Grand Cañon District , with Atlas*, in *Monographs of the United States Geological Survey*, vol. 2 (Washington, D.C.: Government Printing Office, 1882).

38 Dutton, *Tertiary History*, 39.

39 Williams, *Notes on the Underground*, 88.

40 Deleuze and Guattari, *A Thousand Plateaus*, 361–74.

41 "Vatnajökull (the sound of)," Katie Paterson, project description, http://www.katiepaterson.org/vatnajokull/.

42 "We call it the Cretaceous acoustic effect, because ocean acidification forced by global warming appears to be leading us back to the similar ocean acoustic conditions as those that existed 110 million years ago, during the Age of Dinosaurs." "Dinosaur-Era Acoustics: Global Warming May Give Oceans the 'Sound' of the Cretaceous," *Science Daily*, October 18, 2012, http://www.sciencedaily.com/.

43 See Florian Dombois, homepage, for project information, http://www.floriandombois.net/.

44 For Wolfgang Ernst, time-critical media are able to measure events of such time scales not necessarily directly perceptible to the human being. However, time-critical media themselves also operate in such ways. In Ernst's words, "with techno-mathematical computing where minimal temporal moments become critical for the success of the whole process of internal calculation and human-machine communication ('interrupt'), time-criticality becomes

a new object of epistemological attention in the economy of knowledge. When culture is rather counted than narrated, time-criticality needs to be focussed by process-oriented (thus dynamic) media archaeology." Jussi Parikka, "Ernst on Time-Critical Media: A Mini-Interview," blog post, *Machinology*, March 18, 2013, http://jussiparikka.net/2013/03/18/ernst-on -microtemporality-a-mini-interview/. See also Wolfgang Ernst, "From Media History to Zeitkritik," trans. Guido Schenkel, *Theory, Culture, and Society* 30, no. 6 (2013): 132–46.

45 This resonates with Lynn Margulis's understanding of Gaia theory. Also, for an extended discussion of related issues concerning Deleuze's shortcomings in the context of a geophilosophy, see Woodard, *On an Ungrounded Earth*. Leaning on Grant, Woodard points out the possible somaphilia lurking in Deleuze's account of the earth, as well as the dangers of other sorts of stabilizing moves that do not go far enough in terms of granting a vital agency to the earth: "This is to say nothing of Husserl's ark-ization of the earth (the earth as the 'original ark,' where the Earth is flung back in time to its pre-Copernican state as merely the bounds of experience), as over-romanticized ground *(Boden)*, or of what Heidegger would call *Offenheit*, or openness, as Meleau-Ponty *[sic]* shows. It is such images of Earth as both dead body and mute cradle that we set out to destroy with digging machines, massive energy weapons, and total ecological collapse. These images perform a dual criminal function: one, to stabilize thinking, and two, to give gravity to anthropocentric thinking and being" (6).

46 Kahn, *Earth Sound Earth Signal*.

47 A lot of Kahn's arguments regarding the epistemological function of early technological media devices are also present in Wolfgang Ernst's media archaeology. See Ernst, *Digital Memory and the Archive*.

48 Kahn, *Earth Sound Earth Signal*, 255.

49 "An *earth circuit* was open to the sounds of the earth and to other, non-natural sounds, whereas a *metallic circuit* was closed onto its own technological loop. Most often the sounds in an open circuit were thought of as noises, but they were also listened to aesthetically and observed and measured as scientific phenomena." Kahn, *Earth Sound Earth Signal*, 256.

50 Bruno Latour, *What Is the Style of Matters of Concern?* (Amsterdam: Van Gorcum, 2008).

51 Transmediale/Resource: Residency project Critical Infrastructure, http:// www.transmediale.de/resource/residency-project.

52 The project was initiated by Jonathan Kemp and then co-organized by Kemp, Jordan, and Howse. http://crystalworld.org.uk/.

53 Delanda, *Deleuze: History and Science*, 87. See also Matthew Fuller, "The Garden of Earthly Delights," *Mute*, September 19, 2012, http://www.meta mute.org/editorial/articles/garden-earthly-delights.

54 The_crystal_world:space:publicity project, http://crystal.xxn.org.uk/wiki/ doku.php?id=the_crystal_world:space:publicity.

55 Fuller, "Garden of Earthly Delights."

56 Martin Howse, "The Earthcodes Project: Substract/Shifting the Site of Execution," microresearchlab, http://www.1010.co.uk/org/earthcode.html.

57 *Encyclopædia Britannica*, s.v. "Earth Current." Among such mentioned pioneers were Barlow and Walker, interested in diurnal variations and, for instance, the influence of the ground in earth currents.

58 See Friedrich Kittler, "Dracula's Legacy," in *Literature, Media, Information Systems*, ed. John Johnston, 50–84 (Amsterdam: G+B Arts International, 1997).

59 Howse, "The Earthcodes Project." Importantly, soil also has a history. Gradually, during the nineteenth century, in geology, the discussions that saw it only as residue of rocks gave way to alternative versions that granted soil a status, life, and history of its own. One can approach this by reading the transformations in soil science and geology. The soil becomes a heterogeneous assemblage itself. See Denizen, "Three Holes in the Geological Present," in *Architecture in the Anthropocene: Encounters among Design, Deep Time, Science, and Philosophy*, ed. Etienne Turpin, 35–43 (Ann Arbor, Mich.: Open Humanities Press, 2013).

60 Cf. Jussi Parikka, *Digital Contagions: A Media Archaeology of Computer Viruses* (New York: Peter Lang, 2007).

61 Smithson, "A Sedimentation of the Mind," 106.

62 Ibid.

63 Manuel Delanda speaks of "metallic affects" pointing to the role of metals as catalysts of chemical reactions. To paraphrase Delanda, the metallic affect refers to the molecular potential for change in the real composition of chemical interactions. Catalysts themselves are useful for that purpose because they don't change in those reactions. What's more is how the metallic is infused with life more generally. This new materialist perspective promises to extend the list of material entities that usually counted (labor, space, clothes, food) into a molecular level of reactions. Indeed, the metals in our bodies and brains are conductive elements as much as they are in technological assemblages, cutting through a range of different level phenomena. Methodologically, this relates to the new materialist assemblage theory that is interested in reality of entities and their processes irrespective of scale,

aiming to correct the human-centered focus of earlier material philosophies. Delanda, *Deleuze: History and Science*, 78.

64 Wark, *Beach beneath the Street*, 29.

65 Paul Lloyd Sargent, "Landscapes of Erasure: The Removal—and Persistence—of Place," in Ellsworth and Kruse, *Making the Geologic Now*, 108. Also discussions in architecture and the Anthropocene are forcing us to rethink cities and geology: "The image of the city, in particular, as a thing that is made *of* geology or *on* geology, increasingly has to contend with the idea of the city as a thing that *makes* geology, in the forms of nuclear fuel, dammed rivers, atmospheric carbon, and other metabolic products of urbanization whose impacts will stretch into future epochs." Denizen, "Three Holes in the Geological Present," 29.

66 Ibid.

67 See Sargent, "Landscapes of Erasure," 109. "Over time in urban, rural, and even 'wild' space, rivers are diverted, ponds drained, malls constructed, casinos imploded, forests burned, crops grown, oceans polluted, reservoirs created, clouds seeded, cathedrals erected, villages sacked, neighborhoods gentrified, libraries filled, satellites launched, histories forgotten, immigrants deported, businesses turned over, invasive species introduced, indigenous people displaced, and landmarks renamed."

68 Debord, as quoted in Wark, *Beach beneath the Street*, 28.

69 Wark, *Beach beneath the Street*, 28.

70 Pynchon, *The Crying of Lot 49* (New York: Harper and Row, 1966), 181–82.

71 In the sense used by Félix Guattari.

72 Cf. Eugene Thacker on Fritz Leiber and the theme of the unhuman. Thacker, "Black Infinity," 173–80.

73 Cf. Jane Bennett's proposal to see vital matter as parallel to historical materialism in *Vibrant Matter*, 63.

4. Dust and the Exhausted Life

1 Christian Neal MilNeil, "Inner-City Glaciers," in Ellsworth and Kruse, *Making the Geologic Now*, 79–81.

2 Ibid., 79.

3 Negarestani, *Cyclonopedia*. See Gary Genosko, "The New Fundamental Elements of a Contested Planet," talk presented at the Earth, Air, Water: Matter and Meaning in Rituals conference, Victoria College, University of Toronto, June 2013. A case to underline this argument: Cold War nuclear testing culture was tightly linked with climate research. The radioactive fallout from nuclear tests sometimes penetrated the stratosphere, and tracking the

aftereffects of the blast was instrumental to understanding the global circulation of microparticles, including carbon-14. The earth traces of, for instance, carbon became agents through which to understand the global dynamics of the planet, rather ironically through the assistance of nuclear detonations, themselves made possible by advanced computing. See Edwards, *Vast Machine*, 209.

4 "Today, African dust carries with it metals and microbes, persistent organic pollutants and pesticides, and these contaminants fall onto the declining reefs of the Caribbean Ocean. A pathogenic fungus, known to cause sea fan disease and coral mortality in these warm pale waters, originated from Sahel soil in Mali." GinaRae LaCerva, "The History of Dust," *Feedback* blog, http://openhumanitiespress.org/feedback/newecologies/dust/.

5 James P. Sterba, "In Coral Layers Scientists Find a History of the World," *New York Times*, August 10, 1982.

6 Colby Chamberlain, "Something in the Air," *Cabinet* 35 (Fall 2009), http://cabinetmagazine.org/issues/35/chamberlain.php.

7 Steven Connor, "Pulverulence," *Cabinet* 35 (Fall 2009), http://cabinetmagazine.org/issues/35/connor.php.

8 The fictional Dr. Hamid Parsani, in Negarestani, *Cyclonopedia*.

9 Susan Sontag, *Illness as Metaphor* (New York: Farrar, Straus, Giroux, 1977), 13.

10 Jennifer Gabrys, "Telepathically Urban," in *Circulation and the City: Essays on Urban Culture*, ed. Alexandra Boutros and Will Straw (Montreal: McGill-Queen's University Press, 2008), 49.

11 Jonathan M. Bloom, *Paper before Print: The History and Impact of Paper in the Islamic World* (New Haven, Conn.: Yale University Press, 2001), 129.

12 Ned Rossiter, "Dirt Research," in *Depletion Design: A Glossary of Network Ecologies*, ed. Carolin Wiedemann and Soenke Zehle (Amsterdam: Institute of Network Cultures, 2012), 44.

13 See Peter Sloterdijk, *Bubbles. Spheres Volume I: Microspherology*, trans. Wieland Hoban (Los Angeles, Calif.: Semiotext(e), 2011).

14 Connor, "Pulverulence."

15 Ibid.

16 http://phonestory.org/.

17 The iPhone 5 launch and shipping of millions of phones in the first days was accompanied by strikes at the Foxconn factories in Zhengzhou and earlier clashes in Taiyuan. See Adam Gabbatt, "Foxconn Workers on iPhone 5 Line Strike in China, Rights Group Says," *The Guardian*, October 5, 2012, http://www.guardian.co.uk/. Such problems in production are cleaned away from Apple's immaculately polished marketing material that emphasizes the human-sized ergonomics of its products.

18   See Graham Harwood's texts and in general YoHa's 2008 project *Aluminium*, http://www.yoha.co.uk/aluminium. Modern industrialism and its fascist aesthetics (referring to futurism as a sort of an archaeology of the political resonances of the chemical) are distributed as part of the everyday: "Aluminium xmas trees, pots and pans, door and window frames, wall cladding, roofing, awnings, high tension power lines, wires, cables, components for television, radios, computers, refrigerators and air-conditioner, cans, bottle tops, foil wrap, foil semi-rigid containers, kettles and saucepans, propellers, aeroplane, gearboxes, motor parts, tennis racquets and Zepplins [*sic*]." A key scholarly work on aluminum is Mimi Sheller, *Aluminum Dreams: The Making of Light Modernity* (Cambridge, Mass.: MIT Press, 2014).

19   See http://www.phonestory.org/.

20   Nick Dyer-Witheford and Greig de Peuter, *Games of Empire: Global Capitalism and Video Games* (Minneapolis: University of Minnesota Press, 2009), 199.

21   Franco "Bifo" Berardi, *Precarious Rhapsody: Semiocapitalism and the Pathologies of the Post-Alpha Generation* (London: Minor Compositions, 2009), 69.

22   Dyer-Witheford and de Peuter, *Games of Empire*, 38.

23   Franco "Bifo" Berardi, "Exhaustion/Depression," in Wiedemann and Zehle, *Depletion Design*, 77–82.

24   http://i-mine.org/.

25   Vilém Flusser, *Into the Universe of Technical Images*, trans. Nancy Ann Roth (Minneapolis: University of Minnesota Press, 2011), 112.

26   See Pasi Väliaho, *Mapping the Moving Image: Gesture, Thought, and Cinema circa 1900* (Amsterdam: Amsterdam University Press, 2010).

27   Daniel Paul Schreber, *Memoirs of My Nervous Illness*, trans. Ida Macalpine and Richard Hunter (London: W. M. Dawson, 1955).

28   Kittler, *Discourse Networks 1800/1900*. Thank you to Darren Wershler for alerting me to the conceptual link between lungs, bodies, Schreber, and Kittler, in a way that finds another expression in Franz Kafka's Penal Colony (*Strafkolonie*, 1920) and its horrific machine that treats the body as an inscription surface.

29   Kittler, *Discourse Networks 1800/1900*, 292.

30   Geoffrey Winthrop-Young, *Kittler and the Media* (Cambridge: Polity, 2011), 121.

31   Jim Puckett and Ted Smith, eds., *Exporting Harm: The High-Tech Trashing of Asia*, report prepared by the Basel Action Network and Silicon Valley Toxics Coalition, February 25, 2002, http://www.ban.org/E-waste/technotrashfinal comp.pdf.

32 See John McNeill, *Something New under the Sun.*

33 Maxwell and Miller, *Greening the Media,* 46–47.

34 Ibid., 47.

35 Ibid., 53.

36 See also Jussi Parikka, *What Is Media Archaeology?* (Cambridge: Polity, 2012), 163–64.

37 Manuel Delanda interviewed in Dolphjin and van der Tuin, *New Materialism,* 41.

38 Jason W. Moore, "Crisis: Ecological or World-Ecological?," in Wiedemann and Zehle, *Depletion Design,* 73–76.

39 Yann Moulier Boutang, *Cognitive Capitalism,* trans. Ed Emery (Cambridge: Polity, 2012), 19.

40 The estimates about "peak oil" vary, demonstrating the complex epistemologies and trouble in measuring such geologic data but also the economic stakes in the question. According to some worst-case estimates, also in recent research, peak oil could be reached even before 2020. Besides the fact that we need to be aware of the wider energy contexts of media technologies, of course, the dependence on oil has major consequences across sectors where it is hard to play the game of which one is the most important to worry about. The report identified that "major industrial sectors were at risk, including food and food processing, primary agriculture, metals and metals processing, and transport." Hence it is no wonder that a recent report suggests not only the reduction of movement of people and things but also a different sort of fertilizer agriculture, more reliant on organic farming. In general, what is suggested is a lifestyle change that is more about localities and decentralization, to paraphrase the text. Nafeez Ahmed, "Imminent Peak Oil Could Burst US, Global Economic Bubble—Study," *The Guardian,* November 19, 2013, http://www.theguardian.com/.

41 See Hans-Erik Larsen, *The Aesthetics of the Elements* (Aarhus, Denmark: Aarhus University Press, 1996). David Macauley, *Elemental Philosophy: Earth, Air, Fire, and Water as Environmental Ideas* (Albany: State University of New York Press, 2010). See also Ryan Bishop on Bashir Makhoul's video art through the Empedoclean elements' lenses. Bishop, "The Elemental Work of Palestinian Video Art," in *Palestinian Video Art: Constellation of the Moving Image,* ed. Bashir Makhoul, 88–109 (Jerusalem: Al-Hoash/Third Text, 2013).

42 Genosko, "New Fundamental Elements of a Contested Planet."

43 YoHa, *Coal Fired Computers* project, http://yoha.co.uk/cfc.

44 This is also the epigraph to Peter Sloterdijk, *Terror from the Air,* trans. Amy Patton and Steve Corcoran (Los Angeles: Semiotext(e), 2009).

45 Maxwell and Miller, *Greening the Media,* 79.

46 Ibid., 73–74.

47 Jennifer Gabrys, *Digital Rubbish: A Natural History of Electronics* (Ann Arbor: University of Michigan Press, 2011), 139.

48 Matthew Fuller, "Pits to Bits: Interview with Graham Harwood," July 2010, http://www.spc.org/fuller/interviews/pits-to-bits-interview-with-graham -harwood/.

49 http://www.yoha.co.uk/aluminium.

50 Raqs, with Respect to Residue, 2005, quoted on the Aluminium project web page, http://www.yoha.co.uk/node/536. On the "residual" in media, see also Charles R. Acland, ed., *Residual Media* (Minneapolis: University of Minnesota Press, 2007).

51 See, e.g., Huhtamo and Parikka, *Media Archaeology.* Parikka, *What Is Media Archaeology?*

52 Negarestani, *Cyclonopedia,* 88.

53 Consider also smart dust, important not least for emerging military applications, on which I won't go into detail here. Smart dust is not, however, restricted to military applications—all the talk of smart cities demonstrates how the possibility of equipping urban environments in such smartness presents a new paradigm of controlled environments. If smart dust is the marker of the creative informational city—in that it joins together creative brains and the city itself (thus the city becomes brainy, communicative)— then we also need to remember the dumb dust that entangles itself with information and creativity: it is partly the residue of information technology smartness, yet we still need to be aware of its qualities as creative, effective matter (to follow Negarestani's philosophical idea). See Brendan I. Koerner, "What Is Smart Dust Anyway?," *Wired,* June 2003, and Gabrys's excellent historical insight into smart dust and cities, "Telepathically Urban."

54 See Dolphijn and van der Tuin, *New Materialism.* See also, e.g., Milla Tiainen, "Revisiting the Voice in Media and as Medium: New Materialist Propositions," *Necsus,* no. 4 (Autumn 2013), http://www.necsus-ejms.org/revisiting -the-voice-in-media-and-as-medium-new-materialist-propositions/.

55 Ned Rossiter, "Logistics, Labour, and New Regimes of Knowledge Production," http://nedrossiter.org/?p=260.

56 Ibid. See also Maxwell and Miller, *Greening the Media,* 89.

57 Fuller, "Pits to Bits."

58 Ibid.

59 Quoted in Maxwell and Miller, *Greening the Media,* 37.

60 Delanda, *A Thousand Years of Nonlinear History.*

61 Matteo Pasquinelli, *Animal Spirits: A Bestiary of the Commons* (Amsterdam: NAi/Institute of Network Cultures, 2008).

62 Franco "Bifo" Berardi, *The Uprising: On Poetry and Finance* (Cambridge, Mass.: MIT Press/Semiotext(e), 2012), 25.

63 Peter Sloterdijk, *Terror from the Air,* 10.

5. Fossil Futures

1 Seth Denizen, "Three Holes in the Geological Present," in Turpin, *Architecture in the Anthropocene,* 40.

2 Rachel Armstrong, "Why Synthetic Soil Holds the Key to a Sustainable Future," *Guardian Professional,* January 17, 2014, http://www.theguardian.com/.

3 See Gary Genosko, "The New Fundamental Elements of a Contested Planet," talk presented at the Earth, Air, Water: Matter and Meaning in Rituals conference, Victoria College, University of Toronto, June 2013.

4 Alexis C. Madrigal, "Not Even Silicon Valley Escapes History," *The Atlantic,* July 23, 2013, http://www.theatlantic.com/. See also the Silicon Valley Toxics Coalition, http://svtc.org/.

5 Moira Johnston, "High Tech, High Risk and High Life in Silicon Valley," *National Geographic,* October 1982, 459.

6 See David Naguib Pellow and Lisa Sun-Hee Park, *The Silicon Valley of Dreams: Environmental Injustice, Immigrant Workers, and the High-Tech Global Economy* (New York: New York University Press, 2002).

7 Jennifer Gabrys, *Digital Rubbish,* 26.

8 Johnston, "High Tech, High Risk," 459. See also Christine A. Finn, *Artifacts: An Archaeologist's Year in Silicon Valley* (Cambridge, Mass.: MIT Press, 2001).

9 Sean Hollister, "Protestors Block Silicon Valley Shuttles, Smash Google Bus Window," *The Verge,* December 20, 2013, http://www.theverge.com/.

10 Joe Heitzeberg, "Shenzhen Is Like Living in a City-Sized TechShop," *Hack Things,* May 2, 2013, http://www.hackthings.com/shenzhen-is-like-living-in-a-city-sized-techshop/.

11 Pellow and Park, *Silicon Valley of Dreams,* 4.

12 Jay Goldberg, "Hardware Is Dead," *Venturebeat,* September 15, 2012, http://venturebeat.com/2012/09/15/hardware-is-dead/.

13 Bruce Sterling, "The Dead Media Project: A Modest Proposal and a Public Appeal," http://www.deadmedia.org/modest-proposal.html.

14 Goldberg, "Hardware Is Dead."

15 Ibid.

16   Heitzeberg, "Shenzhen Is Like Living in a City-Sized TechShop."

17   John Vidal, "Toxic 'e-Waste' Dumped in Poor Nations, Says United Nations," *The Observer*, December 14, 2013, http://www.theguardian.com/.

18   Step—solving the e-waste problem, http://www.step-initiative.org/.

19   See Martin J. S. Rudwick, *Georges Cuvier, Fossil Bones, and Geological Catastrophes: New Interpretations and Primary Texts* (Chicago: University of Chicago Press, 1997).

20   Gabrys, *Digital Rubbish*, 5. Gabrys on Benjamin: "Benjamin, in his practice of natural history, at once drew on but departed from the usual, more scientific practice of natural history. While he was fascinated by nineteenth-century depictions of and obsessions with natural history and fossil hunting, he interpreted these historical records of the earth's deep time as a renewed temporal vantage point from which to assess practices of consumption. Obsolete objects returned to a kind of prehistory when they fell out of circulation, at which time they could be examined as resonant material residues—fossils—of economic practices. He reflected on the progress narratives that were woven through Victorian natural histories (and economies) and effectively inverted these progress narratives in order to demonstrate the contingency and transience of commodity worlds" (6). See also the chapter on "Natural History: Fossils" in Susan Buck-Morss, *The Dialectics of Seeing: Walter Benjamin and the Arcades Project*, 58–77 (Cambridge, Mass.: MIT Press, 1991).

21   Gabrys, *Digital Rubbish*, 7.

22   Peters, "Space, Time, and Communication Theory."

23   Charles Lyell, *Principles of Geology* (London: John Murray, 1830), 1. Online facsimile at http://www.esp.org/books/lyell/principles/facsimile/. The monument is the crucial figure in Michel Foucault's archaeology, differentiating it from the historiographical tracking of stories. For Foucault, it is the persistence of the past in the present as a concrete monument that is of interest to the archaeologist. This idea is picked up by Wolfgang Ernst in his media archaeology, which tries to follow this nondiscursive line offered by Foucault. Ernst: "Like the media analyst, who gazes at objects in the same way as the ethnologist records the practices of a remote society, the antiquarian intends to achieve a *monumental* relation to the past. This method aims to avoid prematurely interpreting archival or archaeological evidence as documents of history but rather isolates this data into discrete series in order to rearrange them and open them for different configurations." Ernst, *Digital Memory and the Archive*, 44.

24   Ilana Halperin, "Autobiographical Trace Fossils," in Ellsworth and Kruse, *Making the Geologic Now*, 154.

25   Stephen Jay Gould, *Time's Arrow, Time's Cycle: Myth and Metaphor in the Discovery of Geologic Time* (Cambridge, Mass.: Harvard University Press, 1987), 86.

26   Stephen Jay Gould, *Punctuated Equilibrium* (Cambridge, Mass.: Harvard University Press, 2007).

27   Gould, *Time's Arrow, Time's Cycle*, 98–102.

28   Paul Virilio, *Bunker Archaeology*, trans. George Collins (New York: Princeton Architectural Press, 1994), 56.

29   Williams, *Notes on the Underground*, 43.

30   Stoppani, "First Period of the Anthropozoic Era," 40. "A new era has then begun with man. Let us admit, though eccentric it might be, the supposition that a strange intelligence should come to study the Earth in a day when human progeny, such as populated ancient worlds, has disappeared completely. Could he study our epoch's geology on the basis of which the splendid edifice of gone worlds' science was built? Could he, from the pattern of floods, from the distribution of animals and plants, from the traces left by the free forces of nature, deduct the true, natural conditions of the world? Maybe he could; but always and only by putting in all his calculations this new element, human spirit. At this condition, as we, for instance, explain the mounds of terrestrial animals' bones in the deep of the sea, he, too, could explain the mounds of sea shells that savage prehistoric men built on the coasts that they inhabited. But if current geology, to understand finished epochs, has to study nature irrespective of man, future geology, to understand our own epoch, should study man irrespective of nature. So that future geologist, wishing to study our epoch's geology, would end up narrating the history of human intelligence. That is why I believe the epoch of man should be given dignity of a separate new era" (40).

31   Gould, *Time's Arrow, Time's Cycle*, 175–76.

32   "By second nature I mean the space of the material transformation of nature by collective labor. Second nature is a space of fragmentation, alienation, class struggle. In many ways, the space of the vector really is a third nature, from which the second nature of our built environments can be managed and organized, as a standing reserve, just as second nature treats nature as its standing reserve." Wark, "Escape from the Dual Empire."

33   Wark, *Telesthesia*, 34–35.

34   Walter Benjamin, *The Arcades Project*, trans. Howard Eiland and Kevin MacLaughlin (Cambridge, Mass.: Belknap Press of Harvard University Press, 1999), 540.

35   Manuel Delanda, *War in the Age of Intelligent Machines* (New York: Zone Books, 1991), 2–3.

36 Chatonsky, as quoted in Kevin Thome de Souza, "Gregory Chatonsky, Art as an Archaeology of the Future: An Interview," *Amusement*, February 15, 2013, http://www.amusement.net/.

37 See, e.g., Paul Virilio, *The Original Accident*, trans. Julie Rose (Cambridge: Polity, 2006). See also Gabrys on museum of failure in her *Digital Rubbish*.

38 De Souza, "Gregory Chatonsky."

39 Gary Cook, "Clean I.T. Means Clean Suppliers, Too," *New York Times*, Opinion, September 23, 2012, http://www.nytimes.com/.

40 Fredric Jameson, *Archaeologies of the Future* (London: Verso, 2005), xii.

41 Derek Hales, "Design Fictions: An Introduction and a Provisional Taxonomy," *Digital Creativity* 24, no. 1 (2013): 7. On imaginary media, see Eric Kluitenberg, *The Book of Imaginary Media* (Rotterdam: NAi, 2006). Eric Kluitenberg, "On the Archaeology of Imaginary Media," in Huhtamo and Parikka, *Media Archaeology*, 48–69. See also Richard Barbrook, *Imaginary Futures: From Thinking Machines to the Global Village* (London: Pluto Press, 2007).

42 http://paleofuture.gizmodo.com/.

43 See Zielinski, *[. . . After the Media]*.

44 Paul Virilio, *Grey Ecology*, trans. Drew Burk, ed. Hubertus von Amelunxen (New York: Atropos Press, 2009).

45 Steven J. Jackson, "Rethinking Repair," in *Media Technologies: Essays on Communication, Materiality, and Society*, ed. Tarleton Gillespie (Cambridge, Mass.: MIT Press, 2013), 221. Lisa Parks, "Media Fixes: Thoughts on Repair Culture," *Flow* 19 (2013), http://flowtv.org/2013/12/media-fixes-thoughts-on-repair-cultures/.

46 Parks, "Media Fixes."

47 Brooke Belisle, "Trevor Paglen's Frontier Photography," in Ellsworth and Kruse, *Making the Geologic Now*, 147.

48 Paglen, "The Last Pictures."

49 Ryan Bishop, "How to Talk to a Heavenly Body," talk presented at transmediale 2013, February 2013, Berlin.

50 *The Last Pictures* project Web site, http://creativetime.org/projects/the-last-pictures/. See also Trevor Paglen, *The Last Pictures* (Berkeley: University of California Press/Creative Time Books, 2012). Paglen's interest in the geopolitics of satellite technologies as part of our visual culture has continued in more recent projects, such as *Nonfunctional Satellite*, which was exhibited at Protocinema in Istanbul in 2013.

51 Paglen, "The Last Pictures," 508.

52 Understood in the sense suggested by Paul Virilio: a move from the geographically fixed local times to global times of accelerated technological speeds

surpassing the affective and cognitive coordinates of the human. Paul Virilio, *Open Sky*, trans. Julie Rose (London: Verso, 1997). Richard G. Smith, "Escape Velocity," in *The Virilio Dictionary*, ed. John Armitage (Edinburgh: Edinburgh University Press, 2013), 79–80.

53 Katarina Damjanov, "Lunar Cemetary: Global Heterotopia and Biopolitics of Death," *Leonardo* 46, no. 2 (2013): 159–62. See also Parks, "Orbital Ruins," *NECSUS—European Journal of Media Studies*, no. 4 (Autumn 2013), http://www.necsus-ejms.org/orbital-ruins/.

54 Luke Harding, "Russia to Boost Military Presence in Arctic as Canada Plots North Pole Claim," *The Guardian*, December 10, 2013, http://www.theguardian.com/.

55 Richard Seymour, "Why Outer Space Really Is the Final Frontier for Capitalism," *The Guardian*, Comment Is Free, December 20, 2013, http://www.theguardian.com/.

56 Marc Kaufman, "The Promise and Perils of Mining Asteroids," *National Geographic*, January 22, 2013, http://news.nationalgeographic.com/. Adam Mann, "Tech Billionaires Plan Audacious Mission to Mine Asteroids," *Wired*, April 23, 2012, http://www.wired.com/. Although some more recent accounts are not as optimistic as to the viability of asteroid mining. Liat Clark, "Study: Asteroid Mining Might Not Be Commercially Viable," *Wired* (UK), January 14, 2014, http://www.wired.co.uk/.

57 Parks, *Cultures in Orbit.*

58 Belisle, "Trevor Paglen's Frontier Photography," 145–49.

59 Bishop, "Project 'Transparent Earth.'"

60 Katie Drummond, "Pentagon-Backed Venture Aims for 'Google-Underground,'" *Wired*, March 8, 2010, http://www.wired.com/. Bishop, "Project 'Transparent Earth.'"

61 smudge studio (Elizabeth Ellsworth + Jamie Kruse), "The Uneven Time of Space Debris: An Interview with Trevor Paglen," in Ellsworth and Kruse, *Making the Geologic Now*, 150–51.

62 Herschel, as quoted in Peters, "Space, Time, and Communication Theory." As Belisle notes, regarding early pioneers such as Herschel, "echoing with contemporaneous geological arguments, his view unsettled notions of a fixed and perfect universe, arguing it was unimaginably old and vast, and still changing." Belisle, "Trevor Paglen's Frontier Photography."

63 Meillassoux, *After Finitude*, 10.

64 Ibid.

65 Ibid., 14.

66 See Galloway et al., *Excommunication*, 49.

67 Tim Morton, "Zero Landscapes in the Time of Hyperobjects," quoted in Ellsworth and Kruse, *Making the Geologic Now*, 221.

68 See Ernst, *Digital Memory and the Archive*. In general, my use of the notion of "temporeality" is in debt to Ernst.

69 Mél Hogan, "Facebook's Data Storage Centers as the Archive's Underbelly," *Television and New Media*, online first, November 14, 2013.

Afterword

1 Steffen et al., "The Anthropocene," 616.

2 See Nest, *Coltan*, 8–9.

3 Huber, "Dig More Coal." The actual estimates of how much power, and what sort, computers and the Internet consume vary greatly. For a recent Greenpeace report, see "How Clean Is Your Cloud?," April 17, 2012, http://www .greenpeace.org/international/en/publications/Campaign-reports/Climate -Reports/How-Clean-is-Your-Cloud/.

4 Huber, "Dig More Coal."

5 Caillois, as quoted in the introduction by Marguerite Yourcenar to *The Writing of Stones*, trans. Barbara Bray (Charlottesville: University Press of Virginia, 1985), xvi.

6 Babbage, as quoted in Peters, "Space, Time, and Communication Theory."

7 Bishop, "Project 'Transparent Earth,'" 278.

8 Part of the Haus der Kulturen der Welt's important *Anthropocene* project (2013–14) in Berlin, curated by Anselm Franke. The Otolith Group's *Medium Earth* was part of the program in the end of 2014 from October to December.

9 Otolith Group, *Medium Earth*, The Roy and Edna Disney/CalArts Theater (REDCAT), Los Angeles, 2013, http://www.redcat.org/exhibition/otolith -group.

10 Kahn, *Earth Sound Earth Signal*, 23.

Appendix

1 The authors would like to thank Amelia Guimarin, Tony D. Sampson, Lesley Walters, and the three referees for their valuable feedback. Garnet Hertz would like to thank Mark Poster, Peter Krapp, Cécile Whiting, and Robert Nideffer for feedback on earlier versions on this essay. Hertz is supported by the National Science Foundation grant 0808783 and the following organizations at UC Irvine: the Center for Computer Games and Virtual Worlds, the Institute for Software Research, and the California Institute for Telecommunications and Information Technology. No endorsement implied. Jussi Parikka

is grateful to the feedback from audiences at University of Wisconsin–Milwaukee, Wayne State University Detroit, and Coventry University.

Environmental Protection Agency, "Fact Sheet: Management of Electronic Waste in the United States," EPA 530-F-08-014, July 2008.

2 Jonathan Sterne, "Out with the Trash: On the Future of New Media," in *Residual Media*, ed. Charles R. Acland (Minneapolis: University of Minnesota Press, 2007), 17.

3 Erkki Huhtamo, "Thinkering with Media: On the Art of Paul DeMarinis," in *Paul DeMarinis/Buried in Noise*, ed. Ingrid Beirer, Sabine Himmelsbach, and Carsten Seiffarth, 33–46 (Berlin: Kehrer, 2010).

4 Bernard London, "Ending the Depression through Planned Obsolescence," pamphlet, 1932. Reproduced in "How Consumer Society Is Made to Break," http://www.adbusters.org/category/tags/obsolescence.

5 Brooks Stevens, talk at Midland (Minneapolis), 1954, http://www.mam.org/collection/archives/brooks/bio.php.

6 Victor Lebow, "Price Competition in 1955," *New York University Journal of Retailing* 31, no. 1 (1955): 7.

7 For example, Apple's iPod personal audio players and similar devices are manufactured with no user-serviceable parts inside, including their batteries. After approximately three years of use, the lithium-polymer battery will no longer work and the device will need to be either professionally serviced or discarded.

8 For a more detailed account of the history, theory, and contexts even in electronic warfare of the black box, see Philipp von Hilgers, "The History of the Black Box: The Clash of a Thing and Its Concept," *Cultural Politics* 7, no. 1 (2011): 41–58.

9 Diane Waldman, *Collage, Assemblage, and the Found Object* (New York: Harry N. Abrams, 1992), 17. Calvin Tomkins, *Duchamp: A Biography* (New York: Holt, 1998), 181. On media art historical writing concerning the early avant-garde, see, for example, Erkki Huhtamo, "Twin-Touch-Test-Redux: Media Archaeological Approach to Art, Interactivity, and Tactility," in *MediaArtHistories*, ed. Oliver Grau, 71–101 (Cambridge, Mass.: MIT Press, 2007), and Dieter Daniels, "Duchamp: Interface: Turing: A Hypothetical Encounter between the Bachelor Machine and the Universal Machine," in ibid., 103–36.

10 David Joselit, *American Art since 1945* (New York: Thames and Hudson, 2003), 126; Edward A. Shanken, *Art and Electronic Media* (London: Phaidon, 2009).

11 Q. Reed Ghazala, "The Folk Music of Chance Electronics, Circuit-Bending the Modern Coconut," *Leonardo Music Journal* 14 (2004): 97–104.

12 John Markoff, *What the Dormouse Said: How the Sixties Counterculture Shaped the Personal Computer Industry* (New York: Penguin, 2005).

13 Michel de Certeau, *The Practice of Everyday Life,* trans. Steven Rendall (Berkeley: University of California Press, 2002), xiv.

14 In 1995, Richard Barbrook and Andy Cameron coined the phrase "Californian Ideology" in an essay by the same title, which provided a genealogy of the concept of the Internet as a placeless and universalizing utopia, with information technologies as emancipatory, limitless, and beyond geography. See http://www.hrc.wmin.ac.uk/theory-californianideology-main.html.

15 Cf. Charles R. Acland, "Introduction: Residual Media," in Acland, *Residual Media,* xx.

16 Wolfgang Ernst, *Digital Memory and the Archive,* ed. Jussi Parikka (Minneapolis: University of Minnesota Press, 2013), 37–54.

17 See Eric Kluitenberg, ed., *The Book of Imaginary Media* (Rotterdam: Nai, 2006); Eric Kluitenberg, "On the Archaeology of Imaginary Media," in *Media Archaeology: Approaches, Applications, Implications,* ed. Erkki Huhtamo and Jussi Parikka, 48–69 (Berkeley: University of California Press, 2011).

18 Jay David Bolter and Richard Grusin, *Remediation: Understanding New Media* (Cambridge, Mass.: MIT Press, 1999).

19 For more information, see Bruno Latour, *Pandora's Hope: Essays on the Reality of Science Studies* (Cambridge, Mass.: Harvard University Press, 1999). See also Eugene Thacker, introduction to *Protocol: How Control Exists after Decentralization,* by Alex Galloway (Cambridge, Mass.: MIT Press, 2004), xiii.

20 Albert Borgmann, *Holding on to Reality: The Nature of Information at the Turn of the Millennium* (Chicago: University of Chicago Press, 1999), 176. For a relevant discussion of infrastructure, see Susan Leigh Star and Karen Ruhleder, "Steps toward an Ecology of Infrastructure: Design and Access for Large Information Spaces," *Information Systems Research* 7, no. 1 (1996): 63–92.

21 Latour, *Pandora's Hope,* 185.

22 Garnet Hertz, personal correspondence, October 20, 2009.

23 Erkki Huhtamo, "Time-Traveling in the Gallery: An Archaeological Approach in Media Art," in *Immersed in Technology: Art and Virtual Environments,* ed. Mary Anne Moser with Douglas McLeod (Cambridge, Mass.: MIT Press, 1996), 243.

24 Erkki Huhtamo, "Thinkering with Media: The Art of Paul DeMarinis," in *Paul DeMarinis, Buried in Noise* (Berlin: Kehrer, 2011).

25 Gutta-percha is a natural latex rubber made from tropical trees native to Southeast Asia and northern Australasia. Columbite tantalite, or "coltan," is a dull black metallic ore, primarily from the eastern Democratic Republic of

the Congo, whose export has been cited as helping to finance the present-day conflict in Congo.

26 Félix Guattari, *The Three Ecologies*, trans. Ian Pindar and Paul Sutton (London: Athlone Press, 2000).

27 Sean Cubitt, interviewed by Simon Mills, *Framed*, http://www.ada.net.nz/library/framed-sean-cubitt/.

28 Such hidden but completely real and material "epistemologies of everyday life" are investigated in a media archaeological vein by the Institute for Algorhythmics, http://www.algorhythmics.com/.

29 Manuel DeLanda, *A Thousand Years of Non-Linear History* (New York: Zone Books, 1997).

INDEX

abacus, 87–88

abstract geology, 5, 66

acoustic media. *See* soundscapes

actor-network theory, 97–102; media archaeology and, 147–50

Aeneid (Virgil), 14

aesthetics: art of geology and, 68–72; psychogeophysics and, 60–81

affect theory, 97–102; telofossils and, 120–25

Africa: political economy of dust and labor in, 105–7, 179n4; repair culture in, 125

Against the Day (Pynchon), 55–57

Agricola, Georgius, 80–81

agriculture: soil technology and, 53–54

alchemy: history of, 56–58

Allen, Jamie, 28, 73

aluminum dust: health risks of, 89–96, 101–2, 180n18

Aluminum project (YoHa), 89, 180n18

ammoniac (synthetic compound), 53

animal aesthetics, 61–67

Anthrobscene, 17–25, 159n47; industrialization and, 53–54; plate tectonics and, 81; soundscapes and, 70–71

Anthropocene discourse, viii–xi, 16–25; architecture and, 178n65; deep time concepts and, 42–45; dust and, 83–85; environmental damage of media technology and, 45–54; fossil production and, 109–15; geocentric perspective on, 40; geology of art and, 69; "obscenity" of, 159n47; outer space fossils and, 129–31

anthropocentrism: new materialism and, 97–98; psychogeophysics and, 67

antiterrorism: surveillance mechanisms in response to, 30

archaeological history: fossil records and, 115–19; media archaeology and, 2; *Telofossils* (exhibition) and, 120–25

Archaeologies of the Future (Jameson), 123

arche-fossil, 131–35

and, 168n53; Zielinski's deep time discourse and, 39–45; zombie media and, 48, 141–53
media art: deep time and, 39–45, 52–54
medianatures: animal aesthetics and, 63; geology of morals and, 165n25; temporality and, 6–16
media technology: climate change and, 60–61; deep time mobilization discourse and, 35–36; ecology of deep time and, 37–45; geology of morals and, 165n25; geophysics of, viii
media temporalities, 131–35
Medium Earth installation (Otolith), 139
Meillassoux, Quentin, 133
Memoirs of My Nervous Illness (Schreber), 94
Mendelev periodic table, 74
metallic affects: Delanda's concept of, 22–23, 177n63
metals and metallurgy: art of geology and, 77–78; dust from, 87–88; environmental impact of, 46–47; geological materiality and, 22–23, 34–35; health risks for workers in, 89–96; photography and, 55
meteorology: media techniques and, 12–13
microresearchlab projects, 8–9, 27, 28, 73–81
military operations: media-arche-fossil concept and, 131–33; outer space fossils and, 128–31; smart dust and, 182n53
Miller, Toby, 95–96, 100
MilNeil, Christian Neal, 83–84

"Mineral Loads or Veins and Their Bearings" (Diderot and D'Alembert), 44
mining: computer technology and, 138–40; dust and, 85; environmental impact of, 46–52; games involving, 92–96; perception of underground and, 173n21; residue elements from, 96–102; technological culture and role of, 33–34, 168n52
Minter, Adam, 47–48
Molleindustria game company, 89–90
Moore, Jason W., 98–99
morals: geology of, 164n25
Morton, Tim, 63, 135
Mumford, Lewis, 14–15, 25–26, 168n52
Mute magazine, 61, 65, 173n24
mythology: underground in, 173n21

Nam June Paik, 144
nanomaterials: computer culture and, 36–37; dust and, 86–88; geology of media and, 138–40
national parks: art of geology and, 68–69
nation-states: media technology and, 52–54
nature: culture and, x
natureculture concept, 13–16
Negarestani, Reza, 34, 83, 98, 102, 106, 161n68
new materialism: design, fabrication, and standardization of, 36–37; political economy of dust and labor and, 103–7; residue elements in, 96–102
Nietzsche, Friedrich, 93–94, 165n25

(continued from page ii)

Jussi Parikka is professor in technological culture and aesthetics at Winchester School of Art, University of Southampton. He is author of *Digital Contagions: A Media Archaeology of Computer Viruses, What Is Media Archaeology?* and *Insect Media: An Archaeology of Animals and Technology* (Minnesota, 2010); editor of *Medianatures: Materiality of Information Technology and Electronic Waste* and *Digital Media and the Archive* (Minnesota, 2013); and coeditor of *The Spam Book: On Viruses, Porn, and Other Anomalies from the Dark Side of Digital Culture* and *Media Archaeology: Approaches, Applications, and Implications.*